EMPOWERING RELATIONSHIPS

SHAKTI DURGA

Revised Edition Published April 2026 by
Higher Guidance Pty Ltd
First Edition Published May 2012
213 Martinsville Road, Cooranbong NSW 2265
Australia www.shantimission.org
Previous Publications:
Ignite Your Spirit 2004
Child of God 2006
Spiritual Mastery 2008
Dimensions of Wealth 2009
Letters to Initiates Vol 1 2011
Published by Higher Guidance Pty Ltd

Shakti Durga
National Library of Australia Cataloguing-in-Publishing Data
Durga, Shakti 1961-
Empowering Relationships / Shakti Durga
1st edition
Bibliography
ISBN 978-0-9871091-1-8
1. Interpersonal Relations 2. Spirituality II Title.
302

Acknowledgements

This is an important addition to the materials written for the Path of Ease and Grace Seminar series. The contents have been road tested through my own life, which has transformed greatly over the past 30 years. There are many stories contained in this book, all of which are composites and representative of possibly a dozen people who had similar experiences. Thus, the circumstances described and the changes that took place using the tools are factual, but all of the names are fictitious.

The principles of multi-dimensionality help us to have real tools with which to work on ourselves and bring desired change into our lives. We really can ignite our spirits and have fabulous, uplifting, supportive relationships in all parts of our lives.

I would like to thank Adi Dass for her priceless administrative support, Chandradevi, Lalitha Durga, Hecate Ma and Bhu Devi for proofreading.

I dedicate this book to my beloved, Shiva Kata Tjuta, to my parents and children and to the initiates and disciples within Shanti Mission, with gratitude for the priceless relationships, which are such a source of joy and happiness.

Shiva and I hold a vision of spiritually developed and empowered people making a difference to the quality of life throughout many levels and branches of family, community, industry, government and charitable enterprise. By learning tools for peace, we can be empowered to raise the vibration of what is happening in our world, improving conditions for everyone who is willing to embrace a higher quality of life. Then we can all live in peace.

Contents

PART

1

INTRODUCTION

Chapter

1

EMPOWERING RELATIONSHIPS

Life on Earth carries the necessity for experiences which help us to understand and discover ourselves. Much of this is done through a primary mechanism, which is: relationships.

The relationships that are discussed in this book and the tools given are not limited to romantic relationships or marriage. This is a book about how to improve relationships with people at work, relatives and friends, with people who previously have been very tricky to deal with *as well as* improving our love life. The tools contained here if practiced properly will transform your life. They will make bad relationships better and good relationships Divine. You will learn how to take even serious relationship problems and diminish or eliminate them. In short, through practicing the tools in this book you will learn to become a self-empowered peacemaker.

To me relationships are a key to real enlightenment. When we master ourselves through relationships, we have road tested theories and turned them into wisdom. Almost anyone can manage superficial relationships, but what about longer term, deep and vibrant relationships that keep getting better as the years go by?

A solid relationship has lots of energy, and a thought form of 'us' not me. There is confidence that if issues come up, we will be able to resolve them. There is a sense of freedom to be who we want to be and a general sense of feeling supported and loved. We have a sense of wellbeing. We feel safe, valued, appreciated, able to express our individuality, pursue the highest destiny that we might be able to imagine, and the relationship is the bedrock that supports both parties.

Relationships are the advanced class of life, and having good relationships is a sign that a person has integrated and absorbed spiritual teachings, whatever their path, and are living in accordance with Universal principles.

We develop a relationship with the people around us, and also with the Divine, with Saints, Gurus, Sages or teachers who help us get to know our selves better. The Divine is love, so whenever we feel love, we are feeling the Divine. That ineffable, non-physical reality, which is the source of all things, is the ultimate love of every life, and seeing the Divine in every person is part of the journey to realisation of the Divine within us.

Becoming comfortable and committed to the Divine by whatever flavour or path we choose, is to take part in the ultimate relationship, with the Eternal Father/Mother. This book is about that as well.

The Empowering Part of Relationships

Personal empowerment is the ability that we have to be the captain of our own ship. It means that I can direct my life the way that I would like it to be. I can find meaning, satisfaction, creativity, joy, material security, a great career and hopefully some peace and happiness. Along with all that, I can enjoy caring and loving relationships.

There are two kinds of power, internal (feminine or Yin) and external (masculine or Yang).

External power is the kind that depends for its validity upon circumstances that are outside of the individual. This includes one's class, wealth, position, seniority in office, social standing, media profile and so on. For millennia the external power-field was slanted against women, who were not regarded as citizens. We had no voting rights, could not own property or hold public office, and were considered by and large to be the chattels of the father and then the husband. It was impossible for a woman to have any external or masculine power of her own. Thus, all of her efforts needed to go to support her husband, who *could* hold that kind of power.

External power, whether held by a man or a woman, demands that we adhere to the structured codes, rules of conduct and behaviour demanded by society. Mess up and you will not be able to retain the external circumstance through which that power was yours. Lose the external circumstance, and you have lost your power. No one will jump anymore at your command: you are no longer in control. Because of this, there is a lot of stress associated with getting and holding onto external power. We have to control everything and everyone so that we can feel that we are safe in the life we have created.

Internal or yin (feminine) power is the capacity to be magnetic to good things. It is the optimism of a person who has deep trust and faith within themselves and for all of life. It is there irrespective of any external factor. Nothing can diminish it. We no longer have to struggle to stay in control, because inside we are filled with a bubbling wellspring of energy, connectedness and trust in the flow of life.

Internal power is the province of the spiritually connected, mentally and emotionally skilled person that can handle differences of opinion, and who communicates effectively. The internally potent are able to be assertive, not aggressive or passive. They are able to face situations that might give rise to conflict with confidence and with respect for themselves and their beloved. They can open *'don't go there'* topics, get rid of the stale quality that attaches to relationships from time to time, and challenge entrenched habits in a way that makes a positive difference. This internal power is a quality of spirit, born of the virtues. It arises from self-respect, self-acceptance and self-love. It contains within it a deep feeling of connectedness to the Source, to the Earth, to life itself. It comes from stillness, not from frenetic activity. It is what most of us are looking for.

Revolution

The 1960's and 1970's saw a social revolution in which the defined stereotypical roles of men and women were at least partially disintegrated and the expected roles, particularly for women, underwent a tremendous transformation. Most people are no doubt grateful for the freedoms and basic human rights that this revolution gave to the disenfranchised half of the population. Women, like men, can now access external power. They can become the Premier, Prime Minister, sit on boards of large companies, earn big money and own property. In these settings they can be as empowered as a man. However, relationships seem if anything, more fraught than ever, and the social revolution of 50 years ago does not appear to have provided the happy solution for how to live that was envisaged at the time. What went wrong?

It would appear that there has been little really learned about internal (feminine) power. Neither men nor women have paid much attention to that, and so *both* are often disempowered at a core level, and this shows up most acutely in personal relationships.

Everyone has internal power, but not everyone recognises it or knows how to use it. Just as we have to work hard to establish external power, we can do some work on ourselves to cultivate internal power. When we have done that, nothing and no one can ever take it from us. It will change our lives and change the quality of our relationships for the better.

When something goes wrong for a person with little training in internalised power, it is a calamity. The person with little yin power (even if they hold worldly or external power) is likely to find someone to blame, or to beat him/herself up and engage in caustic self-talk when there is a glitch in their plans. This might be a hangover from childhood, when significant elders treated them this way, or were highly critical.

We have come a long way in our social dynamics, at least on the external stage. However, things are unlikely to really come into balance and harmony in a new way until we come to terms with our internal dynamics. Our power to have a loving and deliciously amazing relationship is already within us: we just need to do some excavating to discover this for ourselves and turn our life into a Divine gift. That is what this book is about. May you enjoy the journey, and experience the zing and joy, all the colour and flavour of really empowering relationships.

Making It Real: Choose a Relationship to Renovate

As you read on, think of a tricky relationship. It may be your current relationship, a relationship with your ex, a friend, a difficult relative or someone at work. The more challenging the relationship you chose to work on, the more amazed you will be about the results as you work through the exercises in Empowering Relationships. Notice how the paradigm discussed and the exercises that are included can help you to change and refine your own experiences.

In this book, the other person in the relationship that you have chosen to work will be referred to as 'the beloved'. See if you can identify any of the factors that we will explore together in your nominated relationship and use this book as a manifesto for change.

A workbook has also been created for use with this text, as have a number of meditation and self-healing CD's. These are available online through www.shantimission.org or through our Harmony Centres. You can also come along to Empowering Relationships seminars, held at Shanti Mission Harmony Centres and online, where the principles in this book are filled with the shakti (spiritual energy) of our teachers. This will infuse you with energy and give you a 'leg up' to a life more filled with ease and grace.

Chapter

2

RELATIONSHIPS: A MULTI-DIMENSIONAL PERSPECTIVE

Why do we attract the people that we do in relationships? Why do some intelligent, well-educated and seemingly rational people have such a hard time being in good relationships?

Much of what goes on in relationships and which either makes or breaks them is not really physical. So many factors come into play, including people's moods, motivations, compatibility, chemistry, memories, expectations, and the energy, spark, spirit or lack of it in the relationship. Emotions, feelings, attractions, trust and intimacy; these are not things that we can bang a nail into or investigate fully through our 5 senses. Exploring these things takes us beyond the purely physical world.

To have happy and empowered relationships, it is really helpful to look at the dimensions of human experience that are non-physical.

Practically, there are five dimensions, including the physical dimension, which have a great impact upon our capacity to relate, be happy and fulfilled in relationships. These are the:

1. Divine essence
2. Soul
3. Mind (also called the Astral Field)
4. Energy Field
5. Physical life and body

All of these levels of reality affect us, even if we don't know about them. When we understand the dimensions that together create our reality, we can see that there are areas in which, through lack of consciousness, we might have some relationship blockages. Awareness allows us to work out our problems, and intelligent, consistent application of the laws of the dimensions, help us to bring desired change into our lives. A lot of suffering, heart ache, emotional angst and confusion can be alleviated this way. Even serious relationship problems can be healed and peace restored to our hearts and minds.

Each of the five dimensions exists within us as well as without. We cannot see our non-physical self under a physical magnification device because *it is not physical*. Our invisible self *can* be perceived through clairvoyant observation and intuitive means when we are sufficiently developed in our consciousness and etheric body. With spiritual training much will be revealed that will revolutionise our relationships and our lives.

The V Diagram

Below is a model explaining multi-dimensionality. Imagine that the V diagram represents you. At the bottom, like the tip of the iceberg, is our physical self. It is the only visible part, and so we can mistakenly believe that *'this is who I am,'* when really, it is only a tiny part of who we are. A short description of the dimensions as they apply to relationships is given here. More detail about how to use this framework to create love, joy, happiness peace and personal empowerment within relationships follows as this book unfolds.

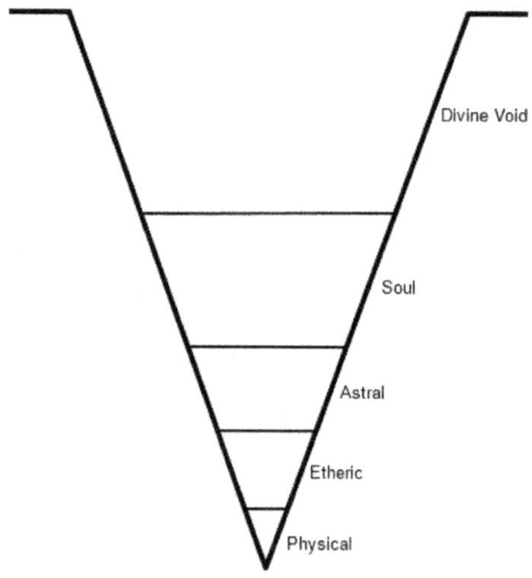

The Physical Dimension

The physical dimension is experienced through the five senses. It can be seen in terms of physical matter and energy, more or less as these are understood by science. The interaction of four elements; fire, earth, water and air create matter in the physical world. These elements are known in science as heat, solid, liquid and gas.

The physical world has to do with things that happen within space and time.

It has its own laws that can't be ignored. In this realm for instance, there are laws of momentum and inertia. It can take a lot of energy to get something moving, but when you do, it will keep moving in the same direction until something else happens to change that. Once you get going, things keep happening much the same way in relationships as well, because of momentum and inertia. We get into patterns of behaviour, and not all of them are good.

In relationships the physical dimension is expressed through spending actual time together. The way that we speak to each other, the physical gestures, giving or with-holding affection in the form of smiles, hugs and use of body language; all of these things affect our experiences. In the physical dimension we can threaten or reassure, find security and get our needs met, or experience a terrible lack. If we do nothing, things stay the same. If we always do what we have always done, we will always get what we have always got.

How we negotiate the physical dimension will have a bearing upon the quality of our relationships and the spirit with which we are able to live. There can be no doubt that the way we treat people, our skill or lack of it in relating is crucial to relationship happiness. Later we will look at ways to be skilful, particularly in the area of communication and the art of listening.

The Energy Field (Etheric Dimension)

The etheric dimension is the dimension of subtle energy or Chi. Our etheric body comprises our aura, chakras, and the meridians. The aura is like a big bubble around us, keeping our energy in, and many other kinds of energy filtered out. The chakras are whirling vortices of energy that have specific functions, and the meridians are the lines of energy that join it all together. My first book, Ignite Your Spirit, is all about this dimension and you can refer to that for more information.

The aura and chakras are responsible for putting fresh energy into us, and pulling stale energy out. If your etheric body is full of garbage it will not work properly. It is like trying to run your clothes dryer when you have not cleaned out the filter for a year or two. Eventually it will break. Dull, polluted auras and chakras cause physical, psychological and spiritual problems for us. If we want to be successful, happy, healthy, strong, vital and energetic, it is a good idea to learn about the etheric body and look after it.

The chakras and the aura are invaluable tools for relating. They are the antennae that help us to instantly feel when something is not right, when there has just been an argument in a room that looks otherwise normal, when there is a danger around the corner. It is the energy pouring into us that causes the hair to stand up on the backs of our necks, or on our arms, when we hear exquisite music, or when in the presence of energy from another dimension. Our chakras and aura are our hardware for the endless minutia of stimuli that come to us not through body language or through our minds, but through frequencies of energy.

People who have issues in their etheric bodies tend to have unsatisfying and perplexing relationships. They often misread other people and find it difficult to get on the same wavelength as others. They can be living in the past, enmeshed in cords of energy that prevent a fresh flow of healing energy coming into their hearts and minds, breathing new life into ever-changing, ever-growing relationships.

If we want to change our relationships, then given the law of inertia that applies in the physical world, we are going to have to muster sufficient energy to do that. The etheric dimension is the dimension of energy. We can clean out and grow our etheric body to spring clean our relationships. We can learn to transform our experiences of other people as we cut old energetic cords that bound us to deadening, stultifying or annoying past experiences. We can set ourselves free to become more present to the here and now and to appreciate the beloved through a new and fresh lens.

We can also learn about and heal the relationship itself, which over time develops its own unique energy. This third energy field (i.e., mine, the beloveds, and the energy of our relationship itself) can hold us back from change, growth and new experiences. Or, it can be cultivated so as to continue deepening our connection based on who we are now, not who we were 10 (or 30) years ago when we first got together. We will do this in chapter 28.

Mind: Astral Dimension

The astral dimension is the non-physical realm of thoughts, feelings and beliefs. The astral dimension contains things that are largely created by the minds of mankind. Our minds are unconsciously affected by all of the activity and thinking patterns of our family, community and species on a daily basis. The astral dimension influences our thoughts, beliefs, moods, decisions, relationships, happiness, stress levels, self-esteem, choices and futures.

Tides of emotion, somewhat like weather patterns, flow through the astral field all the time and affect us in powerful yet subtle ways. When we are clear, even turbulent patterns seem to mysteriously pass us by. When we are filled with astral and etheric garbage, negative thoughts and beliefs, we can get very caught up in hurricanes of thought forms and difficult, powerful emotions that buffet us around and can make us feel very unsafe, sometimes even causing pain or harm to ourselves or others.

We are more often focussed in the astral realm than we are in the physical realm. We are usually thinking thoughts and feeling feelings that have nothing to do with what is currently going on around us. Think about driving the car. Are we focused on the steering wheel, road, speed, scenery, other cars, or is all that happening automatically while we plan our day? Astrally, we are frequently in our future (planning, anticipating, getting stressed) or in the past (remembering, feeling guilty, worrying about what we could have said or done, being conscious of memories). Either way, we are not mentally in the physical world of 'now'.

Most people are not very conscious about what they are thinking and not concerned about it. They imagine that they are entitled to think and believe what they like, because it is no one else's business. *Wrong.* When we learn even basic clairvoyance, it is obvious that *thoughts and beliefs are things.* They flow all around us and clog up our aura and chakras. Our dominant beliefs are like neon lights in the aura, proclaiming to everyone who comes near us what we believe and expect.

We unerringly attract to us through the Law of Attraction that which our deeply held beliefs say we are going to. Thought is creative, as it templates subtle energy and causes patterns to form in the astral dimension which our souls then cause to be attracted to us.

Managing our thoughts and training our minds to think positive and wholesome thoughts is one of the biggest jobs that we need to do in order to create better relationships. Finding out what our subconscious is up to and how it is working either for us or against us is also important when mastering this fascinating dimension of ourselves. We will look at thoughts and beliefs about relationships and also look at hidden contracts of expectation that may be holding us back from seeing the good things that are going on around us, even if they are not the same as what we might have been expecting.

The Soul

The soul dimension is our home, it is where we live when we die, and it is where a part of us lives all the time. Our Higher Soul inhabits this dimension and extends a portion down through the other dimensions into what we think of as reality, the physical world. Our physical, astral and etheric bodies are part of our Soul, in a similar way to how toes and legs and arms are a part of our physical body.

Our soul is the ultimate cause of all that we experience in relationships. The soul also has an agenda, which involves the cultivation of wisdom and self-realisation. When we get in touch with it through accessing our intuition and start to appreciate what we really are, all kinds of things make sense and we can discern meaning in our experiences, even the horrible ones. This allows us to bear misfortune with greater grace and also allows us to head off many issues and problems on account of a deepened insight. We can align with our soul's agenda and relate from an expanded perspective rather than from the limited, localised moment in which we find ourselves.

The laws that pertain to the soul realm and which govern the inner and worldly life of humans are dealt with in my previous book *Spiritual Mastery*. Knowing the laws of the inner world is as important to us as knowing the basic laws of physics in the physical world. Working against the laws of the soul is like expecting water to run up hill. It won't, even if we want it to. When we know what the laws are that form the fabric of the dimensions in which we live, we can start to work *with* the forces of creation instead of unwittingly working against them. Consequently, life gets a lot easier.

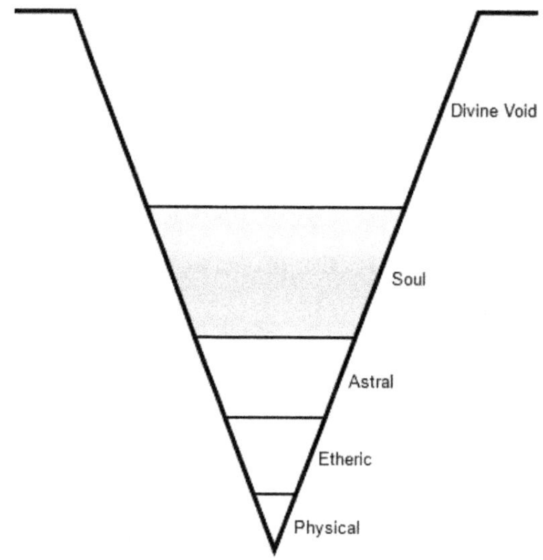

Divine Dimension

The Divine dimension is a void, there is nothing in it, and it is the essence of being. It is pure consciousness and pure love. The Holy Spirit, Mother / Father God, Shiva, Allah, Durga, Brahma, Jehovah, Shekinah, the Creative Force, Universal Energy; all of the names of God are describing the same thing and are used interchangeably in this book.

If you think you are experiencing this dimension, or even the dimension of the soul, you are not. Thinking is an astral experience. During experiences of Samadhi, usually occurring after years of meditation and spiritual training, this level can be consciously experienced, but the experience is more of the nature of bliss than a thought. At this level all is pure consciousness and pure potency or shakti. There is immense love and creative potential and a kind of non-thought awareness that is crystal clear, like seeing the deepest level of what is.

Everything that ever was and ever will be flows from here. The Divine Void is not bounded in any way, and stretches to everyone who ever was or who ever will be. Here there is true oneness. There is no difference between you and me, as we are one continuous field. The extending arms on the side of the V diagram are there to remind us that at this level, we are in unity with everyone else. We do not live in splendid isolation, even when we think we do. Like waves on an ocean, we are part of the one amazing whole.

For years debate has raged as to whether the Divine is inside us or outside of us. Both arguments are true. The voltage we can manage is activated already inside us. There is always more to discover.

Every cell of our being and of all things, contains some Divine Void energy. In science it is known as the quantum field. The unlimited potential reality of the Divine and how much we can turn up the Divine frequency within us depends upon the robustness and development of our mind, chakra system, the degree to which our kundalini energy is active, our level of ethical and moral steadfastness and other factors.

Within us is the power to raise our vibration and embody more Divine energy and grace that is so infinitely available. To learn more about Shiva/ Allah/Jehovah and experience the majesty of Divine wealth there is only one place to look: inside.

Book Series

I have written much more about the etheric dimension in my book *Ignite Your Spirit,* and about the soul and astral dimensions in *Soul Connection.* The laws of the soul are dealt with in Spiritual Mastery. The way in which the various dimensions of our being link together to help us manifest what we want on Earth through increasingly miraculous circumstances is set out in *Dimensions of Wealth.*

In *Empowering Relationships* we will look at key multi-dimensional factors in establishing and maintaining excellence in relationships, even in ones that have been tricky up until now. To avoid repetition of key concepts, you are referred to these earlier books so as to understand the profound implications of working in a multi-dimensional framework more deeply than it will be discussed in this book.

Chapter

3

Relationship Phases and Intimacy

Like love, relationships have various stages and phases. Each is different and important. A dance goes on in all relationships between unity or connectedness and self-ness or separateness. The most crucial relationship is often that with our lover/spouse but just about any important relationship will go through these phases.

One of the things that long term relationships rise and fall on is their capacity to cultivate intimacy. Intimacy can be thought of as: *in-to-me-see*. Intimacy involves personal disclosure, trust and the drawing together of two people. It is about caring, building relationship, sharing, respect, tenderness, closeness and familiarity. Intimacy provides friendship, warmth and oneness, as well as time for each other.

In a sexual relationship it is intimacy that is the key to long-term romance and satisfying sexuality. Through relationships we are looking to see how to realise oneness, while paradoxically finding more of our authentic self at the same time. When we do this, through the dance that intimacy takes us on, what we are actually doing is realising more love. Love is Divine, so we are actually realising our Divine essence.

Intimacy is often confused with sexuality. Sexuality is just one type of intimacy and sometimes there can be sexuality with no intimacy at all. Sometimes people engage in sexual relationships with total strangers, trying to find intimacy. What actually happens is that this kind of relating undermines our self-esteem and diminishes our energy. Thus it is a poor choice of relating and very rarely do we find any actual intimacy, which is what we really crave.

Intimacy is also confused with intense feelings or infatuation. People in the honeymoon phase of any relationship often have very strong desires and feelings concerning the beloved, but this is not intimacy either. Intimacy is something that develops over time.

Intimacy flowers in a relationship like waves flowing onto a beach. Over time the tide goes in and out. It is important not to let the tide go too far out and also we don't want the tide of intimacy swamping us. Some balance is required. A long term relationship without intimacy means that the spark will erode, and we will end up living separate lives, perhaps looking like a couple but really we are more like flat mates.

In order to really understand intimacy we are going to look at 4 phases of relating.

4 Phases of Relating

The four phases of relating are:

1. **Honeymoon phase.** This is when everything is rosy and we are enjoying a rapid drawing together, there is lots of energy flowing and life is wonderful.

2. **Individual Differences phase**. This is when the honeymoon starts to come to an end and we recognise that the beloved has faults, the affairs of everyday life intervene and we slow down from the headlong merging we experienced during the honeymoon phase. Each person may face a raft of inherited issues from their upbringing.

3. **Conflict phase**. This comes as each person tries to assert their will in the relationship, differences have to be sorted out and each person battles with authenticity, assertiveness, putting their point of view, styles of interpersonal relating and styles of conflict resolution. You only really know the calibre of a person when you have disagreed with them. Various forms of dysfunctional behaviour only really show up when we disagree. To live in peace, we actually need to learn how to do deal with conflict.

4. **Separation or Golden Afterglow phase**. If we do not handle our differences and conflict well, then sooner or later the relationship may end up failing. We will move into separation, and the sweet love we knew may turn sour. If we handle phases one to three well, energy will continue to flow in the relationship, and we will end up closer together than ever before. This will create a 'golden glow', which cycles us back into the honeymoon phase again.

Through repetitively cycling through these phases in our relationships, we grow in love, closeness and intimacy. The alternative is that we do not handle the phases very well, and we move further and further apart, until the energy in the relationship dies right down, we are less and less satisfied, and feel quite separate.

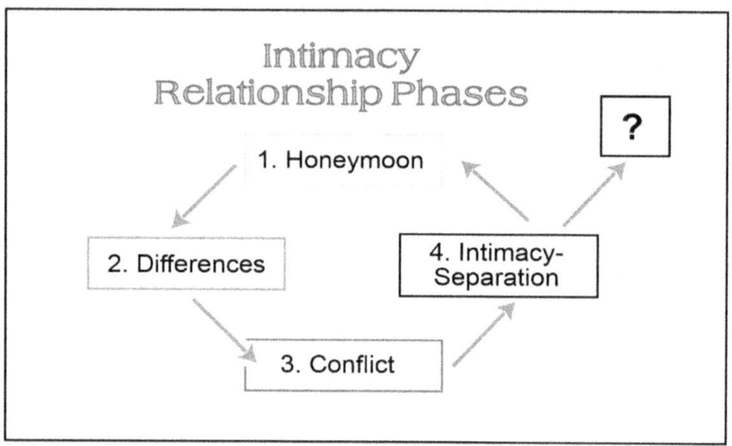

Phase One: The Honeymoon

The honeymoon phase of a relationship is the delicious, rosy and romantic part at the beginning of a relationship. When as two individuals we have just gazed lovingly at each other for the first time (perhaps across a crowded bar), it is sometimes love at first sight. We start to date. We are mad keen about each other. Often when speaking of love, people are actually speaking about the strong physical and romantic attraction that takes place at the beginning of a relationship. In the context of romantic relationships, love and lust are often confused.

The honeymoon phase can be filled with infatuation, and is when the desire to merge and the sexual attraction is intense. There is a very strong desire to please and engage with the beloved. We want to make a good impression and move into a closer relationship.

Things are novel. The beloved is still a mystery. There is lots of discovery and optimism. During the honeymoon phase we are revealing the parts of ourselves that we want to bring into union, and the beloved is doing the same. There is much to share. This generally feels satisfying, expansive, and moves the two of us towards a deeper state of intimacy. The two are becoming as one, whole and feeling complete in each other.

Falling in love feels good, others often say we look fantastic or have a rosy glow. We feel optimistic and hopeful. The beloved is a gift from the Divine. We are bedazzled by the light of the beloved and see none of the faults and they don't see any of ours. We see all of the good characteristics of our new friend or new prospective partner. This is a phase where we most recognise the reflection of our own beauty. You could bring home Godzilla and think they were great while your friends and family are freaking out about it. Sometimes there is not a lot of discernment even in otherwise sensible people. Infatuation can be a bit obsessive, and involves our ego in a dance of excitement, which can capture our spirit and make everything else seem relatively unimportant.

Each person tends to make a big effort, and to be accepting of the other. There is a strong pull to be agreeable, to fit in with what the beloved wants. Each puts their best foot forward to be attractive and desirable. She always has her makeup in place, he washes the car before taking her out in it. She offers to cook: he foregoes Saturday night at the football with his mates to take her to the movies. She cancels lunch with the girls to meet with the beloved and so on.

People sometimes go to surprising lengths during this stage to impress and delight each other. There is nothing wrong with that, it is just that we might not be able to keep it up forever. It can create expectations that later on might be hard to live up to!

In this phase, both parties are revealing themselves and being vulnerable to the extent that they want to. The revealing of the self at this early stage has no emotional price attached to it, because what we share are only the things that we want to share, that we are quite happy to talk about to anyone. Our challenges, growing edges and insecurities are as yet well disguised. Any skeletons in the closet and our inner-most secrets, dreams and fears can remain hidden. We keep the conversation light, and talk about the weather. What job do you have? What is your star sign? Where do you come from? What is your favourite food, what do you like to watch on TV?

At this early stage there is no real investment in each other (kids, mortgages, joint friends) and plenty of freedom. They have their life and we have ours. We have autonomy. We are an *addition* to each other's life but we have our *own* life as well.

Oh really?

At this stage of the game, each person can disclose whatever they like about themselves from their own idiosyncratic point of view, because all that is discussed is history and our concepts of how things were. We don't know if the beloved sees things that have happened in their life with accurate perception, or whether they are wildly distorted in their recollection of events. We just don't know much about them. We can also be a bit gullible in our assessment of others, because we so want people to be a certain way. Our astral impression of who or what we conceive the perfect match to be can be overlaid upon a person who is actually not that at all.

What boundaries?

People sometimes give away a lot in the honeymoon phase, as they are trying to look attractive and be enticing to a new friend/partner. Sometimes boundaries are lacking. Boundaries are what keep us safe, and if we don't really have boundaries then we may create awkwardness or even danger for ourselves. Conversely, some people have boundaries that are so close to them that they are generally difficult and inflexible. Other people have virtually no boundaries, and a symptom of that is the tendency to want to disclose everything about themselves to the first person they meet. This can be taken advantage of, and can also push people away.

Pushing back boundaries too early in a relationship is often associated with lack of self-respect, self-love and self-confidence. Conversely people who fail to open to the beloved and remain aloof, closed and distant are not going to be able to cultivate much intimacy in relationship.

The honeymoon phase is characterised by our desire to move closer to each other, to show our desirability and to engage. The key thing is the revealing of the self, or *in-to-me-see* that we offer to the beloved. Some people are not afraid of intimacy, whereas other people feel quite threatened and have difficulty in trusting. Learning to trust, and learning who to trust, is something that comes as we get to trust and love ourselves more and open our hearts and minds to the world of intuition and the vast wisdom of our spirit.

Slowly, over time each party can start to reveal the deeper truths about themselves. They might share a fear, or give voice to a situation in which they feel vulnerable. As the trust builds, disclosure builds, and the relationship builds. Intimacy grows.

When one or both parties get to a place that they are at the end of their comfort zone about self-revelation, this is really when the energy of the honeymoon phase starts to dwindle. Suddenly we want to pull back, and that is the first turning of the tide of intimacy.

When the intensity of the honeymoon phase is in full swing, enjoy it! This phase, which does not usually last more than 6-12 months, may not be the best time to make major decisions such as whether or not to get married to each other. It is however, heaps of fun.

Honeymoon Phase Tools for Self-Empowerment

1. Be authentic. Don't try to be a chameleon, know that you are perfect as you are and that if the beloved cannot see that, then they are not the beloved for you!

2. Avoid feeling desperate. Many amazing people get the feeling that a bird in the hand is worth two in the bush: I better latch onto this relationship in case there is nothing better out there. Don't sell yourself short!

3. Work on your self-esteem and self-love. We will share tools for doing this as we explore the fascinating world of the inner child.

4. Work on your boundaries: not too little, not too much. The art of boundaries is discussed in chapter 14.

5. Don't fall in love with someone's potential. They may not ever decide to realise it. Will you be happy with the person just as they are, if they never change?

6. Be aware of the Law of Attraction. Whomever we attract to ourselves is telling us something about a hidden part of our own being. Knowing this, we can work on that part so as to bring optimal relationship results into our life.

Phase Two: Individual Differences

The next phase of relating after the honeymoon phase is when we start to become very aware of the differences between us. This can be a confronting stage, but we are still trying our best to be sweet, accommodating, patient and so on. There can still be romance and attraction at this stage (and hopefully forever) but other factors come into play. Cracks start to occur in our conception of our 'perfect' beloved, who is now seeming much more ordinary.

In this phase, and sometimes earlier, patterns of behaviour become entrenched, and either or both parties can be unhappy with the result. We might have fallen into roles with each other, but now it is getting a bit tedious.

Intimacy slow down

When we get to the end of where we feel comfortable continuing to reveal more of the inner truth of ourselves to the beloved, the relationship will start to run out of intimacy. This can happen irrespective of whether we are having sex with them or not. As we said before, sex and intimacy are not the same thing. You can have intimacy without sex, and you can have sex without intimacy. However, our sex life will be better when we have intimacy as well, and that is what keeps the physical aspect of relationships alive and getting better year after year, rather than fizzling out when the initial flush of energy created by newness has passed.

When we stop revealing more of the truth of ourselves to the beloved, the energy of intimacy wanes and the tide of intimacy goes out. This can feel lonely or even frightening, particularly after the enveloping high tide of the honeymoon period. It can take work to turn it back again, work that might take us through conflict and then into a new and even more golden afterglow.

Time to get real

Competing priorities can make the period following the honeymoon phase a tricky time. We see if we really have enough in common to work our way through the things that are different. We find that there are many parts of our life that we have put on hold so as to spend time with the new Mr/Ms Wonderful. The demands of our usual life have not gone away and require some attention. We go out with our girlfriends; he goes out with his mates. We have to work late; he has sport. She is not sure she wants to go to the pub with him and the guys every Friday night, and she misses going out with her girlfriends and so she goes out with them instead. He may feel rejected "What do you mean you don't want to go out with me on Friday night?"

Relationships can be all very fine when we don't actually live together or spend a great deal of time together. But when we do, there will inevitably be different approaches to how we should do things, which can be frustrating. Whereas in the honeymoon phase there is loads of space between us, by stage two the lives, friends, finances and living arrangements are often meshed, creating plenty of opportunity to bump into each other. When this happens, our skills in emotional mastery are invaluable, but relatively few people have good emotional training. Thus, many ructions can occur, sometimes becoming extremely intense and unskilful.

With familiarity comes a *lack* of newness and the discovery of the ordinary about our beloved. We see the undies on the floor and the mess in the fridge, and the housework, daily life and competing priorities all complicate the idyllic honeymoon phase. We have heard each other's stories, and now we are hearing them for the fifth time and they are getting less interesting. She doesn't actually wear makeup and high heels all the time and is a lot less glamorous in real life than on date nights. We start to see each other in our usual world, not our special, *making-it-all-beautiful* world.

The newness, zing and energy of the honeymoon slows down to be replaced by organisational management of two lives meshing together. Sorting things out into manageable and mutually acceptable patterns starts to occur.

It is inevitable that sooner or later the parties to a relationship will disagree about something (or many things!). There are no two people on the planet who are the same as each other, and so there is next to no possibility of finding someone who will agree with you on everything.

Julia and Noel

In the honeymoon phase of their relationship, Julia loved cooking for Noel, going to the market after work, carefully choosing and buying food and wine and it was a really enjoyable act of love. Then in the differences phase she started to think "you know it would be really nice if you would do the cooking once in a while". But she didn't say that, she didn't reveal it as she thought that it might sound selfish or uncaring. Worried about what he might think if she suggested he help, she just said nothing. Her energy changed a little, and Noel did not know why. He didn't know she was feeling resentful of doing the cooking because she had not said so. This created the first emotional or energetic block between them, as she was now withholding something about how she felt or what she needed. She feared his reaction, or even rejection.

Meanwhile Noel was thinking "I used to love cooking. I wish she would let me cook, but I don't want to hurt her feelings or seem ungrateful so I won't say anything".

Both are trying to be nice, but this lack of authenticity gives rise to a wedge between them that is the first chink in the cultivation of intimacy.

Small things that annoy us can be ok for a while, but when the same small things are still happening week after week, year after year they can become sources of long standing and unspoken resentments. Parties can 'act out' their frustration. Before you know it each party is feeling dissatisfied. In the end, either the parties become increasingly inauthentic, or there is a conflict.

Differences arise just because both people have their own view of what should happen and their own set of priorities and tastes. Often the divergent views are neither right nor wrong, they are just an example of individual variation in attitude, preference, consciousness, life experience and expectation.

A difference of opinion can arise over anything, such as whether to watch the movie on Netflix or the one on Prime, or which restaurant to go to for dinner. Which school should we send our kids to? Whose family do we visit for Christmas lunch this year?

The more passionate attachment we feel concerning our position, the greater is the possibility of a conflict arising because of it. The issue then becomes our attachment, which is a spiritual issue, and dealing with things at the spiritual root cause goes a long way to resolving conflict and freeing us to have much happier, energised and enjoyable relationships.

Importantly, we can disagree without having a conflict. We can get skilful at expressing our selves in a non-judgmental, non-aggressive and peaceful way, and we can use tools from the five dimensions of reality to do this.

> ### *Individual Differences Phase Tools for Self Empowerment*
>
> 1. Take note of the influences you received in childhood when we look at contracts of expectations and core beliefs and do the exercises. Know what is driving your assumptions and judgments about how you think things ought to be in relationships.
> 2. Through our relationships and the differences, we see in others, we are meeting parts of ourselves that we have not had the opportunity to learn about before.
> 3. Enjoy the differences: when we work through our judgments about them, it is often our differences that are endearing. When we kill off that which is different between us, we kill off what it was that attracted us to that person in the first place. They will no longer be authentically themselves.
> 4. Do not seek to reform your beloved. They will only resent it and blame you for making their life a prison. Instead, work on transformation of the self, which will transform your relationship. This will miraculously cause differences in what you observe in your beloved.
> 5. Use affirmations to clarify and create in the Astral field the kinds of things that you would like to create in your life.

Phase Three: Conflict

Even really skilful people who are being authentic, and who understand about individual differences, are going to experience some degree of conflict in relationships at some stage. Conflict is necessary to a healthy relationship, in the same way that pruning is necessary for a healthy rosebush. Peacemakers become skilful and effective at making a positive difference in relationships and the world, not by avoiding conflict but by being *good at resolving it* in a way that brings positive change, and a win/win situation for all involved.

Conflict does not have to be negative. It can be the catalyst for change and the removal of old, stale energy that brings a breath of fresh air to everyone involved.

Conflict usually involves an emotional charge and can sometimes be experienced as the butting of heads as two different opinions or paradigms meet. There is often a conscious or unconscious competition for seemingly scarce resources. The resource being fought over at the end of the day is *energy*, expressed physically (time and money), mentally (beliefs) or emotionally (attitudes, respect, judgments). Our ego and its fear of not getting our own way is what fuels conflict. Our higher soul is the vehicle through which conflict can be healed.

A conflict can emerge for all kinds of reasons, but it is often what happens when a difference is not handled well. Conflict then is an emotional and energetic (astral and etheric) response to the difference.

Where there is a large degree of conflict there can be crazy decision making in respect of the difference. Conflict has the capacity to be destructive whereas a difference of opinion is just that. Learning to manage conflict is a skill, which we all need. The skills are spiritual, mental, emotional and physical. This book is packed with ideas about how to learn and use these skills so that you become more empowered in your relationships and in your life.

If people are very skilful, conflict will resolve in a wonderful way, but there is a small likelihood that it will amount to anything more than an unsatisfactory compromise if we lack relationship skills. Compromise is not optimal as neither party is truly happy with the outcome and it has a deadening effect energetically. Compromise comes from the mindset that the only choices are the ones we have thought of already. Actually, our consciousness can be expanded and our range of choices increased through meditation and the consequent raising of our vibration through spiritual practices. Einstein said: you cannot solve problems at the level of consciousness that created them. This holds true in relationships as well as other parts of life. We can raise our vibration and find a win-win outcome, which can be done if both parties are committed to doing so and can trust each other to follow the process to its conclusion. Vibration is such an important relationship concept that it has its own chapter below.

Some people like conflict. It is a delicious adrenalin rush for some people. They will manufacture differences of opinion just so they can get upset about something. You say A they say B. But if you said B then they would say A, just to be disagreeable. Conflict can be generated so as to provide a dumping ground for feelings of aggression and anger. This is an example of a toxic relationship.

Sometimes as a lawyer I saw parties disagree who were really just wanting to be in conflict. There were obvious solutions to the difference of opinion, but due to the conflict, neither party would back down. I remember going to the Family court because neither party would settle a multi-million dollar divorce dispute because both of them wanted the wagon wheels in the front garden! The resulting delays and lawyers' bills would have been enough to purchase hundreds of old wagon wheels, but neither side would back down.

Conversely, some people can be so frightened of conflict that they never share their real feelings and thoughts in a relationship. In effect, they end up living a lie. They just go along with what their beloved wants them to do, seemingly happy but withering inside. Eventually something will happen to bring this situation to a head, but it might take years of suffering before that happens.

Lack of authenticity can be a function of people-pleasing, something that often starts in the honeymoon phase of the relationship and then just carries on. The person who does the pleasing is not authentic, but fears conflict so much that they end up living the life the other person wants to live, sacrificing their own desires and dreams to support that of their partner. In many cases this avoidance of conflict and living an inauthentic life leads to internal issues that can affect emotional functioning, and even our health. The energy of the relationship is undermined.

Interestingly, during or after conflict both parties sometimes have an identical complaint against each other, and both see each other as aggressive and unreasonable, or cold and disinterested. What we give out we get back.

This third stage of relationship is where things get serious. It is where relationships may fling apart, or where we might go into avoidance and get inauthentic. It is where our skills or lack of them can mean the difference between escalating a small disagreement into world war three or clearing potential conflict quickly.

Do I know you?

You don't really know a person until you have disagreed with them. The unrefined or unskilful person goes straight into blame, accusation and seeks to control the behaviour of the other person. They intensify the situation by lack of skilfulness, use heavy and controlling language, threaten, get sanctimonious, bring up all kinds of unrelated issues or make personal attacks in order to 'win'. This may occur as an aggressive interaction, (verbally or even physically) or it may be a passive attack by which they seek to undermine and frustrate you over a period of time. Passive aggression is just as destructive and egoic as the more direct type of aggression, and the victim is just as dysfunctional as the aggressor! Getting out of these roles and unhelpful learned behaviours is part of the joy of becoming empowered in relationships.

The quality of the disagreement is a good indication of the spiritual realisation and emotional intelligence of the people concerned. The more spiritually realised a person becomes, the more able they are to be skilful in all of the phases of relationship. They might experience conflict, but they can hose it down instead of fuelling it. They can return their hearts and minds to peace and love very quickly and avoid slipping into blame, whereas the less spiritually realised person may hold grudges and resentments for years or even lifetimes.

Conflict Phase Tools for Self Empowerment

1. Rules of Combat

When we are in the conflict stage of relating, it is important that we have a framework in which to operate. It would be ideal if you could discuss a possible framework with your beloved when you are getting on well and seek to stick to it.

Disagreement is much more productive and will create traction in your relationships if it can proceed with some rules in place. For instance, there could be rules such as:

- Neither of you bring up former disagreements when discussing a present one.
- That you do not break things, throw things or hit things (including each other) during the discussion.
- Neither will walk out.
- Each person can speak for several minutes without interruption, and then listen while the other responds.
- You will not name call, or bring other peoples opinions into it.

Such rules as these lead to civilised disagreements where both people can say what they mean and hear what the other point of view might be.

It is a good idea to take time out before resuming the discussion to allow both parties time and space to think over the other persons view, then come to a decision if possible which both will stick to.

When agreements can be adhered to or at least consciously renegotiated, progress can be made. Without the capacity to make progress on issues that arise in relationships, the feeling becomes one of being trapped, frustrated, powerless and hopeless.

It can be good to formulate rules when things are going well rather than trying to do it during a conflict!

2. Communication Style

Our communication style alone can be a major source of conflict. How to communicate is not taught at school and we only learn it from our families and early influences. Often the very kinds of communication styles that we abhor as kids are the very ones that we ourselves use when we are under pressure in later life. In Part 5 we will look at how to communicate and what to avoid so as to keep conflict to a minimum.

3. Self-esteem

Our ability to disagree and remain empowered and at peace is fundamentally affected by our level of self-esteem. If we do not accept, respect, love and trust ourselves, we will be more likely to disrespect, distrust, reject and judge others. We actually pull from others a reciprocal lack of acceptance, respect, love and trust. Miracles happen in relationships just by adjusting our own levels of self-love and respect. The entire Path of Ease and Grace[1] and all of the training given in Shanti Mission[2] is designed to help people to have more self-esteem. The ultimate in self-esteem is to understand that we are souls having human

---

[1] The Path of Ease and Grace is a series of seminars in which the teachings of Shakti Durga are shared by Her senior disciples (all highly trained teachers) in an experiential and multi-dimensional way.

[2] Shanti Mission Harmony Centres Ltd, founded by Shakti Durga and her life partner Shiva Kata Tjuta (Hugh Keller) is a visionary organisation dedicated to peace. The Harmony Centres are educational institutions where spiritual training and empowerment seminars are conducted by donation.

experiences, and that we are Divine children of God. The realisation of that goes a long way to raising our self-esteem and helping us to live in accordance with the laws of the spirit.

4. Power Games

Conflict thrives in an environment of power games. Bickering is an expression of power games being played between people. When we find ourselves arguing over the right way to make a salad dressing, we are wise to understand we are playing a power game. Who cares? We will look more closely at power games in chapter 21. Power games are a way of taking the energy of the situation and controlling it.

5. Control Issues

Someone who lives in fear will try to control the behaviour of others so as to minimise their own exposure to pain. This is a person who is over responsible for others and who is not willing to allow others to grow. Such a person is often a controlling parent or spouse, and will become vehement and unreasonable if you want to do something that they do not agree with. Learning to flow and trust is an important relationship skill, which we will look at in the section on parenting the inner child as well as in the section on the drama triad.

6. Assertiveness

For intimacy to develop we have to be authentic with each other. Often we are scared of saying something because we worry about upsetting the other person or that what we say will come out wrong, or we will be judged. Assertiveness is the resting place between passivity, and aggression, both of which are destructive to intimacy. Learning how to cultivate assertiveness is an important skill for a peacemaker and is dealt with in chapter 24.

7. Need to be Right

A person with poor self-esteem is not game to make a mistake. Their personal assessment of self is already so low that a mistake would lead to feelings of guilt and shame. They will argue that black is white so as to avoid the inescapable conclusion that they might be wrong about something.

The need to be right is fuel for conflict. Who is right is neither here nor there, because everyone lives in their own universe. I once heard a married couple arguing about whether or not they had enjoyed their recent vacation: one said they had and the other said they hadn't. He accused her of lying about it! What motive would she have for lying about whether or not she had enjoyed her holiday? This was simply an example of different people having different experiences of the same set of facts. Each was describing their *consciousness* rather than what actually transpired, and that is usually the case.

A great game to play is to decide that whatever your partner says, for three days you will agree that they are right. No matter what. See what happens. It takes the wind out of loads of disputes and will alter the dynamics of your own perception and thus of your relationship. Naturally, if there is a hugely important issue that needs further discussion, ask whether you can defer that discussion until a few days so you can think about it (and finish this exercise).

8. Consciousness

Someone with limited consciousness will see that there is only one way to do things and that is their own way. As they grow in multi-dimensional awareness they will see that there are a multitude of correct courses of action, each of which has a different colour and flavour. Learning to expand our consciousness requires that we break out of the limiting beliefs that have been programmed into us. You will learn more about this later, but also see my other books *Child of God* and *Dimensions of Wealth*, which have substantial information as to how to change the way that you think, so as to be more skilful and successful in your life.

9. Needs being Unmet

Conflict occurs when people fear that their needs are not being met. All kinds of crazy behaviour will then ensue as they seek by any means to get other people to meet their needs. Many get controlling as they do not know any better way than forcing the beloved to meet their needs, rather than learning skills through which they can meet more of their own needs. Later, when we look at the Inner Child and Parent paradigm, we will look at certain key basic human needs, and some tools to learn how to more effectively meet our own needs, by parenting our own inner child.

10. The Energy Factor

When conflict arises in our life, we can learn to dissolve it. We can use energy healing techniques to free ourselves from chakral congestion and imbalance. We also show you how to get the anger out of the system.

Anger, like any emotion is just energy, and we can learn to be effective managers of this energy. Combined with forgiveness exercises, this is a great way to bring harmony and raise the vibration of your situation. In the workbook we will be learning how to clean out the aura, meridians of energy and the chakras, which are where our relationship patterns are held.

11. The Soul Factor

At the end of the day if we are coming from our ego or lower nature, we will be more aggressive, territorial, selfish and demanding than if we are anchored in the soul of our being. Learning to appreciate and utilise the vast gift of grace that is our soul is the essence of how we can manage our lives, our conflicts, and our relationships in a way that promotes inner and outer peace, wellbeing, happiness and love.

12. The Mirror

Through the lens of the higher soul, all of life is just an amazing interactive mirror through which certain 'seeds' within the soul play out as interactions with other souls. These create circumstances that lead us to learn, grow, balance our karma and become more enlightened. How this mirroring process works is described below in chapter 26.

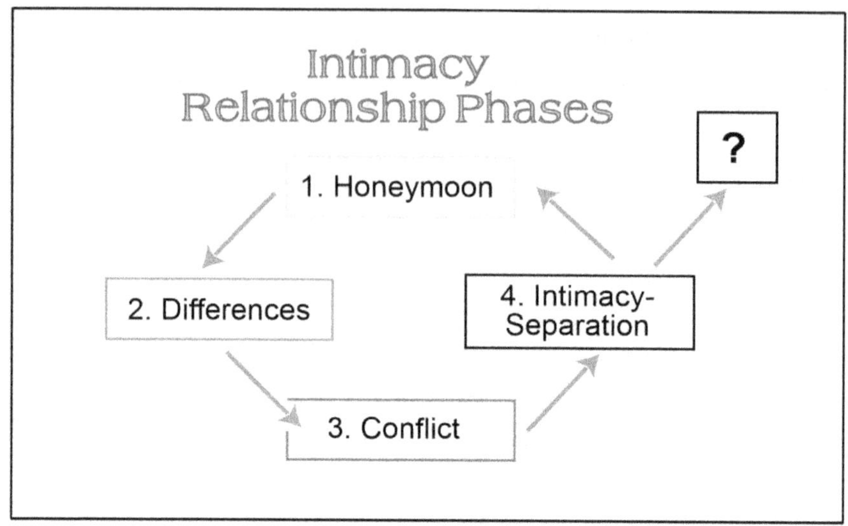

Phase Four: Separation or Golden Afterglow

The way that we handle dispute and conflict has a direct bearing on what the long-term prospects of the relationship will be. There are three possible scenarios.

The first option is that the parties separate or divorce. Failing to handle conflict within a relationship means it will eventually spill over into the difficult transition period of separation or divorce. All of the unresolved hurts as well as grief, fear and anxiety fuels a volatile divorce environment. There is often a strong fear of loss in which neither party is very stable, grounded or centered. Because of this the parties are not able to think or function at their best. Communication is often done through the lens of pain and fear, or breaks down altogether and is only conducted through the lawyers.

The unresolved conflict which brought the marriage to an end fuels further conflict and additional dispute as each party seeks to control the outcome and defend themselves against the other person who they often come to see as the person in the wrong. Tolerance and grace and even manners disappear as verbal and emotional blows are traded.

The second outcome is that the conflict is swept under the carpet and is not really dealt with at all. This exists as a nail in the coffin of a close and loving, empowered relationship. Nevertheless, the relation-*ship* still floats, but it has been damaged. There is a reserve in the relationship that can deaden closeness and cause each party to be wary of the other. This will undermine both intimacy and sexual energy in the relationship. While the relationship is still there in form, people may start to drift apart. They lead more separate lives, skirt around difficult subjects, avoid certain areas all together, and end up with a lot of stuck energy and buried frustration.

If conflict is resolved cleanly and thoroughly, this heralds a deeper connection of comfort, trust, friendship and connection. Couples (or friends) who can effectively disagree are in a strong position to be truly themselves, and know that they can assert their own views in a safe environment. They are able to build up trust and thus open to deeper intimacy.

This scenario, which can arise from conflict has the effect of clearing the air, adding to our understanding of each other, and bringing us even closer together than we were before the conflict occurred. This is the desired outcome from conflict. Here we have met a part of self and of our beloved that we have never known about or accepted before. If the conflict is thoroughly healed, the relationship will spiral back to phase one, the honeymoon phase, and the cycle will start again.

'*Parampara*' develops between people who are in a long-term intimate relationship. Parampara is a Sanskrit word for the state of likeness that occurs between people who are devoted to each other. It is often associated with the way that a disciple will resemble their guru, but it is also evident in the way that couples that are very happy together can start to look like each other. Even if they physically don't look the same there is something about them that makes them look like they are a couple. That develops through unity. If you can achieve that in relationships then you are doing well.

Cycling through Phases

If we can come through conflict cleanly, then we spiral back into the honeymoon phase again where everything is once more beautiful and full of magic. There is more energy and potency in the relationship even than there was at the beginning, the sex is fantastic and everything seems amazing. This is a truly golden phase.

Over a period of time, these four phases of honeymoon, individual differences, conflict and golden after-glow are repeated again and again. At different times more energy is found in stage one or two and at others, stage three needs to be dealt with again. This leads to stage four, which tends to lead back to stage one.

Everyday there are high tides and low tides at the beach. Intimacy has its own tides as well. The tide comes in and everything is rosy. We are together and intimate, connecting and coming closer. Then the tide goes out. We once more seek our own individuality and to lead our own life. That which is not already sorted out arises so we can move past more of our fears and blind spots, and bring more of our self into consciousness. There is a clearing of the air and deeper understanding. The tide turns and once again we engage in intimacy as love grows.

PART

2

WHAT IS
ON YOUR MIND?

Chapter

4

MY RELATIONSHIP THOUGHTS

Some of what happens in relationships is physical. But much of what happens in relationships takes place within our minds. The quality of our thoughts and how we utilise our minds can have a large bearing on our success or otherwise in relationships.

Right now we are going to search within our minds for help in understanding our actions, motivations and drives in relationships. This first written exercise is a good starting place: to get the most from the subsequent pages please answer these questions before proceeding further into Empowering Relationships. It is important to assess what we have already created, before we go on to create something better. Knowing what we like and what we dislike about relationships lets us know where we may benefit from making some changes.

1. What comes into my head when I think about relationships?

2. What does my reality look like in this area?

3. What are the good bits?

4. What are the frustrating bits?

5. How important is it for me to experience something different in the field of relationships?

6. Am I prepared to step outside my comfort zone and try something new?

7. What do I *want* to experience in my most important relationships that I don't experience right now.

8. Do I believe that is possible? (Yes / No)

9. What might I have to do or be to experience what I *want* to experience?

Chapter

5

CONTRACTS OF EXPECTATION AND CORE BELIEFS

When it comes to relationships or any other part of life, we are preprogrammed by our upbringing to have certain beliefs and expectations about how things will be. Many of the things that affect us in relationships are so deeply held within us that we might even have difficulty identifying what the factors are. Each family has its own unwritten rules and expectations, and when we merge with another person in an intimate relationship, we are taking on not only them, but their conditioning. They, like us, will probably be a bit hazy about all that this entails.

Expectations, an Often Unconscious Problem

In the workplace, most people are hired pursuant to a written contract. That document is often nothing but a broad outline of what the job entails, and the more senior one becomes, the less detail is likely to be in the document about how to go about fulfilling ones contractual obligations, and meeting corporate objectives.

Some contracts of expectation are obvious because it is written in your job specification. Other expectations are more subtle, here is where the cultural aspect of the situation can come in. As a new recruit or new manager, you may only ever find out about the unwritten expectations of the group when you do something outside of them. This is interpreted as you having 'done the wrong thing'.

When we form relationships with others, whether at home or at work, there is no up-front written agreement! Certain expectations arise in terms of who will do what during the course of the relationship. Humans are creatures of habit. As soon as a pattern is established, both parties can take for granted that this is the way things are. It can bring up a lot of resistance if we try to bring about a change in the way things are done.

There is a natural tendency to assume things. Part of our assumption is that other people will do things the same way as we do. We assume that others will have the same kinds of expectations as us. Our relationship expectations are a function of our prior experiences. Our experiences can be as richly different as is Shakespearian poetry and a technical manual. To assume that other people will be the same as us, is just plain wrong. Not even two people brought up in the same house together have a matching set of expectations. The fact is, we are all different.

When we are in the beginning phase of a relationship, there is usually an attempt made on both sides to fit in. Both are trying to find common ground. While the search for oneness and the desire to merge continues, there is usually goodwill.

Our unwritten expectations are often not conscious in the beginning and we only find out about them when someone does something or reacts to a situation in a completely unexpected way. This can cause us to experience not only a clash of differing expectations, but an attempt, sometimes mutual, to get the other one to see things our way, not their way. When our expectations are not met, we can feel aggrieved. It can cause stress and conflict can arise.

A difference of opinion between two people can cause their invisible contracts of expectation to become more evident. Because we did not understand that the other person has an entirely different set of expectations, there can be total miscommunication and misunderstanding, which can become heated depending upon the level of emotional skilfulness of the individuals concerned.

Years ago people went into marriage with the belief that the woman would stay home and raise children and the man would support the family. It was not necessary to discuss it, as it was so obvious. Roles were rigidly defined. Now things are more complicated. We have many unspoken contracts of expectation, which are often not even conscious. We do not even realise that we have these until something happens that we didn't expect. This confusion can happen to anyone but is particularly noticeable for people who marry partners from different ethnic or racial backgrounds. The contracts of expectation vary greatly.

Imagine a marriage where one partner comes from a large family and therefore automatically expects that (s)he will have a large family. This is so obvious to that person that it is not even something worthy of discussion. Five years into the marriage the topic of beginning a family is raised and the other partner only wants to have one child, or none.

When it is then discussed each party may be shocked to hear the perspective of the other one, because they assumed that their own conditioning would automatically be what the other person would want as well.

When we are in the honeymoon phase of a relationship, we make lots of assumptions. It is only when we discuss things or when circumstances are upon us that we find that how much our views are different.

Our expectations can get us all tied up in knots. Lots of expectations about how things will be are based upon what we experienced as our 'reality' when we were kids. Roles and traditions get deeply ingrained within us.

Working Mum

Karen was raised in a family where mum stayed home. Karen is a career woman and thinks that she will always be so. When she has children she finds that much to her surprise she feels great guilt at working and she feels confused about her role. Conscious and unconscious forces may be at work here, the unconscious force telling her that she should not be working has been laid down during her formative childhood years. Her turmoil may be reflected back to her from her family or partner, making her situation even more difficult to penetrate. It may well look like others are putting pressure on her to stay home, when really they are just unconsciously mirroring back to her what is within her own internal landscape. The seed of this issue is within Karen's own being.

Karen really needs to get clear in her own mind what her choices might be. Separating herself out from her childhood experience and being in the now requires courage and a lot of clarity. She can cut cords to the past and get some IYS therapy to help move the stale energy. She can become aware of the deep veins of conditioning that sit within her. Through becoming more internally aware, she is able to make real changes in her own attitude. Instead of feeling conflicted, she can use spiritual tools such as affirmations to help her embed her considered choice more deeply in her consciousness. This will make her world of home and work much easier to manage. As she becomes more comfortable internally with her own choice, and her mind gets clear about it both consciously and unconsciously, she will find that others may become more supportive of her decision, even when they were not previously.

Growing up, Families, and their Impact on our Expectations

Our relationships with our parents and the relationship between our parents usually provide us with our first imprinting about relationships. From these, we are imprinted with what we can expect our own grown up relationships to be like. Whether these relationships were wholesome or troubled may have a profound effect upon the way in which the journey of our life unfolds. What are the roles of men and women? Can I trust people? How is conflict managed? How do I get what I want or need? What do I learn is my role in life? Am I the pleaser, the jester, the rebel, the 'can do' person, or the responsible one?

More assumptions and conditioning then gets fed into us in our relationships with our school friends, our teachers, other mentors, sports coaches, team mates, siblings and their friends, other relatives, grandparents and the people who live in the same community we do.

Relationship networks are highly complex. Two people who come from the same family may experience growing up in different ways. In our childhood, we learn to cope, assert ourselves, or withdraw, hide, and stay in the background. Patterns that develop early can have a big effect upon events that will unfold later. Different roles form within the family, and playing our role is often second nature not only during those formative years, but in later relationships as well. Even if we resented our role, we may find we reproduce it in adult relationships, as well as patterns of behaviour modelled by our parents. Even if we didn't like them and swore we would never be like that, we may have difficulty untangling ourselves from complex webs of early relationship patterning. This can be playing out decades later when we are all grown up (or even getting a bit wrinkly).

Taken for Granted

Expectations can continue to form during adult relationships. Things can get out of hand when one party continually tries to please another, and takes on more and more roles, tasks and responsibility. Whereas in the beginning it was intended as a one-off experience, it becomes commonplace for them do it and no-one says thank you. That which was previously given as an additional thing, is now expected from them and viewed as their job.

Terry

Terry was married to Jo, and used to buy her flowers every Friday night on the way home from work. After doing this for some months, he forgets to buy them, and she is disappointed because she expected him to give her flowers. Instead of a gift, it is a part of the contract now. By not doing it, he has 'done the wrong thing'. Jo feels unloved.

Habits are a doorway through which people take each other for granted. The bar can be raised in terms of performance, and there may be little or no appreciation shown for the effort required.

In the case of Terry and Jo, a person with relationship skills might choose to be grateful for all of the flowers they had already received and if they needed flowers, they could buy them themselves. If Jo had poor relationship skills she might feel unappreciated and even start to fantasise that Terry has found another woman because he stopped buying flowers. The scope for the mind to become a runaway train in relationships, taking something trivial and turning it into a drama, is very great.

Searching your Memory Banks

The exercise below is designed to help us become more conscious of our conditioning. We are going to look at our mum and our dad, and at our own experiences so far in relationships. If you were not raised by your biological mum or dad, then just focus upon the main male or female role model that you had growing up. Please answer these questions as fully as you can because you might be amazed at how patterns were instigated way back in the early years of your life.

Beliefs About Relationships

Learning From Female Role Model, Mother

How did Mum understand her position within her *society*, its limitations privileges and responsibilities?

What do I perceive Mum thought her role was in the *family*?

What were the advantages and disadvantages to her of her societal and family role?

What do I perceive that her personal limitations were?

What do I perceive that her personal strengths were?

What did I notice about my mother and how she dealt with being in a *marriage* or *intimate relationship*?

What *"commandments"* does it look like she lived by in a relationship?

Do I have the *same* beliefs as her in some areas? Which ones?

How did she *react under pressure* or when upset?

When under pressure, *do I react in a similar way* to how Mum would have reacted?

Learning From Male Role Model, Father

How did Dad understand his position within his *society*, its limitations, privileges and responsibilities?

What do I perceive Dad thought his role was in the *family*?

What were the advantages and disadvantages to him of his societal and family role?

What do I perceive that his *personal limitations* were?

What do I perceive that his *personal strengths* were?

What did I notice about my father and how he dealt with being in a *marriage* or *intimate relationship*?

What '*commandments*' does it look like he lived by when it came to being in a relationship?

Do I have the *same beliefs* as him in some areas? Which ones?

How did he *react under pressure* or when upset?

When under pressure, *do I react in a similar way* to how Dad would have reacted?

Learning from My Experiences so far in Relationships

How do I see my role in Society and the broader community?

How do I see my role in my family?

How do I see my role in relationships?

What commonly arise as problem patterns in my intimate relationships?

What commonly arise as benefits or positive patterns in my intimate relationships?

What have *partners* praised me for in relationships?

What have *partners* criticised me for in relationships? (you don't have to agree with the criticism, just note it)

What have *I learnt* from being in partnership, about myself and my relating skills?

What *now* are *my perceived strengths* in relationships? List 6 strengths you have to offer in relating.

What are *now my perceived areas of weakness* in relationships?

List 6 weaknesses or areas of challenge you have to offer in relating.

What *conscious* beliefs do I hold now about *relationships*?

Completing this exercise as thoughtfully as possible is often an eye opening experience. Many things that have been unconscious for us become more conscious and we can see how we have developed the kinds of expectations that we have of relationships.

Often recognising the patterns that we took on from our parents can be enough to start the process of release of those patterns if they are not serving us. Many things we regard as issues are just a result of our conditioning, and are neither right nor wrong and are about us and not others. This of itself is a great start for moving ahead in our relationships because it helps us to broaden our perspective and look at other possibilities.

Assessing my Expectations

Looking closely at the answers to the questions above about your mum, dad and your own relationships, can you see any imprinted expectations that might be playing out in your current (or most recent) relationship?

I realise that I expect my partner...
I realise that I expect myself....

When we get clear about some of the unconscious things that are driving us in relationships, we have a better chance of making changes. Often we will think it is our beloved who has strange beliefs, set ways and peculiar habits, but how long is it since we looked at our own? Truly, if an alien were to arrive on Earth and live with a hundred different families for a week at a time, it may come to the conclusion that we are all insane. Conventions are just that. They are not right or wrong. They are just what we are used to.

Chapter

6

AFFIRMING A
BETTER RELATIONSHIP

The physical world is, to a large extent, revealed to us in accordance with how we believe that it will be. This is particularly true in our relationships. Our thinking is not done in the physical world, it is done in the powerful astral world. Most of the time, most people think about the way things are, and form judgments about it. To some degree, thinking about what has already manifested is a waste of the immense power that our astral bodies have. The astral field is where things are created as thoughts first, before they spill over into the 'reality' of the physical world.

If we are having problems in our relationships, particularly if they are significant or heated issues, then it is quite difficult for most people to refrain from thinking about it. We actually get caught in an astral thought loop through which it can become difficult to think of anything else!

For those who have spiritual training in mental purification and discipline, there is another option. Instead of thinking about what is (particularly if we do not like it) we start the creative wheels in motion by thinking of what 'could be.'

The more we think about a thing,
the more likely it is to manifest.

When we think about our problems,
we help solidify them in place.

When we think instead of solutions,
we start to create a way forward.

Sometimes people say to me: is it not avoiding reality to train your mind to think of what you want instead of about what is happening to you? My response is: I am not asking you to lose touch with reality. I am not asking that you become ungrounded and delusional. One must be aware of the physical dimension of our life. However, one has the capacity to be a creator being. When we use our minds as mere sense organs, just giving us stimuli as to what is going on in our world, we miss the whole point of having a mind in the first place. The point of a mind is that it is an instrument of action and creation. As well as being able to help keep you in touch with your physical surroundings, the mind can be employed to create new circumstances.

The things that we are programmed to think and expect may or may not support us in having a really great relationship. One simple tool that can be surprisingly helpful to change this is the use of affirmation.

An affirmation is a positive statement repeated over and over again. It is a clear phrase or sentence, which affirms the opposite of what our usual limiting or negative thought might be. It is conscious self-talk that affirms what we *want* to think rather than what we are *already* thinking. The point of using affirmations is to retrain the way our brain thinks. Thoughts affect our reality. Therefore, a well-designed affirmation that is used regularly is likely to bring change to our lives.

The best affirmations are those which turn your negative thoughts upside down as you affirm the exact opposite of your previous idea about things. If you think people are unreliable, you affirm that people are reliable. If you think it is hard to get respect then affirm how easy it is. If you think you your partner doesn't understand you, affirm that s/he does. When we say positive things like "I am successful and loveable" we raise our vibration. The higher our vibration, the easier creating positive change becomes.

If something is not broken we should not try to fix it. You do not need to use affirmations in areas where you are already content with yourself or your life. Affirmations are best employed as a tool to change our experience in some area where we feel discontented or that we could achieve more and would like to do so.

A well designed affirmation is one that directly addresses the root cause of our lack or perceived inadequacy. A good affirmation is "I have a fabulous relationship that gets better every week". If you are someone who often thinks that they are not as good as other people, then a better affirmation might be "I am worthy of a fabulous relationship that gets better every week". Putting the concept of worth in there not only deals with the outcome you want, which is a fabulous relationship, it also deals with the problem that may well underlie your lack of relationship: the thought that you don't deserve it.

No Idle Thoughts

It should be remembered that we are thinking thoughts constantly. There is no point diligently repeating our affirmations for 10 minutes per day, if for the other 23 hours and 50 minutes, we are thinking thoughts that are our old pattern. This cancels out our 10 minutes of practice, and throws us way back into our old life experience.

I have used affirmations to great effect in my life and continue to use them in any areas where I find that my reality is falling short of my preferred life experience. The more we use them, the easier and more effective they are at creating change.

When working with affirmations, it pays to find out what your brain is really getting up to when you are not paying attention to it. Every thought creates, and serves either to reinforce or break down a core belief. It is a useful and interesting exercise to set a phone or wrist watch alarm to go off every 15 minutes for 3 days to record what we are thinking when it rings. This gives fascinating feedback about what our thoughts are doing when we would not normally be actually listening to them.

Every Thought is a Prayer

Prayer is a powerful way to affect your reality. It is a conversation with the Divine. Every prayer is heard and the universe goes straight into the mode of answering your prayer. The problem is that prayer happens not only when you kneel down in a church to pray. Prayer is happening constantly. *Every thought is a prayer.* Every thought you think is heard by the Divinely conscious universe in which we reside, and so you are in effect praying for the things you are thinking about.

The angelic beings who serve us by bringing to us what we pray for, do not distinguish between the praying-on-your-knees prayers and your ordinary thoughts. They regard you as Holy, and as a creator being that they are there to serve. While no one is perfect in the thought department, it is quite important if you want to live a life of ease and grace that you stop thinking garbage.

The good news is that thoughts of a high vibration are much more powerful than thoughts of a low vibration. Whenever you catch yourself thinking rubbish, you can erase it, a skill which is taught in our *Yoga of the Mind* seminar. This will have the effect of using energy from your soul to rub out your astral (mental and emotional) mess. Then you use an affirmation to put in place what you actually want to experience. With a bit of practice this approach becomes second nature.

A Safe Place to Park your Brain

Have you ever noticed that when you get into certain challenging situations, or when certain people treat you rudely, you go into a really negative tailspin of anger and negative thinking? You try to fall asleep at night, but your mind has a terrier-like grip on the negative situation and will not stop thinking about it? This can happen if we have an argument with our beloved. When we are trying to consciously change our relationship reality, this issue needs special attention.

One of the best things I ever discovered is that if you use a really good affirmation often enough, it starts to play by itself in your head. You will just be thinking of nothing in particular and suddenly in your head is the thought, "I am so loved, valued and appreciated". This is exciting! It means your mind is beginning to act like an *instrument of creation* instead of a bolting horse or instrument of destruction.

By creating a 'safe place to park your brain' when you are in a good space, you can then have a really valuable tool to help you through difficult times. When you wake up in the night worried about a situation, just make your brain focus on the affirmation that you have practiced so often. Every time it wanders off, just bring it back to the affirmation and give yourself permission to fall asleep again, knowing that you are doing all that you can in that moment to change your reality, not keep rehashing the old one.

The more you can really identify the underlying cause of a relationship issue, the more effective an affirmation in relation to it will be. Effective relationship affirmations might include:

I am loved, honoured and valued in all of my relationships.

*I accept caring and nurturing as a normal part of my life
because I deserve it.*

My partner is loving, committed, intimate and charming.

I am safe, valued and it is easy for me to be myself in my relationships.

I deserve to have a magnificent relationship in my life now.

My relationships are fulfilling, fun and fabulous.

*I have a partner who matches me physically, mentally, emotionally and
spiritually and I am so blessed.*

My relationships get better every day.

*I accept, respect, love and trust myself and my partner accepts,
respects, loves and trusts me too.*

I deserve love, and I am so happy to have an amazing relationship now.

By consistent use of an affirmation, you create deep furrows in your brain that thoughts just automatically want to think. Our biology supports habit. To change habit requires that we be deliberate for a while with our thinking. By doing this you can create a safe place to park your brain so that it doesn't go off like popcorn the first time you are faced with adversity or challenges. Keep it steady. Make it go into a familiar pattern of thought. Instead of thinking about how much a person peeves you, think, "Isn't it wonderful that I am so respected and loved and my life flows with ease and grace".

In the Empowering Relationships workbook you have the opportunity to create more relationship affirmations that are more tailored to your own circumstances. What you discovered about yourself when you looked at your family of origin and how they did things may inform some very potent affirmations designed to help bring in a new reality for you.

As an aside, one of the most helpful things a Guru can do for a disciple is to hold a high vision of them. Parents often do this for their children as well. By holding a high vision of the disciple, the Guru helps them to manifest their dreams.

The key to mastery in relationships is to understand that relationships are taking place more in the Astral, Etheric and Soul realms than in the Physical realm. If we only look in the world of results, the physical dimension, how are we going to understand the unseen roots of causation in our life?

Interplay of Thoughts and Emotions

In the next chapter we are going to look at emotions. Before we do, it is worth considering the relationship that exists between these two factors in creation, which are thought and emotion.

A thought, when viewed clairvoyantly, is a container of energy, which resembles a particular shape. In order for it to manifest into the physical world, it has to be filled with energy. The energy with which most people fill their thoughts is the energy of emotion.

Whatever emotion we feel when we are creating a particular thought will be the dominant emotion that fills it. When we are experiencing that thing on Earth when it manifests, we will feel happy about it, or disappointed about it or angry or whatever, depending upon what quality or vibration of energy went into its creation when it was still within the inner world of formation.

An even more potent method of working with the mind is to learn to rub out old dysfunctional thoughts or thoughts that were filled with a low vibrational emotion. Then, we can energise new brighter ones into our consciousness. How to do this is taught in *Yoga of the Mind* and you can read about that in my *Child of God* book.

I have found that it has been important over the years to keep coming back to watching my thoughts about relationships. The more empowered I become, the more care I feel that I need to take with the way I hold my thoughts about people.

When we dissolve thoughts, we are setting free the emotional energy that sits within them. This helps us to feel lighter and clearer, and sets us free to take a fresh look at ourselves and our lives. The effect can be miraculous, particularly in the arena of relating.

PART

3

EMOTIONS AND THEIR MANAGEMENT

Chapter

7

EMOTION AND RELATIONSHIP CHALLENGES

When it comes to relationships there are so many issues and situations to manage that sometimes one could wonder why it is that we bother in the first place. Over the years we have had thousands of people through our relationship seminars and at a point where we ask: "What are the main challenges in relationships?"

The answers include:

- Not feeling respected
- Feeling undervalued
- Feeling overly responsible for others
- Feeling inadequate, rescuing
- Control issues
- Criticism, vilification
- Neediness, (their own or other people's)
- Co-dependence

- Difficulty speaking our truth and being authentic
- Loss of self-identity
- Abandonment
- Distrust
- Manipulation
- Others acting out
- People-pleasing
- Betrayal
- Rejection
- Addiction
- Arrogance
- Low self-esteem
- Rejection
- Fear of intimacy
- Fear (of a large range of things)
- Coldness t Judgment t Guilt t Defensiveness
- Denial
- Suppression of emotions
- Resentment
- Martyrdom
- Fear of conflict
- Blame
- Avoidance of challenges
- Subservience
- Expectations
- Loss of identity
- Loss of freedom
- Need to be right
- Possessiveness
- Violence

All of this creates an emotional soup that can be challenging and confusing to deal with. Few of us have had great role-models of remaining empowered in relationships when we experience any of these things. Most of us have our own stuff to deal with, let alone having to deal with all our partner's unresolved issues as well.

In my grandmother's day, a way of coping was simply not to talk about things, to have a stiff upper lip, and to just 'get on with it'. Untold sorrow was masked and hidden under a veil of secrecy. Emotions were by and large suppressed. Time has shown that this is unhealthy, and now we are trying to address our emotional issues through diverse means which include books, self-help classes, psychotherapy, medication, self-medication and so on.

Most people even today are not very good at emotions, and either avoid them by engaging in strategies which deflect them, such as being too busy for them. Or, they suppress them, which can affect our health and wellbeing as well as our levels of vitality. Often they blame others for the way they are feeling: "I feel like this because of something you did." The other game that is played is projecting how we are feeling onto another person and believing that it is them who has this feeling, not us.

By far one of the most difficult parts of relationships is taking personal responsibility for how we are feeling. Being skilful in action and in conversation, even when we are feeling strong emotion is a core relationship skill. Parenting the inner child is a clear and workable paradigm in which we can find support and derive better understanding of what is going on and how to deal with it.

Working out what is ours and what is theirs, and finding real, authentic methods to deal with difficult situations in relationships has been a 25 year obsession of mine! Having been married and then divorced twice I am happy to say that I enjoy a 12 year relationship (as of 2012) with Shiva Kata

Tjuta which continues to grow in intimacy and love. The tools in this book are ones that I have used to turn my own relationship patterns around and to be empowered in relationships. One of the best and most useful, practical methods I have ever come across for dealing with emotions is the art of self-parenting. Before diving into that topic, let's just consider for a moment from a multi-dimensional perspective precisely what emotions are, and then see what our own emotional patterns might be.

Emotions

Emotions are forms of energy. They exist in an endless sea, flowing not only from us, but to us from the planets of our solar system, from people, from animals, and so on. They exist on a kind of scale that ranges from very refined and beautiful emotions that we enjoy feeling, such as love, peace, bliss. On the other end of the scale are some very dense and unpleasant emotions that are not fun to experience such as guilt, shame and blame.

In the Divine dimension of our being there are no emotions, there is just constant ecstasy. This is impersonal in that here there is no preference for any particular person, philosophy or event, as they all emanated long ago from here. The bliss remains in place no matter what happens, no matter what we might think, say or do. World wars do not change the peace and stillness of this dimension. It just is. It contains no thoughts at all but is an endless sea of awareness and potency. Because of the lack of any form of recognisable emotion, or conditioned emotional response, and the lack of co-dependence, favouritism or preference, one could say from the perspective of the ego that this is a cold realm. And yet it contains everything, is the source of everything, and is blissful, still and empty.

In the Soul dimension emotions are all expressed in their blazing glory, in a way that is unified and constant. Love, Joy, Happiness, Peace, Bliss and Contentment for example, are always just that. At the dimension of our soul, we too can have these feelings as our bedrock, helping us to define who we are and stretch into a magnificent golden age of tranquillity and grace. We can reach into and through this realm by meditation, prayer, and listening to the quiet voice of the Divine that issues forth through our soul rather than through our minds.

In the Astral and Physical dimensions we have the inescapable law of polarity to deal with. The law of polarity says that everything must have its opposite. In the physical dimension, summer must have winter, day needs night, up needs down and thin needs fat in order to exist. In the Astral dimension every theory developed generates an opposing theory, somewhere, somehow. Just look at the literature telling us what we ought to eat! Every opinion will generate someone who disagrees with it.

In the Astral world, every emotion has an opposite. Whereas in the Soul dimension we experience love, joy, happiness, peace, bliss and contentment, in the Astral dimension these flow through as having a bright and dull end of their own spectrum. The bright end of the emotional spectrum of contentment is contentment. The dull end is discontent. Bliss generates agony when it is turned right down in volume. Peace in its relative absence creates animosity/anxiety, happiness gives rise to sadness, joy creates sorrow and love creates hatred or fear as it drops from the soul dimension into the Astral and Physical dimensions. Whilst ever we have one end, we have the other as well, somewhere in the world.

Having said that, our own thoughts, words actions and karma will determine where on the spectrums we exist and experience our lives. Usually we go up and down, and experience a large range of emotions over time, and even during a single day. As Buddha said, life is suffering, and he found a way through that to the soul dimension where the suffering did not exist. He then left a pathway through his teachings for others to find that same place. Other great souls from many traditions have done this too.

In our school we believe that although every life must have its share of suffering, we are capable of becoming skilled in how to live our lives through a multi-dimensional focus. With skilfulness, even serious problems can be diminished. Without skilfulness, small problems become big ones on account of the way we handle them and the energy that we ourselves feed into them.

Because of spiritual skilfulness, we are capable of creating a life that is filled with as much ease and grace as possible. Relationships are the perfect laboratory to learn about ourselves, and the multi-dimensional world we live in. We are Divine Souls here on Earth having a human educational experience called life. When we learn the rules of the game and play by them, all kinds of great things start to emerge – even out of situations that looked really grim.

While we are embodied we are always going to experience the astral field because it is the dimension in which we think. Thus, we are always going to be challenged by both ends of the emotional spectrum in our lives. The thing is, how are we going to handle it?

In the moment it might be accurate to say, "The reason I am angry is because you never help with the washing up". It looks as though there is an external reason for my distress. However, what has really happened is that an event has occurred which I am astrally programmed to respond to in a certain way. I might be programmed to feel for example anger, or blame in that situation. Yet there is a deeper level of truth that we can access.

We have the capacity to choose emotional responses to a whole range of stimuli. Most often we stick to a predictably small bandwidth of emotional responses, such as, if you forget to put out the garbage I am going to feel frustrated and angry. Such responses are a result of our programming, not an inescapable reality. What people say and what they do *seems* as though it affects us emotionally. Actually what is happening is that one of our belief systems is being triggered. Our belief might be "I will know I am respected if I have help with the household duties". Thus, if you don't help me with the washing up, or put out the garbage, I will feel disrespected and it is that rather than the washing up that causes me to be upset.

Any event itself is emotionally neutral and emotions are event neutral.

Our belief system creates a habitual emotional response that is only ever changed if we decide consciously to change either ourselves, or our beliefs.

While my feeling response to not being helped with the washing up might be resentment, another person might feel gratitude and joy that they just had a meal to eat. Our expectations and assumptions are once again at play, bringing forth various emotional responses, which we usually lay at the feet of others and say, "You made me feel like this!"

When we learn to parent our inner child, we can learn to respect ourselves and become more considered about our emotional responses. This is a process, and like a spiral will go round and round, producing scenarios in which we get to see if we have really done it yet. Over time we will notice that our response is changing, that we are able to nurture, comfort and respect ourselves as an internal reality in any situation. Because our internal landscape changes, the response that we pull from others will change as well. They will start to respect us, even though nothing different may have happened in the physical world. Astrally, things are going to be different because we are learning some better skills in dealing with our feelings. Before you know it your beloved is offering to do the chores and you will not need to remind them! Even when they occasionally forget, you can choose to feel gratitude for all the time they remembered instead of anger at this little piece of imperfection. The game is done, you have learned self-respect and now life is different.

The art of self-parenting is a means by which we can learn to accept, respect, love and trust ourselves. Then, if another person does or does not do something we are expecting, we do not have to feel that a basic human need of ours is not being met. We can provide our own acceptance, respect and so on. We are not co-dependent upon another person to meet that need, or to feel validated. Learning what our needs actually are and how to meet them will change your life, help with emotions and improve all of your relationships.

Emotions are powerful and can be overwhelming. That is no doubt why there is a cultural tendency to suppress emotions, or to avoid them, or to blame others when we feel emotions we do not like. This pattern of trying to control or disown emotions can actually reinforce experiences of anxiety and depression as well as depleting our flow of energy. Even worse, bad emotional patterns make relating hell on roller skates!

In the workbook you have the opportunity to do an emotional self-assessment, to see just where you are currently at in the field of emotions. Later when we look at the self-parenting model we will come back and use the information you have just recorded in the workbook, to complete another exercise. It does not matter what your answers are, or how much or little skill you feel you have in this area. We can all learn and grow. The most important thing is to decide that now is the time to do so.

Chapter

8

FEELINGS AS MESSENGERS

When we are fully in touch with our emotions, we have access to a lot of information about the world in which we live than we do when we are not in touch with our emotions. Emotional literacy allows us to expand our range of perception. While it might be strange and even feel a bit threatening to begin with, learning to feel and respond to emotion as a valued part of life will help us live with more ease and grace. Even with difficult emotions, we can learn to respond to them positively and skilfully.

It is normal and natural to feel and experience the full range of emotions and this is part of the human condition. Many times, however, our gender, cultural background, or childhood conditioning interferes with the process of our emotional literacy. The term, 'emotional intelligence' means having access to and the ability to accurately read, this full range of emotions. It also means being able to either ask for, or put in place ourselves, appropriate responses for the emotions we are feeling, that will help us to return to a happy, stable place.

Our feelings are very good messengers, or signals, that all is well or that something is not right, or that something is required for us to return to a state of equilibrium. That something may be external to us, or it may be internal, within us. Often it is both.

We cannot make much headway with all this if we do not understand what it is that our feelings are trying to convey. When we misread our feelings, we might not put in place what we need, and we might also send out a misleading message to others about our emotional state. We are then unlikely to have others respond to our needs in a way that is other than what we may need.

There are some parts of life that are so complex and so unable to be dealt with using pure reason, that we cannot hope to rely upon it for optimal results. Luckily we have been given another tool with which to progress. This is our feelings, which are the seat of our intuition and inner guidance system.

Our feelings help us handle all kinds of things. Whether or not we should be in a relationship with another person comes down in the end to how we feel about it. You could tick all the list of things that you want in a partner, and still there would be something missing. There is a 'nothing' where there should be a 'something'. The feelings are not there. The heart is not engaged.

Feelings also help us to know where we stand in times of conflict and stressful situations.

Change, transition and being in a situation where there is no precedent to help us, when we don't know the terrain and we are not sure how to proceed: this is another time when there are definitely advantages to listening to our gut response, or to put that in other words, we need to assess how we feel about it.

Becoming More Emotionally Literate

Becoming fully emotionally literate is a good ambition, because it will help us know ourselves, understand our various competing inner drives, get a handle on things and then, to communicate clearly and appropriately to others. When we are free of dysfunctional family and gender messages, we are able to appropriately express all of our feelings and find ways of getting what we need. Then we do not have to live in fear of the full expression of feelings, whether ours or other peoples.

In our relationships and in life generally, we need to be able to trust and engage, with all of the emotional states we encounter within ourselves, and be confident responding to the emotional states of others. We especially want to engage the playful, fun-loving, spontaneous, creative, and joyful parts of ourselves, which are part of the 'child' persona which we will be looking at shortly. The child part of you will dare to see things in new ways, be open to new ideas, and spontaneously connect to the awe inspiring beauty of sound, colour, movement, words, or ideas. When (s)he is closed down under a burden of unexpressed feelings, this connection is hard if not impossible to do.

Four Families of Feelings

In modern counselling, one sometimes speaks of there being four families of feelings. The following table shows the Four Families of Feelings and the corresponding needs. You will notice that the family of 'Glad' feelings also includes joyful, peaceful and powerful. Glad is a much larger family than the other three, and ideally we want to spend more time there. This is how it feels to the soul all the time. This is the way the Universe is configured in dimensions beyond the physical one we inhabit, and the astral one in which we do our thinking. When we can transcend our own Astral Maya we find beauty and all of the peace, power and joy that Glad entails.

Our feelings are very good messengers or signals, that something is required for us to return to a state of equilibrium (Glad). So, if we misread our feelings, we might not put in place what we need, and we might also send out a misleading message to others about our emotional state. We are then unlikely to have others respond to our needs in the way we need or want.

Glad	Sad
Happy, cheerful, light hearted, content, joyful, peaceful, powerful,	Gloomy, sombre, grief, melancholy, down, ambivalent, apathetic, despairing, pity,
faith, hope, courage, compassion,	hopelessness, overwhelmed, pressured, lost, helpless, inadequate
contentment, calmness, peace, freedom, fun, gentleness,	**'I am experiencing or anticipating loss.**

gratitude, confidence, self-love, self-motivation, drive, tenacity, perseverance, flexibility, security, sensitivity, openness, success, sympathy, clarity, grounded, warmth, ease, time, relaxation, self awareness, sensuality, intelligence, reason, respect, acceptance of others, tolerance, honesty, strength **'I keep on keeping on' My needs are met.**	**I need space and/or support to grieve, let go, and take in.'** **I need love and acceptance.**
Mad	**Scared**
Upset, furious, irate, sore, indignant, insulted, vindictive, angry, resentful, impatient, annoyed, revengeful, malicious, rage **'I have been violated!** **I need to re-establish my boundaries.'**	Anxious, terrified, worried, frightened, nervous, alarmed, fear, hysterical, panic, trapped, persecuted **'I am in danger!** **I need protection.'** **I need security and then rest.**

Glad

Glad is a state of spiritual equilibrium, which is what we experience when our needs are being met and we are in the flow of the natural energy from the Divine and Soul dimensions. Our soul can fill up with these feelings and shine through, even if our minds are grappling with difficult issues. Feeling happy, content, peaceful and calm as well as the rest of the 'glad' feelings is our birthright.

While we might prefer to feel things from the 'glad' family more than any of the others, it is a mistake to think the others are bad, wrong, unskilful or negative. They are messengers. Each of the feelings we have which are uncomfortable are telling us something. When we learn to feel them without shame or blame, reaction or revulsion, we will be in good shape to hear the message and be more informed in our lives than we were before.

Mad

When we feel angry, resentful, frustrated or vindictive our inner being is trying to tell us something. The basic message is that our boundaries are not in the right place. We might be putting up with things that we should not be. We might be experiencing being disrespected by others. Our anger is not a call to dump and blame. It is a call to listen to what is going on, and learn what needs to be adjusted so that our life path can unfold with more ease and grace and more in alignment with the original blue print of our creation.

Anger is not about just what is going on in the physical world, or just about the other person. The other person is really just a catalyst for us to recognise and deal with some internal dynamic that has come a bit adrift. Perhaps we have not yet learned to respect ourselves. Thus, we are getting disrespected by others, and we feel angry about it. We can blame them, which will probably not achieve very much, or we can look within and give ourselves the respect that we are demanding from others. As our respect increases internally, it gets easier to ask in a normal voice for what we need. How to communicate our needs (and how not to) is dealt with in the communication chapter below. If we start to treat anger as a messenger, we can be informed about our life and our world in a clear and accurate way. Handling it skilfully is important, and it could be that we need to learn some anger management skills or have some healings around anger as well as learning how to get the charge of it out of our bodies before we interact with the beloved. This is also dealt with later.

Sad

The sad family of feelings are trying to tell us something too. They are telling us that I am experiencing loss, and I need to grieve. This is a natural part of life. We experience the cycles of birth and death, creation and destruction. Being able to be fully present to these feelings can take us deep into a new level of peacefulness. It can help us to cultivate a more compassionate heart. Love takes on a new flavour. Things that we might have taken for granted, we now understand to be the precious gifts that they were. Our consciousness adapts and adjusts to a new phase in our lives, one that is immeasurably enriched by the having and losing of something that we now know was of tremendous value to us.

Every time we love, we risk sadness. We risk that the beloved might leave us, or even die before us. The poignancy of this potential serves to keep us properly informed of the gift that they are.

Sadness, grief and other members of the sad family help us to get real perspective about our lives. When we are in a situation where we feel truly sad or grief stricken, it is as if all of the small things that usually irritate us pale into insignificance. Suddenly we know what is important. This feeling helps us to stay in the now, and seems to pierce the veil of everydayness that we can sink into. It encourages us to richly enjoy every precious minute we have without beloveds. In this way we are able to overlook the small things and focus on the things that count.

Scared

When we are feeling scared or anxious, we are getting a message from beyond our usual thoughts telling us we need to protect ourselves, to take care, ensure we are secure and that we are not in danger.

We can get scared of an amazing range of things. Fear seems to be one of those boundless qualities that we encounter in our lives. Like love, fear is an energy that is generative of experiences. Fear lets us know that we are at the edge of our comfort zone in life.

Feeling scared is not all bad. Comfort zones are very amazing things. If we are not challenging them, they shrink. If we face our fears and do something that we want to do anyway, our comfort zone grows. In our relationships we can slip into very narrow comfort zones, and sometimes it is our fears that prevents us from exploring more, getting out more, going deeper, getting more in touch with each other. Dealing with this sensation is an important skill for us all.

As we advance through various stages of spiritual growth, we find that it is in our vulnerability that we attain great things. The only way to be vulnerable is to feel our fear and do it anyway. Progress is not attained by sticking within the realms of what we know. Going beyond the known parameters into an unknown world may bring up fear. Being able to help ourselves through that and keep ourselves safe is a very important life and relationship skill.

His and Hers

The emotional literacy of females and males is not the same. We are sometimes taught very different things about how emotions can be dealt with in accordance with our gender. Even if our families tried to give us a similar sense of things regardless of our gender, the problem is that we 'catch' our emotional responses not from what people say to us, but from how they be.

Females and males are 'caught and taught' lessons about valuing and acting out feelings in very different ways. Generally speaking society gives women permission to exhibit Scared, Sad, and Glad, with little permission to express Mad. Men, on the other hand, are given permission to express Mad and less support to express Scared, Sad, and some men even have a lot of trouble with Glad. When conflict occurs and scared feelings arise, a man may show them as mad. He appears to be angry, when really he is feeling anxious and doesn't know how to say so. When a female is in a situation where her boundaries are undermined and the real underlying feeling she has is mad, she may not have any cultural permission to express this. Instead, she may show her feelings as sad.

Needs

Every person has needs. Obvious ones are fresh air, food, water and shelter. We have emotional needs as well. These may be less obvious, but we truly do need love, approval, acceptance, stimulation, hope and fun.

Our emotional responses are designed to help us identify what our needs might be. As you can see from the table above, when our needs are being met, we feel glad as well as being able to feel the other delicious feelings in the 'Glad' family. This is a great place to be, and is the closest state of consciousness to that which is inherent in our Divine core.

Notice that the three other families of feelings are all telling us something specific is missing. A need is going unmet. With sadness it is love, hope and acceptance that is missing; we are pining for it. With anger it is that boundaries are in the wrong place; we are feeling put upon. With scared we are feeling endangered somehow and what we are needing is protection and rest.

How to get these needs met is a really important question, and perhaps one that we do not consciously focus on too much. Many of us have burdened our relationships with endless unmet needs, and then gotten mad, sad and scared when the beloved does not provide for these needs in the manner that we expect and demand. When we 'outsource' the meeting of our needs to others we become needy and co-dependent. We then have to control others so that they will meet our needs, which we do not know how to meet ourselves. All hell breaks loose, and dysfunctional patterns of manipulation, control and power games sneak in. Eventually the relationship gets untenable and breaks down or remains on foot but is a misery to everyone involved.

Contained in the next few chapters of the book is the best model I have come across for identifying and meeting the needs that everyone has. When we are able to ensure that most of our needs are met from within, and without becoming dependent upon another person, we are more likely to experience the state of Glad rather than the other families of feelings. We can then help others meet their needs too. All of this involves getting to know the vulnerable and emotional part inside, and learning how to look after it. This is the art of self-parenting.

Chapter

9

SELF-PARENTING

Analysing

We are one integrated whole person. For the purposes of having deeper insight about who we are, we can look at various of our component parts. If we wanted to look anatomically at ourselves we could divide our bodies up into the digestive system, the respiratory system, the nervous system and so on. When we looked at dimensions we saw that we had five, and we can examine ourselves from that model. From the perspective of the Etheric dimension alone we can divide ourselves up further, chakra by chakra, so as to understand more about our consciousness and energy.

Here you are about to be presented with another analysis, which I have found extremely helpful in understanding what is driving me from a relationship perspective. This model is not meant to fit precisely into any other models, and it is best not to try and shove it into the V diagram of multi-dimensionality, which we will use elsewhere in the book. Just enjoy and appreciate it for what it is. For interest sake, if you are a student of the Kabbalah, there are a few notes and clues to how we work with transactional analysis within the tree of life. If you have not studied that, just ignore them.

The following analysis is derived from transactional analysis, which was developed in the 1950s and onwards starting with Eric Berne and his famous book *Games People Play* which was published in 1964. It has since been developed and adapted by many people. I learned about it from Barbara and Terry Tebo[3] through their wonderful Free to Be Me programs. Barbara and Terry were my first spiritual mentors and showed me great kindness, love and compassion during a time when I really needed it, during the time when I was experiencing divorce for the first time. Having worked with the paradigm extensively I have amended it to include a fourth persona, the Higher Soul.

Who am I?

When trying to find a way to handle strong emotions and all of the complexities of relating, it has helped me greatly to know that there are really 4 of me living inside my body. What is more, there are 4 of everyone else as well. These four parts of me are:

the adult, the parent, the inner child, the Higher Soul[4].

---

[3] Barbara and Terry are semi-retired now but still offer counselling services and conduct peace seminars from their home in Corlette near Nelson Bay in NSW. Their excellent book Free to be Me and other of their products are highly recommended.

Their website is www.peacefulpeople.com.au

[4] Traditional transactional analysis as developed by Eric Berne does not include any analysis to do with the higher soul, and restricts itself to the child, adult and parent.

When you are in a relationship with someone else, that means there are really 8 of you trying to have a relationship! No wonder it gets so tricky!

The Adult

The adult is the part of us that can plan and take responsibility. It can deal with issues and problems in a realistic, calm and appropriate way. The adult can show leadership, assess situations calmly because it doesn't have emotion. It can co-operate and communicate in a dispassionate way. It can think of ways to make things better, find pathways through problems, and visualise with the mind how to adapt and create positive changes in our life.

The adult is a bit like a human computer, which operates on data fed into it. This data is stored and used for decision making. When you go to buy a new fridge, the adult can compute the various attributes of the available choices, how much money you have and how big it has to be. It will be able to buy the most appropriate one. It is logical. If the facts are up to date then the adult's answers will be timely and accurate.

When people live in this part of themselves to the exclusion of the other parts, they do not feel emotions. This is where the British, stiff upper-lip person lives. Unfortunately, because it has no emotions, it has no compassion or empathy. It is no good at parenting, or relating to anyone! Adult personas read the paper at the breakfast table so that they do not have to talk to anyone. They are very sensible. They have forgotten how to have fun because they have so many responsibilities.

Many people live in their adult self all the time, have stale or failed relationships and miss out on lots of the joy of life. They are dry, boring, dull, closed, rigid, tend to overwork and be over responsible. Everything is serious for the person who lives too much in their adult.

Conversely a person with too little adult cannot commit, plan, act or find the right direction. They may take too many risks, be unrealistic in their expectations or stuck in old cultural paradigms that are quite ridiculous if even a little analysis was brought to bear. There is superstition and reactive behaviour that simply does not make any sense.

The adult places sole reliance upon its logical, analytical, sequence oriented left brain[5]. The reason they cannot fathom emotions is because emotions, like intuition, are not able to be accessed through our left brains. It is the right brain, our creative and intuitive faculty, which we rely on for emotional understanding.

The adult part of us equates to the Kabbalistic Sephira of Hod. Hod is the part of us that is of the mind. Particularly we are referring to the part of the mind that builds form. This part can follow or create maps, create critical flow path diagrams and work for months, or years, following a procedure that will eventually lead to an event, invention or other outcome being produced.

The adult is our propensity to organise and create form.

The adult is able to concentrate and focus the mind.

The adult can use affirmations, will remember to do so, and will continue to use them until the desired result has vested in the physical plane.

---

[5] I have written about the attributes of the left and right brain in a previous book: Chapter 4 *Child of God*. Information about this is freely available on the internet.

The adult keeps a diary and checks his schedule so as to ensure that his actions are efficient and orderly.

The adult can learn and study paradigms of thought, and it is most likely the adult part of you that is reading this sentence.

The adult is the part of us that is good at controlling our physical environment. Birds build nests, beavers build dams, and in so doing they are illustrating some degree of 'adult' in their behaviour. But the things that humans build are truly stupendous. Without our adult analytical self we would not have all of the amenities of modern civilisation, ranging from the building of homes, roads, factories and systems for trains to run, traffic lights to function and airplanes to fly and land safely. We would not have medical technology to help us when we are sick. Computers would never have been invented, nor any form of mechanisation.

In all the adult part of us is very important to modern life. The thing is not to get completely lost in it. Remember, it doesn't know how to relate to others, it doesn't know how to love, and it doesn't have any compassion or kindness. It cannot have fun and does not understand virtues. An adult which has no other part of itself operating would actually become a sociopath, indifferent to the needs, drives or vulnerabilities of others or even the self. A society run just by adults would be a nightmare to live within because it would have no heart.

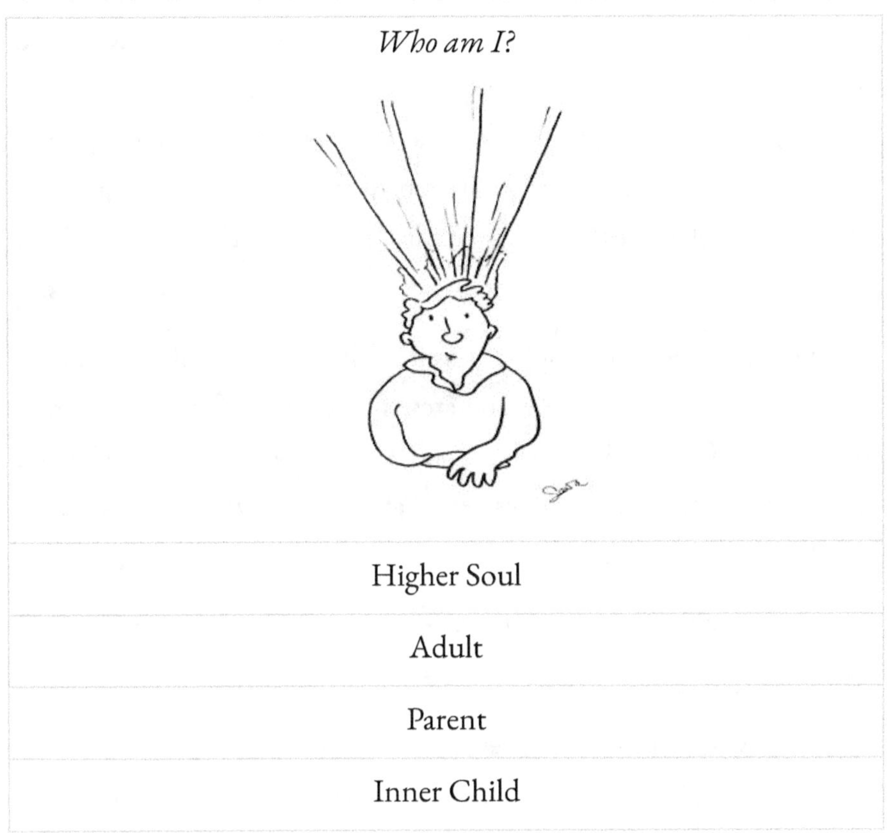

Higher Soul

Adult

Parent

Inner Child

The Parent

The first thing to say is that the parent is not our actual parent/s, but the way in which we have internalised the state of parent-ness from them. The parent is an instinctual, habit-driven, reacting part of ourselves. It is like a tape recorder, a collection of pre-recorded rules for living. When we are acting from our parent, we think and behave as we have internalised (and become one with the behaviours of) one of our parents or someone who took their place. The parent decides *without reasoning* how to react to situations, what is good or bad, and how people should live. The response that comes from the parent is pretty much instant.

The mind is not engaged, there is no logical sequence of thoughts and analysis of the situation. There is simply an instant "bam!" the programmed response that was already inside of us just came out. Whether it was good bad or indifferent is not the issue, it is just our nature, born of a great deal of conditioning over the period of our lifetime.

The parent helps us to solve questions that do not really have a hard and fast answer. The parent operates in the field of norms, morals, expectations, feelings and habit. The adage "If we always do what we have always done we will always get what we have always got" perfectly describes the parent part of us.

Some of the issues that the parent part of us might face include:

- How to relate to others.
- How to balance being responsible with having fun.
- How to behave when you are at a party.
- How to react when your daughter brings home her first boyfriend
- How to resolve conflict.
- How the family should be run.
- What time should you go to bed and get up in the morning.
- Beliefs and decisions around practice and control of sexuality.
- Whether or not you or your family drinks alcohol, attitudes and habits around smoking.
- Whether you are racist, sexist, bigoted, and if so, against whom.
- Who the family votes for (because that's the way we have always voted).
- Where to put boundaries in place in our lives.

- How to respond to someone who is having a tantrum and acting out.
- How the genders respond to each other from a cultural and familiar pattern.
- How to best look after your health and diet and the way you are going to exercise.
- And a host of other social, moral and ethical questions.

When we are in our parent part, we rely on learning that is at least 20 years out of date, because we imbibed these tapes while still a very young child from the people who raised us. Actually, it could be worse. Our parents (or other adults) got these tapes from their parents, who got them from their parents and so on. Thus, these 'solutions' to difficult moral and ethical questions may actually be hundreds of years behind the times! An example here is the Italian and Greek immigrants who came to Australia post war. The culture that they established here is just as it was before they left Europe. A Greek friend of mine seeking to marry in the 1990's had very draconian restrictions placed upon her by her parents. However Greek culture itself in Greece and other parts of Europe had moved on. People had much more freedom in Greece, but this family was still playing the tapes of post war Europe. In an effort to be true to their culture, they parented in a very different way to what would have happened had they actually still been in Greece where much evolution has taken place.

The voice of the parent is the voice of the unconscious, and that is indeed a pretty murky place. There are so many influences of which we are unaware, but which can become conscious and be cleaned up if we are prepared to do some spiritual training.

The voice of the parent can pop out of our mouths when we become parents ourselves and need to discipline our kids. Even if we really didn't like the way our own parents behaved when things went wrong, and we swore we would never be like them, the tapes of the past can over-power us. In the heat of the moment when reacting to something that our own child has done, we say something, which we can't believe we said: "God I sound just like my mother!" Some of these influences may have become a little clearer if you took the exercise in chapter 5 above to do with the effect of your family of origin.

The parent part of ourselves corresponds to the Kabbalistic sephirot of Yesod.

Yesod is called the foundation, and is the way in which all of the forces operating above and below us, through all dimensions of our being, are balanced within us.

Our foundation as people, particularly in our early years is very subject to the consciousness of the group with which we identify. Thus, the parent who happens to be of the upper middle class tribe is subject to the group consciousness of the upper middle class ideal of how we organise ourselves and what is right and not right. The parent who is of a native tribal extraction has a different set of beliefs, expectations, habits and instincts upon which to draw from people who are of Colonial European descent. Modern western culture provides its own sets of habits and instincts and within that each family has its own sets of codes, norms and a kind of moral group-mind as well.

As a matter of real life experience, we know that there are parents who are critical, over-controlling, violent, perfectionist, derisive, difficult, unreasonable, oppressive and who treat their children appallingly. This is a negative parent archetype, and not the way it is naturally meant to be. This parent is coming from the ego, which is lacking refinement.

Some parents lack judgment about their children and behave in a weak way that is non-protective, undisciplined, and non-assertive. They can be disloyal to their children and have no clarity in what they expect. Thus people go astray because the rules are not clear and even if there are rules, they are not fairly and uniformly enforced. This is not an optimal environment for a child, including an inner child.

Likewise we can find parents who are noble and kind, fair and loving. The ideal parent is devoted and nurturing, clear, respectful, has good boundaries, instils good boundaries in their children, is unconditionally loving, giving, supportive and tender. The nurturing parent values others, and creates a safe environment for self and others. This kind of parent is coming more from the soul characteristics of a person who has anchored a lot of spiritual light within themselves and can utilise it effectively in life.

Whether they see themselves as spiritual or not is irrelevant to the fact that they actually are!

A too-much nurturing parent spoils the child by giving too much and cultivating over-dependency in the child. They do whatever the child wants, and in so doing they stop the child growing. They smother the child with indulgence, thereby creating a wilful child who does not contribute, who tends to be selfish and demanding.

When we have too-little nurturing parent we are the kind of person who is impatient, unforgiving, intolerant, doesn't have time, doesn't seem to care and does not support us. We are inattentive and unaware.

We don't mean to be horrible, we are just not awake to having an actual relationship.

Most often we are a mixture of all these things, and so were our parents. In our culture, we are often in too much of a hurry, not present enough and not anywhere skilled enough to parent in an optimal way all the time. We are too physical world focused to notice subtle communication and cues that would allow us to parent in a gentler and more fruitful manner. It really is the case that no matter how hard our parents tried to do the right thing, there are still plenty of phobias, neuroses and kinks in our psychological make up that we can spend an entire lifetime sorting out! Never mind, your own kids will do the same thing no matter what we do, so at the end of the day, let's just do our best.

The Child

The first thing to say about the child is that this does **not** represent **you** as a child. It is not your actual historical self. It is an archetypal part of ourselves that exists within us in the here and now. Even overly serious and very old people have an inner child. Everyone does. Each and every one of us has a three year old hidden just beneath the surface. This part of us wants what it wants, and wants it now. This part of us has needs, and if those needs are not met it will do whatever it takes to get them met. This part is powerful, but not always pretty. In some respects it represents our raw and voracious ego.

The inner child, like most actual three year old children, is playful and cute. It is a part of the self that if expressed well leads us to be charming, curious, adaptable, spontaneous, adventurous, loving, loveable, affectionate, engaging, energised and enthused about life.

People in whom the child is free-spirited and happy are a lot of fun. They find pleasure in everything and are creative as well.

Sometimes for various reasons the spirit of the child has been somewhat crushed and is under expressed. People with this problem are humourless, lack spontaneity, have little imagination, may be sexually inhibited, non-expressive, cold, untouching and withholding of affection. They might tend to keep others at a distance. People whose inner child has been suppressed in this way have difficulty with relationships and generally do not have a good relationship with the self internally.

The child is often an invisible part of us that gets put in a cupboard and forgotten. The child is usually invisible in the workplace, and in proper polite grown-up company.

The child can be seen in social situations where people have permission to let the child out, like at a football game or party. There it can yell and scream, cheer and boo, dance on the table, etc. It is the sexy playmate, the life of the party, the part of ourselves that feels emotions in a very liberated and unrestrained way.

However too much of the child in our lives can lead to cultural or family rules being ignored, immorality, irresponsibility, and they are very frustrating because of their total hedonism and freedom-seeking habits. They spread a wake of destruction and pain and seem to have no idea how to show any restraint. Boundaries are non-existent and their word means nothing because unless it feels good to keep it, they don't.

Some inner children are well socialised, and while they still exhibit lots of playfulness and childish enthusiasm for life, they can be co-operative, share with others, show respect and accept that they cannot always have what they want when they want it. They can let go, surrender, and trust their parent.

Other inner children have never really been socialised very much at all and they become the rebel child. They can be aggressive and do the opposite of anything that you ask them to. They can be spiteful, taunt others, are self-centred and have no sense of being able to fit in with others. They are a royal pain in the neck.

The opposite problem is the inner child who has had such strict parenting that they are over-socialised. They are compliant and afraid to say boo to a goose. They are not assertive and are very dependent. They conform and want to please everyone so that they don't get into trouble. They have lost their spontaneity and can be quite helpless, often falling into victim situations. The over-socialised cannot express how they are feeling, and so often become like volcanoes, holding onto things until they eventually blow their stack and create carnage everywhere.

Each and every inner child has certain needs, which we will look at shortly. When the child's needs are unmet, for instance if the child feels unloved and uncared for, the child's neediness can completely dominate a person's life. This can lead to addictions, inappropriate behaviour, attention seeking, selfish and uncaring reactions, harsh words, violence, depression, anxiety, acting out and a whole heap of self-destructive and self-sabotaging behaviours, all of which are knee jerk reactions by the child to get what it needs. It is like a little baby screaming because it is hungry. However the person doing the screaming might be 40 years old.

When the child feels loved and secure it results in a spontaneous, happy person who is fully alive to each moment and bubbling over with fun and enthusiasm.

Like all children, our inner child needs unconditional acceptance and love from the nurturing parent, as well as good boundaries. All this involves the art of self-parenting. Also like all children, you can't just do this once and put the child back in the cupboard again! It just doesn't work. Self-parenting is a long term commitment to nurturing and caring for ourselves, ensuring that our actual needs are met and providing safety and boundaries for ourselves so that we are able to live with other people in a way that brings inner peace, ease and grace.

The child inside us has a natural understanding of emotions and no fear of feeling them. When we don't get in her way, the child deals with emotions in an honest and direct fashion. Like any three year old, the inner child is capable of feeling great one minute and lousy the next, then fantastic again, all in the space of 5 minutes.

Have you ever been in the presence of a three year old who in a moment of not being able to get her own way, screams at her mother that she hates her? She doesn't really hate her mother, but in that moment she feels hatred and so she momentarily associates the person that has denied her something, with the emotion of hatred. If the child is not attached or socialised into thinking that hatred is bad, there is no snag to cause that emotion to get buried inside her. After a few minutes and some tears, she flows back into feeling happy again and wants to give her mum a hug.

When there is no resistance caused through judgment, all of us have the capacity to snap out of negative emotions reasonably quickly. The catch is that we need to **accept and feel our feelings** first for this natural flow to occur. At the same time our parent steps in to ensure that we do not do or say anything while feeling that emotion that would cause harm to ourselves or others.

In many people the inner child has disappeared, locked away where we cannot feel anything. It is all too scary. The problem is, if we lock away the child, we lock away our capacity for love, joy, happiness, long term good health and wellbeing. The child is very powerful, and has total control over our body. If ignored for too long, (s)he will grab your attention in the only way (s)he knows how. The child will make you sick or will create self-sabotage.

The inner child in Kabbalah relates to the sephirot of Netzach. The

Netzach habitual and instinctive part of who we are, is also a function of the degree to which we embody a mixture of our higher and lower nature in the here and now. Some people would say that humanity is basically selfish and animalistic (features of the lower nature or Ahamkara/ego). Some people would say that humanity is basically altruistic and noble (features of the higher soul, Jiv Atma and Atma).

We could find evidence for the truth of either of these statements (which of course the Adult would do – research being one of its specialities), and for hundreds of states of nobility or lack of it in between the two extremes.

The triad of adult (Hod) parent (Yesod) and child (Netzach) all work together to determine how our lower spiritual vehicle or ego operates in the world. A well-loved and well parented child with good boundaries combined with clear adult analysis and expansive and perceptive parenting will result in an inner Egoic foundation which is robust, enquiring, growth oriented, stable, flexible, contributory, adaptable and happy.

At the same time the higher soul, which is the forces of the Supernal triad of the tree of life coming down through Tiphareth, is always exerting an evolutionary and growth impulse to us. This has to be absorbed into our other selves, and results in refinement, and a spirited, enabled, joyful, loving and radiant self. The idea is to cultivate ourselves internally so that more and more of the time the 'self' that we encounter and identify with becomes the King, who is also the Divine child, of Tiphareth. Tiphareth is the archetype of the Sun, as well as the Son of God. It is as though the emotional and mind part of ourselves are capable of helping us to actually embody our soul self, bringing a sense of innocence, joy, and at the same time empowerment to everything that we think, say and do.

When we are not Relating to our Inner Child

If we ignore our inner child, and/or fail to parent him or her with love and nurturing, we will find that we will become prone to addictions, allergies, sabotage, illness, emotional instability, disastrous relationships, inappropriate behaviour either from self or others, tantrums, depression, disempowerment, loneliness, isolation, co-dependence, exhaustion and poor diet. Life may be fairly tricky.

Sometimes anti-social urges emanate from the inner child. The child lives in the here and now and is not interested in the future. Consequences of actions are not within the ambit of the child, nor does the child have a great awareness of many forms of danger. Imagine that Jack does something to upset Fred. Fred immediately wants to kick Jack because he feels angry at Jack. It is up to Big Fred to stop Little Fred from acting out his feelings in the here and now. Instead, Fred Parent needs to immediately distract Little Fred, or exert strong authority to tell Little

Fred that it is not OK to kick Jack for being rude to him. Big Fred (Parent) might take Little Fred out of the room. Or if Jack is drunk and looking dangerous Fred Parent might take Little Fred out of the room while Fred Adult calls the police.

Susie inner child is having a great time at a party. She is a great dancer and the music is amazing. It is getting late. Susie Parent needs to remind Susie Inner Child that she has to go to work in the morning and if she stays out dancing all night she won't be able to. Susie Inner Child couldn't care less because she is having fun in the here and now and does not want to listen to Susie Parent. Susie Parent needs to get really clear and assertive with Little Susie and insist that she come home now. This does not have to be unpleasant. The degree to which Little Susie listens to Big Susie will reflect the time and effort Susie parent has put into loving, nurturing and respecting herself up to this point in time.

Over time the child comes to trust the parent. Between the parent and child they work out ways to both have fun and stay within boundaries of safety, common sense and the avoidance of negative consequences for themselves and others.

The adult self is the part that most frequently takes us to work, gets us on the train and makes lots of practical, information based decisions. However the adult is influenced by the other parts of self. If the adult tries to stifle the child for too long, the child will become rebellious given the first opportunity when the adult lets his guard down even for a moment. Imagine that Adult Sam has not had a day off in months. Even beautiful Sunday mornings Adult Sam has taken little Sam to work. All little Sam wants to do is go to the beach but neither Adult nor Parent Sam are listening. Suddenly staid Sam is drinking too much at the office party and his guard is down. Out comes little Sam who is sick of the whole work thing. Suddenly Sam is saying a whole lot of things that would have been much better left unsaid. This can have dire consequences for Sam but Little Sam couldn't care less, because little Sam has been locked away so long that Little Sam is enjoying having some fun in an unbridled, unparented kind of way. If Parent Sam had just intervened and said that Little Sam needed a bit of rest and fun to balance out Adult Sam's work life, this probably would not have happened.

Jane is married to Arnold. They live in a nice house and Jane is very house proud. Arnold and Jane both work and they employ a housekeeper, Nancy to help them. She does a really good job but every week she puts all the things from the dishwasher in different locations, so neither Arnold nor Jane know where things are. Neither Arnold nor Jane are very assertive or good at saying what they need. Jane gets huffy and goes around each week peering in all the cupboards and finding things that are out of place and putting them back where they 'should' live according to her parenting tapes. Jane's adult insists that order be restored, whereas Jane's inner child is not at all happy about this because Little Jane needs some attention, which she is not getting as Jane fusses with the cupboards. Little Jane is being ignored all together while Big Jane is busy. Like a kettle getting up a head of steam, over months of not saying anything, Little Jane erupts one day and rings up the housekeeper and abuses her for her continual mistakes and mis-filing of things in kitchen cupboards. The housekeeper quits without notice. Jane then takes months to find a suitable replacement, and goes through 4 housekeepers before she can find one who is as thorough as Nancy was. It puts a lot of pressure on both Arnold, Jane and their relationship in the meantime, as both of them have to do extra work that Nancy used to do.

Jane's inner parent ought to have intervened long before and asked Jane's inner adult to ring the housekeeper and calmly discuss the situation and ways that it could be dealt with. Instead, she did not listen to the voice of her inner child who was feeling dissatisfied. The inner child therefore eventually reacted with no thought for consequences or how others might feel.

Because Jane continually ignores her inner child, her inner child does not trust her. This plays out in Jane's life, making it hard for Jane to be deeply trusting of others. She does not know where this distrust comes from, and thinks it is just how she is. It has ruined quite a few friendships. Actually, it is just how the relationship she has (or doesn't have) with her inner child is. This can be healed.

Child and Child

To have a great relationship a couple need to have inner children who like to play together. If they won't play together, then the relationship is unlikely to last and if it does it will be boring and frustrating. Having fun together and being able to sort out disagreements, to 'get back in the sandpit and play' again is a really valuable attribute for a couple to have.

The Soul Self

Each of us has a soul. It is the difference between a body that is animated and alive and one that is a corpse. It is the essential life force within us, which allows us to think, breathe, move and live.

Our Higher Self is a consciousness that is connected to the whole, in touch with pure Divine essence and able to guide us from a very expanded perspective. Our ability to tune-in to our higher self depends upon the development of our etheric body, particularly our spiritual pillar of light and upper chakras, the clarity of our astral body, and our letting go of attachment to how we think things should be. Someone who is connected to the Higher Self has help in all areas of personality and life. The Higher Soul impulses the parent and child towards loving kindness, personal development, and expansion of consciousness. This also flows from the parent into the mind of the adult and helps with the process of refinement of the mind and clarity of thinking processes. Wholeness is achieved through Divine Union, empowered love of self, and understanding of the Spiritual Laws of reflection and attraction.

Soul guidance comes in a multitude of ways. There is no end to the amount of guidance we get. The tricky part for some is recognising it. For others, they know that they are receiving guidance, but the scary part would be following it, when sometimes that guidance suggests that we do things which logically we might have a problem with. The thing is, the soul is guiding us to learn, grow and progress spiritually. The logical mind is guiding us to feel safe and be in control. The voices of these two parts of us will not always agree, and it can take courage as well as experience to know how to follow guidance in a practical way, given that what we are being asked to do may not sound rational. The best analogy I have heard is the Adult ship's captain who receives guidance through the ship's radio, where an unseen Higher Self is telling him to bear 15 degrees starboard. The captain says "I am the captain of this ship, and who are you to tell me to divert from my charted course?" The answer comes back "I am a light house... turn now or you will be on my rocks!"

So, the captain who then appreciates his predicament, does what needs to be done to turn the ship.

The soul does not actually do the doing, leaving it to the Parent and the Adult logical mind to work out what to do. If they ignore the guidance however the soul can enlist all kinds of supernatural help to create Murphy's Law 'everything that can go wrong does go wrong', which is Universe-speak for "You are going the wrong way!"

The child might co-operate with the soul's guidance, or it might bring up all kinds of fears, whether they are rational or not the child reacts to fears and often acts out in crazy ways. The parent then has to soothe the child and stop it acting out, controlling the child's behaviour so that the child and everyone else is safe.

Our Soul self guides us a lot through the process of synchronicity, which is part of the Law of Grace. The Law of Grace is the opposite of Murphy's law. The Law of Grace says that everything that can go right and flow, will. When 'coincidences' happen all around us, then we are going in the right direction. When things flow in our lives, we are on track with the guidance that is coming from our soul.

Another form of guidance is occurring when you have ended up at the right place at the right time for something amazing to happen. For instance, if you usually take a particular route on your walk home, but one day you decide to vary it seemingly on a whim and you end up bumping into an old friend you had been thinking of. That impulse comes from the soul. Or you find the very thing in a shop that you have been searching for and unable to find elsewhere, and it is on special!

Books can fall off shelves in shops and land on or near you that are perfect for you at this very moment. That is your soul helping you realise things. Being in the flow of the guidance of your soul is a great and natural way to live.

The Soul-self corresponds to the Briatic world of Kabbalah, and to the supernal triad of Kether, Chokmah and Binah. It is about the entire spiritual resources of the guides, spiritual teachers and inner plane Angelic friends that are ceaselessly with us, helping us to learn and grow.

When we have not enough soul, we are unable to embrace mystery, change or move towards being a peacemaker in our lives and relationships. We are unlikely to have much inner peace at the best of times. We don't appreciate that we are part of a magnificent Whole, and our conception of the cycles of life and light are limited or lacking altogether. Life is seen as bounded by the physical world, and we don't have much incentive to better ourselves except where we can see real material or financial gain flowing from it.

When we live in the Soul self too much of the time we can lose track of the practical day-to-day realities of the other dimensions in which we live, including the physical. This is not meant to refer to those amazing priests, nuns, monks and holy people who have renounced worldly life and are entirely devoted to the spirit. Their job is to be in the realms of the Divine, anchoring energy through meditation and prayer that has a beneficial and uplifting effect on the entire human astral field. Here we are simply referring to the householder, who is living in the world and trying at the same time to have a spiritually enriching and emotionally satisfying set of relationships. How to combine spiritual excellence with grounded practicality is what the entire Path of Ease and Grace, of which Empowering Relationships is a module, is all about.

The Soul can control the child easily and lovingly. The problem is that we have to surrender to it in order that it does so.

If the child wants to drink alcohol and likes how that makes it feel, it is up to the parent to decide if this is an appropriate time to do that, and if so, when the child ought to stop drinking because it has had enough.

Some people cannot stop drinking. The child will not submit to any authority and is out of control. This is often in response to life circumstances of stress, emptiness or some other 'negative' emotion that the person does not want to feel. In Alcoholics Anonymous there is a stage where one surrenders to a higher power. There is a recognition that they themselves are not strong enough to stop drinking alcohol and they ask that the higher power intervene. Many who have successfully stopped drinking report that this is actually what happens. The Divine just lifted the desire out of them so that they could live soberly, dealing with life in healthier ways. This happens through our soul.

I have experienced this from time to time with various parts of my life: getting to a stage that things are just too hard. It is like being on a galloping horse heading straight for that big scary hurdle, and wishing with all your might that it would start to gallop backwards. All that is left is praying about it, and the next thing you know you are over the hurdle, looking back thinking: that was not too hard at all was it? This is a time where your higher soul has intervened, and after that we are never the same again.

The soul is also visible in our four-part self in a manner that keeps life fresh and interesting. The soul loves variety. It wants to experience life in a 360 degree learning curve. The soul is not happy with the same old, same old, day in day out, year in year out. That feeling of being in a rut means that our spirit has become trapped and it is time for it to be set free. The soul will begin to impulse us to change, learn and grow. The soul will try first to speak to the parent about it, and if the parent is sensitive to the guidance of the soul then the parent might speak to the adult about how we could work out a new way of living.

If the parent ignores the soul, then it will take desperate measures. It may enlist the help of the inner child to create a scandal, or to rock the boat in some way, possibly through a tantrum or acting out, by which everyone suddenly knows how we feel and there is no turning back. We have 'made our bed' so to speak. While the ego loves to control everything and protect its turf, the higher soul loves change, opportunity and going with the flow of Cosmic intelligence and Divine timing.

In a relationship it is important to have some stimulation that keeps the relationship progressing and growing. Getting out occasionally, doing something different together, meeting new people, having separate hobbies as well as joint ones, these are some strategies that will help prevent the 'rut' which our spirit so resists and which our inner child also has trouble dealing with.

Soul guidance is not available to the adult. The reason for this is that the Adult lives just in the logical and analytical left brain. There is no scope for the entry of Divine awareness here. We just work with what we have already learned. It is very mechanical and not at all connected to feelings, emotions, intuition or guidance. This guidance can come to us intuitively, and will be heard by the parent or child from whom the Adult may hear it as a factor to take into consideration.

The parent can hear guidance if he/she listens for it. Because of expectations, conditioning, attachment to things and outcomes, the parent is sometimes not able to register or follow higher guidance.

Given that soul guidance cannot be accessed by the adult, then if guidance is neglected or ignored by our parent, it has to be processed by the child.

If the only way that an adult and parent can hear the soul is through the child, things may have to get right out of hand before the message is heard. An example is someone who is working really hard in a job that they hate, travelling for hours every day, and they know that the job is destroying their health and peace of mind but they stick at it because they are fearful of what will happen if they don't. The child gets on really well with our soul self. If soul guidance is being ignored by the parent, the child can get upset and close down energy. This can lead to disease, depression and self-sabotage.

Generally the child within is in tune with the Soul, but sometimes like all children there can be rebelliousness and a lack of responsible action in the face of what needs to be done, and this is another reason to learn two things: ***the art of self parenting and how to consciously hear the voice of your Higher Soul.***

Working Foursome

When this foursome is working the way it was all designed, the Higher self gives guidance and direction which is observed by the parent and child. The adult helps the parent to meet the child's needs, so that the child is content and sparkling. Even when the child gets frightened or rebels at the thought of doing what the soul wants, like leaving a job or starting a relationship, or forgiving someone, the parent is there to soothe the child and lead the way. If the parent works out that a certain course has to be adopted because of its beliefs and intuition, the adult will start calculating the steps of how it is that the job will be accomplished and manages the implementation of what the Higher Soul, parent and child require. All in all, when this foursome is working well, we have the perfect basis to now enter into sublime and satisfying relationships.

Relating with Ourselves and Others: Who am I, When?

You are now invited to assess yourself based on the information about the 4 parts of self that are involved in your relationship with your beloved. Refer back to chapter 9 and see if you can identify whether there is not enough, enough or excessive amounts of the following categories of self.

My Analysis of Self

Quality	Not enough	Enough	Excessive
Higher Soul			
Adult			
Parental Boundaries			
Parental Nurturing			
Spirited Child			
Socialised child			

My Analysis of Significant Other

Quality	Not enough	Enough	Excessive
Higher Soul			
Adult			
Parental Boundaries			
Parental Nurturing			
Spirited Child			
Socialised child			

10 things not to let your inner child do alone:

1. The grocery shopping when (s)he is hungry (your cart will be full of ice cream and biscuits).
2. Have control of your credit cards, particularly when the sales are on.
3. Drive when angry.
4. Give feedback to your partner when (s)he is feeling upset.
5. Decide when you have had enough to eat or drink (never).
6. Determine your communication style.
7. Have free reign during an argument.
8. Talk to difficult relatives at Christmas lunch.

9. Deal with scary people and feel unprotected.

10. Extreme sports.

10 things not to let your inner adult do alone:

1. Make love.

2. Decide what to do on your day off (it will want to go to work).

3. Decide what to watch on TV (it will be the news, or a factual documentary with no humour).

4. Plan your diary (you will have no down time).

5. Speak to your teenage children (they will think you are heartless).

6. Decorate the house (it will be bland and colourless).

7. Dress you (you will always wear a suit).

8. Go to a fancy dress party (it won't dress up).

9. Hang out with your friends.

10. Play games (it won't enjoy it and no, the stock market is not a game).

One of the biggest jobs is to get to know and understand the child, and then to take appropriate actions based on what we have learned. The next sections are about the inner child and its needs, then we will go on to study this further in the context of relating.

Chapter

10

THE NEEDS OF
THE INNER CHILD

Every single one of us has basic needs, which have to be met so that we can exist on Earth with some degree of skilfulness and harmony with others. Below are 8 needs that we have identified as being core to a happy person, and a person who is capable of having good, intra-dependent (as opposed to co-dependent) relationships. When these needs go unmet, particularly for a period of time, the inner child will end up sabotaging us in some unpleasant way to get our attention. Generally this is destructive of relationships.

All of us need help from time to time, and this analysis is not meant to suggest that we become isolated and cut off from outside assistance. What it is saying is that we need to develop inner wherewithal so that we can meet these needs ourselves, on a day-to-day basis. A person who in a sustained way, cannot meet their own needs is challenging to live with. They place unconscious burdens on those they relate with and manipulate others to ensure that their needs are met. Much of the time they are not really conscious of what they are doing. This takes the joy out of relating and creates all of the issues of co-dependence, control, use of force to get our own way and so on.

If you have ever been around needy people you will know what it is like. They are so draining, always wanting to be validated and noticed, like a black hole that can never be filled no matter how much attention you give them.

8 Basic Needs that we all have to Fulfill

1. Security
2. Approval
3. Authenticity and Acceptance
4. Hope and Encouragement
5. Love
6. Attention, Stimulation and Physicality 7. Sleep & Rest 8. Fun.

1. Security

This includes physical security such as a roof over your head, enough to eat and drink, and not being physically threatened or abandoned. Women historically relied on their husbands for their need for financial security to be met. The woman would stay at home and keep house as well as look after children, and often provided the emotional security for the household.

Today roles are much less rigid. When one person earns all the money and the other person is financially dependent upon them it can work if they are both mature about it and if both people are generous in their regard for the other. This arrangement requires a good level of trust and communication so that each person can function within reasonable boundaries under this arrangement. There would be a budget for the things that were required every week or month, like mortgage payments, and the other bills like food and utilities. Ideally each would also have a modest personal budget that is just for them and which is not subject to accountability to the partner. This gives a little independence and freedom to each person without upsetting the security of either person.

Sometimes when one party earns the money and the other is dependent the arrangement becomes quite co-dependent. The giver of financial security can feel the need to control every move the other one makes. This is because the financial supporter might be relying on the other party for *emotional* security. Controlling behaviour happens when a person is so scared of not getting their need for security met that they insist everything be done their way so they can feel safe. Often the controlling person believes that they are only being controlling because they love the other person so much, but underneath this is a fear of loss, lack, and not getting needs met.

Love is not controlling, it is enabling, freeing and allowing, so if you are experiencing lots of control issues, look to your inner child and what you are co-creating.

Every person requires access to enough resources including money to be able to meet the very basic physical survival needs. Ensuring that you have this is one way that we learn to parent our inner child. For instance, every person ought have access to some money in a bank account that they are not beholden to others for how it ought to be spent. This does not need to be a big amount of money, just something that enables a basic amount of financial independence. When we are able to do that, we are not in desperate need of an external security provider, even though we might enjoy being provided for in some ways. We are much more secure when we can provide at least some basic physical needs for ourselves.

In some marriages money is used as a means of control. It is important that every person have access to at least some money that they can use as they require it without recourse to the other party. This allows for a degree of autonomy and independence, without which you have a disempowering co-dependent relationship.

Security Strategies:

- Rooting exercise (see *Ignite Your Spirit* book P 88).
- Ensure that you feel secure in your home by locking the doors and windows particularly before you go to sleep.
- Ask the driver to slow down if you feel that they are driving in a dangerous way: be assertive about what you need.
- If you live alone, have the phone number of a trusted person that you can ring or who will ring you once per week to see how you are going.
- Bring your awareness into the now: "I am safe I am secure".
- Pat your arm or put your hands over the solar plexus area to help protect your energy field when you are feeling threatened.
- Have good boundaries about your personal safety and do not allow yourself to be talked into things you do not feel comfortable about.
- Don't let people hit you. If they do it is not OK, it was not your fault and you do not need to put up with it. Get some assistance and get out.

- Have a nice comfy shawl and wrap yourself in it.
- Tell your inner child "it is alright I will look after you" and follow through with that by really looking after yourself.
- Be secure about your values: learn how to operate from values instead of from fears.
- Join 4 groups where you are known and accepted and in which you feel secure.
- Become secure in your Divine relationship.
- Suck on mints or Life Savers whilst you start a new job or when you start doing something for the first time.

2. Approval

Every person on the planet needs approval. When we don't get it, we feel worthless. People will do all kinds of things to gain approval. In domestic violence situations, often the persecutor will undermine the self esteem of the person who is the victim, through verbal criticism and put downs. Often the victim ends up thinking no one would ever want to love them. Then, the persecutor gives occasional approval, for which the victim feels grateful. The victim is able to convince themselves that the violence is an isolated thing and will not continue, of course it usually does. People will stay in the most outlandishly horrible relationships, just so that they get the odd crumb of approval.

Even in ordinary circumstances, approval is a big deal. Many people gain approval by being nice. "Oh, Jane is such a lovely woman, she is always so kind, thoughtful of others, charming and generous." Meanwhile, Jane is exhausted, and feels like she is on a treadmill surrounded by people who need her. Jane ends up getting sick, or having some major sabotage go on in her life.

Most of the time, people don't realise they are giving not for the joy of it, but for approval. They feel good helping others. They are getting their approval need met by people who like being helped, so they just soldier on.

When I was married (the first time) I used to prepare lavish meals. If my husband came home and ate the meal and approved of it I felt great and things were good. But if he rang and said "Sorry, I have to work late" or "I had lunch out so I am not hungry" I would be furious! Looking back I realised that I was not doing this time-consuming cooking because I loved cooking, but because I was seeking approval. By continuing to engage in activities that I was actually doing because I wanted to get approval, I became depleted and empty and in the end got run down and sick.

When you give and give all the time and find yourself getting

exhausted, consider whether your inner child might just be seeking approval.

Real giving is from the heart, not seeking approval, and feeds the person who does it. They are not attached to outcomes. Whether their gift is appreciated or not, is not the issue. If no one ever says thank you, it doesn't matter. We are giving for the joy of it. Giving is a sustaining pleasure for the giver as well as the recipient when there are no needy strings attached to it.

Lucy

Lucy was a very good healer and a lovely woman. She was always the first to offer to help someone in need, was always available by phone for people if they needed someone to talk to. She actually annoyed some people because the minute they complained of any bodily symptom, she was on her feet waving her hands around giving them a healing whether they had asked for it or not. She did anything for anyone, and thought that this was because she was such a nice person, and so loving and giving.

Lucy developed serious lethargy, and was also experiencing problems in her family relationships. She was often the brunt of caustic comments by family members. She did everything for them, but was often really upset because they didn't seem to respect her.

We did some inner child work, and Lucy was unaware she had one. She couldn't find it during meditation, and started to cry. She realised that she was really out of touch with herself. The lethargy was the way the inner child was trying to get her attention.

I asked Lucy to stop meeting everyone else's needs and to start meeting her own. No amount of approval will be enough if we do not approve of ourselves. She came to see that her ardent attempts to help everyone in sight was just approval seeking. It was draining and was creating around her a lot of dysfunctional people whom she had allowed to become dependent on her.

We did a lot of cutting from various people, and she realised that they were not really friends so much as needy people who wanted her energy. Over time as she got on with her inner child and built a relationship with herself, Lucy found that many of her old, needy friends stopped calling her. She started to build new and mutually nurturing relationships, with people who were not needy. The more she approved of herself, the less Lucy was the brunt of other people's criticism. She found that her family members seemed to respect her more. Her energy levels improved.

All it took was for her to find, nurture, love and approve of herself, and her whole life changed.

Approval Strategies:

- Self-talk is critical here. When you are unsure, have just mucked something up or forgotten to do something, avoid self criticism and self condemnation, instead use nurturing self-talk like "It's all right, I approve of me even if no one else seems to".
- Use affirmation tapes or repeat the many affirmations in the relationship healing part of this book like "I accept respect love and trust myself just as I am".
- Use the affirmations from Chapter 6 of this book.
- Teach your child to express his or her anger in ways that your inner parent can feel good about.
- Regard your needs, wants, goals and welfare as being as important as anyone else's.
- Don't try to be perfect. t Learn to say no and still feel loved.
- If you have made a mess of something or hurt others, ask for forgiveness. Whether they give it or not, you have sought to make amends for which you can give yourself approval.
- Give yourself permission to be boring, untidy and unattractive at times.

3. Authenticity and Acceptance

Inner children need to feel accepted. Life is very challenging when we have to prove ourselves all the time. Everyone needs someone who just understands them, accepts them the way they are and doesn't want to change them. The person who is best placed to provide the acceptance is, guess who? You!

Instead of whining about your fat hips, or straggly hair, why not focus on your overall style and beauty. Accept yourself for who you are, and others will too. If you are very self-critical, you will find that others will reflect this back to you and your acceptance barometer will keep going down.

If you do not accept yourself, you will then be forced to seek acceptance externally. Many people join gangs or groups of people that they would not normally condone, because they crave acceptance, and in the group they get it.

It is not just the Hells Angels or the street gangs that take advantage of our need for acceptance. Ivy League types ensure that they join the right clubs, be seen in the right places, drive the right cars and live in the right suburb, so that they are acceptable. It is a need-meeting game. You do not have to play 'keeping up with the Joneses' if you just accept yourself as you are.

When we gain greater self-acceptance, we are able to become more authentic. Many people fear being authentic because they don't think they will be accepted any more.

If we believe that we are only acceptable if we think, act, dress and behave in a certain way, then this is going to be the astral reality that we manufacture in our lives. The truth is, the world will only ever accept us to the level that we ourselves are accepting of the truth of who we are.

When people join monasteries, the organisation often moves people from one geographic location to another. The training that is given in a spiritual institution is generally intense, and causes us to lose some of our culturally conditioned inauthenticity and gain more of who we really are, vast souls having human incarnations. We become so different that family and old friends can have difficulty relating to us and there is a lot of pressure to revert to the 'old you'. To alleviate that pressure and to enable the person to be their authentic selves they are moved to other locations.

We do not have to move away if we do the inner work to change our thoughts and beliefs about who we think we are. Any resistance that we get from others when we follow our authentic truth is in reality just a reflection of some conscious or unconscious resistance and non-acceptance that we hold internally about ourselves. As this changes, so will the response we pull forth from others.

For us to have respect from others, we need to have self-respect first. For us to have healthy self-respect, we are going to need to have self acceptance as well as self-approval. Meeting this need of your inner child will revolutionise your life.

Acceptance Strategies:

- Use affirmations like "It is ok to be different: I still love me" and "My uniqueness is a gift to the world: I am beautiful".
- Accept your body and focus upon its best attributes.
- Accept that there are things you can change and things that you cannot change. Do not try and change the things you cannot change.
- Focus on what you can change, which is yourself.
- Accept other people as they are.

- When you feel the stress of resistance in your body, breathe it out.

- Be real, by being more honest both about your thoughts and your feelings.

- Ensure that your self-talk is respectful and non-judgmental.

4. Hope and Encouragement

Life without hope is intolerable. We will be prone to depression and deep melancholy without hope. One of the hallmarks of an authentic spiritual tradition and spiritual practices is to give us hope.

When life is challenging it can be hard to have hope. Yet without it there is no point to anything.

During the World War II, many prisoners of war were taken and kept in terrible conditions in Japanese and German prisoner of war camps. They were fed inadequately and treated with little human dignity at all. Many lost hope, and simply died. Those that survived on the whole were able to continue to visualise their loved ones at home, and the life that they would eventually return to when the war was over. They did not lose hope, and this powerful force kept them alive and well during the most extreme kinds of deprivations that a person could imagine.

In our relationships it is important to have hope as well. When things have been going badly, it is easy to give up either on the other person, ourselves or the situation. The energy can get so congested that the radiant spirit of hope that is always available goes unnoticed.

Hope Strategies:

- Know that it is always the darkest before the dawn. With any real and important changes, we can sometimes face a barrage of challenges that can seem overwhelming just before there is a breakthrough.

- Pray for help from the Divine by whatever name or style best suits you.

- Keep asking that the highest situation or highest destiny manifest and don't be too attached to what that might look like.

- Have a health check up and make sure that you have not slipped into depression: possibly you may need some counselling or medical treatment to help get through a difficult period.

- Have Ignite Your Spirit therapy: it does what the name says, and helps us return to our natural state of hopefulness.

- Focus on the good in other people.

- Practice the meeting of the other 7 needs as a commitment to yourself, regardless of how you may be feeling.

- Learn to meditate. Do the Pillar of Light meditation (available through Harmony Centres or through the Shanti Mission website) and allow more spiritual energy into your system. Hope will naturally spring eternally when we are in contact with our spirit.

5. Love

Love is splendid, but is often confused with other things, like lust. Love registers through the heart chakra, and has a euphoric quality. Love is one of the most seductive of energies. No one is immune to it.

The inner child needs love. If the inner child doesn't get love, the person can be very bitter. Very 'hard hearted' people have usually been hurt, and so have walled up their heart chakra and cut off all further risk of emotional upset. They have also walled themselves off from love. There is often no pleasing these people. They do not love themselves, so they certainly are not going to love you. They might say they do, they might even think they do, but love for such people will be highly conditional. They will have strong expectations of how you should behave and what you should do to perform your side of a co-dependent contract.

True love has no conditions, and wants only what the other person wants for themselves. We are not capable of that kind of love, unless we really love ourselves. When we love ourselves, we are not needy. We need nothing in return for giving the greatest gift of all.

Usually when you give something away, then you don't have it anymore. Think of a pound of sausages. If I give one to Harry and one to Stuart and one to Carrie and one to Rebecca, I will not have many sausages left. There will be less for me. This is not true of love. The best way to receive love is to give it. Love multiplies the more we give it. You can love many people at once. Love is a multi-faceted reality. Love is God.

Love is allowing, and is not defined by conditions, attachments, judgments or expectations. When our inner child feels love, that love radiates all around us and causes us to have many loving relationships in our life.

The only way we can come in contact with this love is to love ourselves. When we do this we realise that we can love others, and allow others to love us.

Love Strategies:

- Pick up a virtues card each day and focus on that as a daily practice, as all of the virtues combine to create a life filled with love.
- Decide: I love me all the time, even if I am currently experiencing hardships or loss. I am innately loveable.
- Give yourself time each day just to be.
- Meditate, particularly upon the heart chakra, or upon a Guru, Saint, particular name of God or sacred image that has rich meaning for you.
- Practice forgiveness with those you love, and with yourself.
- Talk tenderly and lovingly to yourself.
- Decide that you will learn to love and like yourself more than ever before.
- Teach your inner child the affirmations you are currently choosing to live by.
- Listen to what your child likes and give it to him or her in moderation, providing it doesn't hurt anyone else including your inner parent.
- Support the vibration of love in your house by creating a love-filled temple. Keep it clean and de-cluttered, relaxing and beautiful, full of fresh air and nice flowers or greenery from the garden. To begin with, do these lovely things for yourself. (Later when self-love is established, you can practice bhakti yoga, and

offer all of these things in your mind as gifts of love to the Beloved. First learn to do them for yourself because you are loveable and you deserve it.)

- Try burning essential oils and use sacred music to template the energy in your space. Rose oil is by far the best, but any oil which you love will do.

- Have pieces of rose quartz scattered around in the house, as it vibrates at the frequency of love and in the vast majority of people it activates the heart chakra, the center of love within us.

- Train your mind to remember times in your life when you were really happy, sharing times with loved ones. Feed those memories into your heart chakra.

6. Attention, Stimulation and Physicality

If a young child is ignored, they very soon learn that they can get attention really fast if they misbehave. Toddlers will even throw themselves on the ground if their demands are not met. They make such a fuss, that sometimes people give in to them, just for peace.

One of the really messy bits of ignoring inner child work is that we can fool ourselves into thinking that we don't have needs. We can just keep working 80 hours per week, and ignore the fact that we need love, acceptance, approval and stimulation just like everyone else does. If you ignore your inner child, whose main motivation in life is to have fun, then sooner or later they will break out. You had better watch out!

Career Destruction

Years ago I went in an event called the Great Bar Yacht Race. This was an end of year excuse for a lot of lawyers to drink too much, sail around the harbour, have lunch and sail home again. At the end of the day many people kept partying at an exclusive yacht club. A female barrister who was well known and (until then) respected, decided that it would be a great idea to get her gear off and dance on the table. She certainly ended up getting a lot of attention.

This woman was usually a sedate, hard working and responsible person who diligently worked weekends and went the distance to get good results for her clients. Her inner child had been ignored for years. In fact she never acted as though she knew she had one. Far too much alcohol was the chance her inner child had to jump out of the cupboard and grab all of the attention. She certainly did that. People were talking about it for months. Unfortunately, inner children don't give a toss about consequences. This woman was a laughing stock and found it really difficult to continue in the profession.

When we find our inner child, and give her attention, we then have to parent that child, so as to avoid situations where the child rules our life, making it chaotic.

If you are smart, you will pay yourself
attention regularly and often. This way,

you will be less likely to sabotage your life.

Studies have shown that babies who are handled grow far more rapidly than babies who are fed and kept clean, but not handled. Baby humans need human contact so that they can grow. They need it like plants need sunshine. Big humans need it too. Many people who live alone do not get touched by anyone. This can be a very lonely experience.

As we learn to parent ourselves, we find ways to meet our needs. Get a massage. Get out more, mingle, find nice people who you can just hug from time to time. It is up to the parent to find ways to give stimulation and physical contact to the child. With a little imagination and moving out of your comfort zone, you can achieve anything at all, even getting hugged.

Attention strategies:

- Learn to listen to what your inner child is feeling without judgment.
- Respond to your inner child's communication. This doesn't mean you have to act out whatever it is, but you need to have some response or your inner child will not trust you.
- Praise your inner child often.
- Journaling and channelled writing allow for the free flow of expression from your interior landscape into your conscious mind, where the parent can take care of anything that may have arisen in this dialogue from the child.
- Have a massage or other forms of body work, pay attention to how your body is feeling and look after it.
- Go to the beach. t Exercise. t Sit in the sun and feel it. t Be in nature and feel, smell, listen with all of your senses, whether at the beach, sitting in the sun or being aware of the clouds and the rain: practice being present with your environment and notice what arises within you.

- Hug people and let them hug you.
- Notice: How do I feel? What do I like, what upsets me?
- Nurture yourself when your inner child is in challenging situations.
- Have a manicure, facial and get your hair done. Nurture your physical body.
- Watch what you eat. Pay attention to food, don't go unconscious about it and before you know it you have eaten half a box of biscuits and ten chocolates.
- Create your own supportive network of friends.
- Pat yourself on the arm, actually soothing the inner child.

7. Sleep and Rest

If you don't think sleep is a core human need, then you have never been deprived of it. When my first baby was born, she was premature, and needed to be fed every 2 hours round the clock. She was tiny, and took about an hour to feed each time. That gave me one hour in bed, then one hour feeding. This went on for weeks. I became angry, depressed, teary, frustrated, irrational, tired (what an understatement) and completely unable to meet my own needs let alone anyone else's.

Your inner child might want to stay up all night partying, but the parent knows that work tomorrow is going to be ugly unless we go home now. Exerting control over the child in nurturing ways, and not giving in to their every desire, is as important as knowing their needs. Partying all night is not a need but a desire. Sleep is a need. Get some.

Sleep and Rest Strategies:

- Try and sleep 6-8 hours every night. For best rejuvenation, get a couple hours sleep before midnight, so don't go to bed too late.
- Take a rest after lunch.
- If there is no time to sleep and you are tired, meditate even briefly and this will recharge you.
  Practice sleep hygiene: no screen-based activity, and no high sugar or heavy meals just before bed, no intense activity before bed.
- Have regular bed time.
- Have regular getting up time. Set the alarm and get up, even if you have a nap later.
- Keep bed just for sleeping, don't study and watch TV habitually in bed as the thought forms will gather in the space and invade your mind when you are trying to rest.
- Use soothing chants, Archangelic Space or Om music in your bedroom to help you sleep.
- Get plenty of rest before doing anything new.
- Sit quietly wrapped up in a comforter or blanket.
- Give yourself a bubble bath or lounge in a tub of warm water and bath oils.
- Spend thirty minutes to an hour floating in a swimming pool on a warm sunny day.
- Hang in a hammock for a long time.

8. Fun

For many reasons people can feel guilty about taking time for themselves, just to have fun. Fun is not of any relevance to the adult. It is tolerated by the parent, but the inner child thrives on it. If you let your inner child have some wholesome fun, they will be cooperative and satisfied and will be 'good' while you get on with other parts of your life. Laughing, having a good time, enjoying sports and wholesome interests, feeds our energy and gives us more oomph to deal with other parts of our life.

The buzz you get from surfing, or sailing, or playing bridge, or having hobbies or interests that you pursue just because you love it, is a way to energise your whole life and nurture your inner child.

Fun Strategies:

- Focus on things other than our challenges.
- Try and remember times in the past where you had fun.
- Make a decision that in the future life is going to be fun.
- Today find something, even a small thing that is pleasant.
- 'Borrow' the joy of your loved ones. Feel good for them for the joy in their life.
- Watch comedies (Don't watch disaster movies, don't listen to world news, don't even listen to national news, it is only the bad news!) Watch feel good shows, comedies or documentaries, cooking programs, gardening shows, sport, but not horror or war movies as these will drop your vibration.
- Have sports, hobbies or other interests.
- Enjoy your body including your sexuality.

We have spent some time identifying the needs of the inner child. To make it more real, it's good to meet your inner child by doing the 'Meet Your Inner Child' guided meditation available on the Shanti Mission website.

Parenting in Practice

Picture something that is going on in your life and in your relationship that you are not happy about. You may have said nothing about it because you don't want to seem difficult or uncaring. Yet it is driving you and your inner child nuts. It is a valid conversation to say "I know that you are in the habit of watching 'the Detective' on TV every Thursday night, but I would really like to watch what I want occasionally, can we discuss this?" How we say it is going to be as important as what we say, a topic we will return to later.

This is the very time we need to parent the inner child. Put the child behind you and let the adult or parent do the talking. The child may well want to kick him, for monopolising the TV for the past 6 years. At the same time the child might feel scared of being rejected for rocking the boat. That is why you haven't said anything for the past 6 years.

If I love me even if my partner rejects me, then I am empowered and enabled to say what I need to say. If my inner child is feeling safe and secure that it is not going to be abandoned, then it is OK to say something that may make my beloved mad, because it is my truth. Parenting the inner child is about learning how to speak your truth. Then you can stand up and see what you need to say, in a timely and skilful way. The more you do that, the more your inner child will trust you. The level of self-sabotage in your life will diminish.

In terms of meeting the 8 needs of the child, it is no good saying "Let's have an ice cream", which is a fun thing, if the need of the child is to be safe. You might shut the child up by feeding her ice cream, but the need is still there. Usually this strategy of shutting up the child leads to addiction. We engage in an activity that drowns out the voice of our neediness, and the feelings that we do not want to hear. Instead, we need to work out what is really going on, and develop a strategy to meet the need. When the need is met, the requirement for the addictive behaviour will wane.

Sometimes you are just tired and the need is just sleep. You might have 5 different jobs that you think you need to do, but if the inner child need for sleep is not met then something might happen that sabotages your efforts anyway. That may be just when your computer starts playing up, and starts to reformat everything you have just done and it takes you even longer.

Everything in our life is an extension of us, and the energy we put in them affects how they work. The energy emanating from our inner child is particularly strong, so it is good to be careful with it.

If you are not empowered in your own relationship with your inner child, you can forget being empowered in your relationships with others.

Chapter

11

MEETING YOUR INNER CHILD

In our seminars we do a guided meditation process to get in tune with our inner child. We advise that you get the 'Meet your Inner Child' meditation which can be used regularly to see how your inner child is faring. It provides a means by which the often unnoticed voice of the inner child can be brought into our awareness with safety and ease.

Then, we are going to write a letter to our inner child with our dominant hand. We will do this as the nurturing parent part of ourselves.

After writing a letter to our inner child, we are going to write a response from our inner child to our parent self. This will be written with our non-dominant hand so as to get more in touch with our subconscious landscape. Little children do not write very many words, so the letter from your inner child is likely to be short. Below are examples of letters from the parent to the child and from the child to the parent.

Dear little Fiona,

I know that you are very lonely. I know that you are scared that people are going to hurt you or leave you and so you don't want to let anyone near you. You feel like you have to be brave all the time, and be a good girl and do lots of things you don't like with horrid people and no one loves you very much. I'm from the future and I know better than anyone what you have been through. I love you and want you to be with me always. I will let you be exactly the way you are. I will help you achieve some balance and listen to how you feel and comfort you, keep you company and listen to you. You need never be lonely again. Love, Big Fiona

Example letter from the inner child to the nurturing parent:

Dear Big Ben,

I want to play with you but you are big and scary.

Can I sit on your knee?

Little Ben

In your workbook you are invited to write to your inner child and have them write back to you. It can be very revealing. You can keep an inner child journal for a while and really learn a lot about what is driving you.

The workbook also contains numerous exercises, meditations and opportunities to meet and continue the journey of parenting your inner child with balance and grace. The practical exercises are an important way of really getting the paradigm and how useful it can be for us all. They are also covered in our Empowering Relationships 1 seminar and mentor groups.

Chapter

12

Some Inner Child Practices

Daily Check In

After meeting your inner child in meditation, it is a very good idea to check in with them often, like you would with a real child. This tool for self-empowerment is useless if we get in touch with the child, then ignore them again for the next 3 months. Your inner child will hate you and will not trust you if you do this.

One of the ways that I have found effective at checking in with my inner child is to bring her to mind each evening before I fall asleep. I ask her how she is going and mostly she is fine. This might only take a minute. Sometimes she is not fine and I need to help her or listen to what she is telling me. Then I will think about that and work out how I am going to deal with it. Ignoring it is not really an option because I know that sooner or later it will lead to problems.

Dealing with Scary People or Big Challenges

If you have to do something that is scary, like going to court as a witness, or having a job interview and so forth, ensure that you speak to your inner child and encourage her before you go. Tell her how great she is and how everyone loves her, and how you love her. Let her know that your parent and adult self will do this thing so that she can feel safe and protected. When she is feeling safe, she may show herself as delightful and shine through as appropriate humour, energy and creativity.

The Art of Distraction

If your inner child is used to getting volatile when its needs do not seem to be met, then as the parent, you need to change this behaviour or it will ruin relationships. If your inner child starts to build up a head of steam and it seems like it is going to act out, distract it. Take it out of the room, show it something interesting, do whatever it takes to get the inner child to think about something else and do not let it be destructive or abusive.

At the same time it is important not to ignore the information that the child was giving you. Why was the child angry? What need is not being met? Often the child will lash out when at the root of the issue the child does not feel safe.

How can I take responsibility for that need and not project that need onto others? Time and experience will enable us to become much more skilful in managing our inner child and dealing with the child's anger is a particularly important thing to do. We will look at anger management later in the energy healing section. If anger is your thing, get some healings to try and deal with the charge of energy **and** parent your inner child.

Pat your Arm

Funny as this might sound, I have found it very comforting when Little Kim is upset to pat my arm. It is like stroking a real child. It is very calming and reassuring, takes only a second and connects me to that part of myself in a helpful way. Try it yourself and see.

Small Joyful Detours

I know a professional man who worked very hard in a big city. He spent a lot of time walking around town attending meetings. His inner child loved bulldozers. So whenever there was construction work going on, he would walk via those streets and spend a minute looking through the peep-holes into the construction site and show his inner child the bulldozers and cranes working. Then he would be off for more meetings and his inner child felt loved and appreciated. What slight detour could you make in your busy day that your inner child would love?

Using Virtue Cards to Parent the Inner Child

Get a pack of virtue cards[6]. Pick a card for the inner mother, place it in your left hand. Pick a card for the inner father, place it in your right hand.

This can best be done by shuffling the cards, which adds your energy to them. Close your eyes, asking for Divine guidance through the

---

[6] Virtue cards are created by the Virtues Project. They are available online and are sold in Shanti Mission Harmony Centres as a spiritual development tool.

intuitive selection of the card. Then, without looking, pick the mother card then the father card.

If you feel resistance when you see the card, you know you picked a good one! Follow the tips on the virtues card to help yourself learn how practically you can apply this virtue to your daily life and parenting role. This will have the effect not only of improving the most basic and important relationship in your life (with yourself) it will also raise your vibration. This puts you into a new vibrational 'address' in Vibrational Valley so that life unfolds in a different way.

You can choose two cards like this each day, or even better focus on the same card for at least a week. If you really want to go deep, do a 40 day sadhana (spiritual practice) focusing on the same two virtues, one for the inner mother and one for the inner father, for that entire time. You will learn heaps!

The Fantasy Parent

Sometimes we can have the belief that our life would have been so much better if only we had a different parent or parents. Or, if only Mum had loved me like this, or if only Dad had come to my football matches, or if they had not been so self absorbed, or if they had not been so critical and judgmental… then how different I would be now.

One of our teachers Savitur Dhanvantre has a method of dealing with this thought form. We take the view that we choose our parents prior to incarnating and that there is always a spiritual reason for the choice. This has to do with the need within our soul to grow, balance karma and have a foundation in life, which sets up the paradigm of learning or the classroom that we most need here in Earth school.

A really empowered thing to do is: if you could have any parent in the world, fantasy or real, who would that be and what are the qualities that you admire in them and their parenting role. If you were not protected, you might want a father like a character played by Clint Eastwood or other action hero who fights the bad guys and always wins. If you were not given much nurturing you might want a mum like in Happy Days, or you might chose a Saint or Avatar, whose sterling qualities resound with you.

In a healing Savitur gets his client to imagine those qualities, connect to the inner child and then feel the energy that those qualities have in the chosen fantasy parent. In essence, you are invoking those qualities. Then you start to give these things to your own inner child. This is a practical way of starting to parent your inner child. It is also a powerful way to take responsibility for cultivating the parent that you truly desire. It takes us out of victim consciousness, which is one of the most disempowering states in which we can live, into real empowerment.

He finds that the inner child starts to get a lot of joy and feels heard when we start to cultivate and attend to the inner needs of our beloved little ones in this way.

Chapter

13

BHAKTI YOGA

Yoga means Divine Union. Many people are mostly familiar with the physical branches of yoga such as Hatha yoga. But this is only one part of an incredibly rich and beautiful system for becoming one with the Divine in various ways.

Bhakti yoga is the yoga of love. A Bhakti is someone who wants to serve the beloved. Through nurturing and caring and through the selflessness that develops, the Bhakti attains enlightenment.

One can love God or a spiritual teacher in a devotional way and experience Bhakti. One can love *anyone* and experience bhakti because everyone is Divine, whether conscious of that or not. One can also apply the principles of Bhakti to our partner, seeing God/Goddess in them.

There is a story of an Indian woman who loved her family as though they were each God. She cooked for God, cleaned God's house and did

God's washing. She saw only God in each member of her family, all the time. She attained enlightenment.

In our Western ways, sometimes we fear this kind of selflessness because when we practice it, or when we have done so in the past, it has become messy. Perhaps we have been taken advantage of, or treated like a doormat. Perhaps we have become miserable rather than enlightened by the experience. If this is the case then there are some technical issues that we might want to look at.

Firstly, are we doing the serving of our family and/or partner from a place of selflessness and purity, or are we trying to get approval? If we are angry or upset when they don't notice all the things that we do then it is because we are not getting the approval that we want. This is an opportunity for us to practice parenting our inner child, giving ourselves the approval that we crave. This sets us free to really serve from a place of lightness of heart and delight. When we do that, a great deal of Divine energy comes to and through us, enabling what we are doing.

I once went to stay with a couple in a distant city to teach a Path of Ease and Grace seminar. They were both professional people, but she did all the cooking. She did it with love. She was not looking for approval, she just loved her husband and wanted to prepare stunning healthy food for both him and herself. She cooked with love, and you could taste it in the food. The energy of the food was very strong because of her attitude while making it. Each meal was a total gift. Similarly, he did all the cleaning. While mopping the floor I heard him chanting. He really put the energy and vibration of the Divine into that mopping. The place was spotless, and for him the housework was serving the temple in which he lived with his beloved. Needless to say they had a very happy marriage.

Sometimes we get so busy, and caught up with the things that we have to do, that other things which are possibly more important in the long run are overlooked. When we are on our death bed, it is unlikely that we will be looking back at all the reports that we handed to our boss on time; more likely we will be regretting all of the lost opportunities to tell those we love how much they mean to us and how we wish we had valued our time with them more.

Bhakti yoga really becomes the most satisfying and uplifting when the love that goes into our relationships firstly goes into our primary relationship, which is with ourselves. We ensure that our inner child is told every day how much we love her. We look after her, and do not let her be in situations where she would be devalued or abused. As part of looking after her, we would do affirmations and spiritual work to 'up' our own level of self-respect. The more we respect ourselves, the more others will too. Then we can love and give with all our hearts, and the world will mirror back to us an even greater amount of love and abundance of all kinds than we ever could have imagined.

FAMILY

Are you aware that if we died tomorrow, the company that we are working for could easily replace us in a matter of days.

But the family we left behind will feel the loss for the rest of their lives.

And come to think of it, we pour ourselves more into work than into our own family,

an unwise investment indeed, don't you think?

So what is behind the story?

Do you know what the word FAMILY means?

FAMILY = (F)ATHER (A)ND (M)OTHER (I) (L)OVE (Y)OU

The Wise Spiritual Teacher or Guru

One can obtain endless help from a Guru in becoming empowered in parenting your inner child and learning deep love and devotion to the self and others. If we can learn to love the self as much as we love the Guru, then we will become masters in the art of relationships and love. It will create vast joy and happiness.

At some stages in the Guru/disciple relationship, the inner child of the disciple will want the Guru to parent them. In our school at least, this is not going to happen in the manner that our inner child is necessarily looking for. Guru will provide love, guidance and reassurance. Like a Divine mother, the Guru cares for the disciple with love that is unconditional. This means, no matter what the disciple does, the Guru will still love them. Like a Divine Father, Guru also has boundaries, and is interested in the child becoming strong, independent and functional at all levels, able to take care of their own needs. This means saying no to disciples when necessary in order that the disciple realise their own self-empowerment.

Guru is not a mentor in the usual sense. Guru is someone who can relate with us spiritually, energetically, and in our sleep and dreams as well. When the relationship is working properly it has nothing to do with co-dependence. It is about the way that we can develop inter-dependence which is healthy and satisfying on many different levels. Ever since people stopped living by themselves in caves, our society has been too complex to imagine that any one of us can live without others. So, learning to live inter-dependently instead of co-dependently will revolutionise the way we live and have relationships. People who are interdependent can meet their own needs first, then have plenty of energy with which to help others to learn and grow.

The reason people like being around a Guru is because they are full of love and bliss. They are very spiritually empowered. The inner child loves that. The job of the Guru is to help the disciple to have this same bliss and love within themselves. Much of the inner glory, bliss and radiance that comes to a disciple is placed there through direct energetic transfer from the Guru. This creates inner spiritual brilliance but will take root more easily when the person is parenting their own inner child.

The inner child wants to be the special one, the chosen one, wants to be the one who gets the blessing today, who has the initiation, and who can bask in the glory and notice of the Guru. The Guru sees this as attachment and a bid for co-dependence and will give teachings or behave in such a way as to challenge the perception that the person has.

The challenge is in order for the person to take responsibility for their own inner child, and learn by example how to parent and come from 'cup full'. This can feel a little uncomfortable, and the inner children can want to blame the Guru for making them feel bad, un-chosen and so on. However the Guru is actually doing them a great service.

In our School for the Soul, the most empowered people have all been through this. We talk about this openly, and we keep our relationships clear and empowered. We are there for each other when we really need help, but we do not rescue each other or parent each other's inner children. This does not mean we lack compassion, but we don't sympathise or feel sorry for each other, and we do not sit with each other's victim child. That would be dishonouring of the individual and is very disempowering.

When our cup is empty, we are needy and dependent on others to fill us up. This creates co-dependence. When our cup is full, we can start to send love to the self as well as give it to others. If love is given so that you will give something to me, it is just a contract. It is not unconditional love, and you will feel depleted after the giving unless the other party does their part in the transaction (i.e. I will do this for you if you do this for me). If we have so much love that it spills out of us, we are unaffected by what others might do with that love, and we are always able to give it to ourselves, not needing someone else to do it for us.

Every relationship, every interaction and every conversation is an opportunity to see how my cup is faring, how much am I loving myself and others today in a non-co-dependent, free and giving way. Remember that love is another word for God. However you feel love, you are really feeling the Divine. When you look at a newborn baby, your beloved or when you cuddle your dog, you are feeling God in your heart. Imagine being able to do that no matter what is going on in your life? The Guru can and can teach you to do so as well.

Interdependence

Instead of co-dependence, which has a strangulating effect upon us, physically, mentally, emotionally and spiritually, the idea is to strive for interdependent relationships. These relationships are characterised by respect and love in action. If your partner really wants to go and do something, you let them. You want them to be fulfilled and you can parent your inner child and therefore not be lonely while they are gone. You always have great company: You!

My partner Shiva Kata Tjuta and I, after many years living with this model of reality, have learned to be interdependent rather than codependent. We help each other, love each other, live our own lives and feel free and fulfilled, and yet we have blazingly strong commitment, joyfulness, fun and closeness. We both know that we are really free to pursue that which is important to us, and we both know that we will speak our truth to each other in an assertive way. Occasionally we have a good argument before flowing into the 'golden after-glow' phase again. When the chips are down, we parent our own inner children, and do not demand that the other does it for us. Weirdly enough, our experience has been that generally if one of us is going through some stuff, so is the other one. Thus, we have become very practiced at parenting ourselves during this time and not having to rely on the other one to do it for us.

Kahlil Gibran on Marriage: From The Prophet

You were born together, and together you shall be forevermore.

You shall be together when the white wings of death scatter your days.

Ay, you shall be together even in the silent memory of God.

But let there be spaces in your togetherness,

And let the winds of the heavens dance between you.

Love one another, but make not a bond of love:

Let it rather be a moving sea between the shores of your souls.

Fill each other>s cup but drink not from one cup.

Give one another of your bread but eat not from the same loaf

Sing and dance together and be joyous, but let each one of you be alone,

Even as the strings of a lute are alone though they quiver with the same music.

Give your hearts, but not into each other>s keeping.

For only the hand of Life can contain your hearts.

And stand together yet not too near together:

For the pillars of the temple stand apart,

And the oak tree and the cypress grow not in each other>s shadow.

PART

4

BOUNDARIES

Chapter

14

RELATING OR DEPENDING

Relationships and the Emotion-Child

A lot of the people that we meet in Empowering Relationships seminars have grown out of touch with themselves. Their inner child is no-where to be seen. They have difficulty accepting, respecting, loving and trusting either themselves or other people. The fundamental relationship between parent and child is not working. When this happens, the things that the child needs will be impossible to find within. Thus, the person has to try and find them in other relationships. This creates neediness, and needy people coming into relationships together create classic co-dependence. It ends up being destructive, one way or another. Instead of having a heartfelt relationship of freedom, love, spaciousness and flow, it is a continual dance of "I agree to meet your need for this if you will meet my need for that". Then we try and control each other endlessly so that our needs will be met.

When people become attracted to each other as potential mates, there is a sizing up by each child as to the manner in which the other will parent them. Our child then starts to look to the beloved to meet its needs, instead of looking to its own parent self. Almost instantly, *his* inner child is looking at *her* parent and asking "Will you mother me?" And *her* inner child is looking at *his* parent and asking "Will you father me?" This happens so fast we might barely be conscious of it, but our inner child is always on the look out for how to get its needs met, particularly if we have not attended to it ourselves. This also happens in same sex relationships, and there are times that he does the mothering and she does the fathering: all combinations are possible.

In traditional marriages, the woman mothered both inner children by holding the emotional content of the marriage, cooking and keeping house. The man went to work and provided for and fathered both inner children. The contract of expectations that they had was "I will father you if you will mother me".

In our generation the roles are much less clear-cut. Issues erupt as our inner child gives our power to our lover, because then our inner parent has to fight to get that power back again. It is usually a dirty and none too conscious fight! As we move into wholeness, we are integrating our male and female parts. In doing so we have to learn to care for ourselves rather than having the expectation that someone else is going to do it for us.

Parent to Child Imbalance

In some relationships one party is all parent and the other is all child. This creates a strong attraction at first, but over time is frustrating for both parties. The child persona finds the parent stultifying, and the parent finds the child impossible, and wants to scream "I am not your mother!" This kind of imbalance is difficult to sustain in the long run unless each learns to develop the other parts of self.

Co-dependent relationships can get by OK for a while, until something threatens the inner child's security and the other person does not meet its needs. This can happen for instance if there is a big change in routine. This can lead to relationship disaster if either or both parties are unable to move to meet their *own* needs, at least during a period of crisis. A crisis might be anything from a retrenchment, a bad medical diagnosis, a new baby in the house, a death in the family, and so on.

If the child feels jealous, or if the partner is spending too much time with others, then she or he has no way of dealing with that because Daddy or Mummy is not there and so she or he starts acting out. There is no parent in sight. The relationship between our own parent and child is non-existent and so the child will not listen to us, just as we have not listened to them for years. Things go off the rails.

Imagine a marriage with both parents working, there are kids to look after, both are tired and finding that their own needs are not being met, each is expecting the other to help them and they don't have the energy to do so, and friction has arisen. Each one is pointing to the other to do something, but they lack any excess capacity at that time. Sometimes at this stage, a drama gets created so that the needs of that inner child get attended to. This can take the form of illness, accidents, acting out, aggressiveness or affairs.

While ever we expect our mate to parent our inner child and are incapable of doing it ourselves when the need arises, we are in for a difficult time. Inevitably they will not be there for us. They might leave.

They might die. We live in terror of these kinds of eventualities.

Are You Crazy?

When we expect that someone else is going to parent us and they don't, we are disempowered and feel angry or disappointed. When this happens, our inner child can cause us to behave in ways that we would normally consider to be unacceptable if we saw someone else acting that way.

For example, if a woman has been the emotional provider in a relationship, and suddenly she is sick for weeks on end, she will be unable to meet her husband's expectations. She has to give priority to her own needs. The needs of the husband, which she usually met, are not able to be handled by her, at least for a while. This can cause the inner child of the husband to go berserk, acting selfishly, unreasonably, staying out late at the pub, having affairs, etc. This is all just to get attention and feel loved. If the man learnt to love himself, he would not be dependent on someone else to love him. He would not need to be unreasonable. He would not need to have an affair. He would give love and attention to himself for a while, and create situations where he could help his wife, and provide for her needs until things got better.

Parenting Biological Children

When my kids were little, I found that if I looked after my inner child, then I was able to maintain a sweet(Ish) disposition with them. However if I did not allow myself a bit of time every day just for me, parenting was much harder. I would get a bit frazzled. When this happened, I found it really hard to be patient and understanding with them. They didn't seem all that gorgeous when I was tired irritable and feeling needy. Little Kim (my birth name) could get out of hand, get jealous of the attention that they were getting from Big Kim or anyone else, and it was not pretty.

I found that it was in everyone's best interests when I felt like that to simply announce "Little Kim needs me right now". My children, who are very intelligent, knew that this was a good time to disappear momentarily and find something to do. After a few minutes with Little Kim, telling her everything is OK, giving her some approval and love, and sitting down for a couple of minutes, I was usually fine again.

I realised that I needed to give Little Kim a bit more of my time so that I could avoid falling into 'harassed parent' mode. I then looked in my diary and found some time, which I could cross off and spend just doing whatever I wanted instead of the myriad things I have to do. Having done that, Little Kim was ready to go and play with our real children, and the whole thing only took a few minutes.

Needy People

Needy people can be quite exhausting to be around. Needy people are not able to meet their own needs, and so they MUST find other people to do this for them. This is not wrong, it just is. The consequence of this mode of living is that they will end up in co-dependent relationships and wonder why they are so unfulfilling or fragile. If you are surrounded by needy people you may need to reassess how you allocate your time and energy. The first person whose needs ought be met, are your own. When your own needs are met, you are then able to meet the needs of others. This gets easier over time as we become more skilled and aware. We then get a lot of energy with which we can serve and help other people, which we love to do. For sustained ability to help others, we cannot do so at the expense of caring for ourselves first. This is not selfish. It is how to survive.

Affairs

Lots of people get bent out of shape worrying about whether or not their partner is having an affair. Generally speaking affairs only happen because the inner child of one or both parties in the relationship is totally ignored by its own parent, and is not having his or her needs met. It is not always just the active party who is having the affair that has inner child problems. Often the spouse does too. Affairs are a way that an inner child seeks to get needs met.

Sometimes affairs mean the end of a relationship. Other times, affairs are a catalyst that brings into the open the need for both parties to get a better emotional education. Brick walls can build up as people hide behind their fears of revealing their deep emotions and needs. They are not truly open about themselves, their desires, priorities and expectations. Through counselling, workshops and spiritual awareness, there are many ways that relationships can be rejuvenated, leading people to much deeper states of love and connection than ever before.

The ultimate in love for another person is to want for them whatever makes them happy. If that happiness is found with another person, then we can relinquish them and let them go. This might hurt, but if we can love ourselves, we will soon find a partner who mirrors that love back to us.

When we really give people the freedom to be who they really are, and we are really loving, that has a magnetic quality. It is highly unlikely that anyone is going to want to stray in the face of true love. Not codependent neediness, but real, grace-filled, unconditional love. Real love is embracing, enabling, sometimes scary, ebbs and flows, develops and has different phases. The more we open our heart and allow love to flow within ourselves, the more we can share this love with those around us.

Chapter

15

BOUNDARIES

A boundary is a method of demarcation. Sometimes it can be like a fence, something that keeps us in and others out. In relationships a boundary can be a marker of the place where 'appropriate' and 'inappropriate' meet each other.

Some people live without very many boundaries. Generally this will become uncomfortable, as others seem to trample all over us. Some people live with boundaries that are like the walls of a maximum security prison complex. There is no way you are going to get in, and no way they are going to reach out.

Setting boundaries with the people with whom we relate is a delicate art, and one which needs to be mastered if we are going to have long term happiness.

Basically, the main components of our life are our time and energy. We have a huge range of choices as to what we do with these things. If we have no boundaries, others will hijack our agenda, and before we know it we are living a life that someone else wants us to live, instead of the one we were incarnated to live. We can lose sight of who we are and what our life is about.

Boundaries are part of the security need of our inner child. We need internal boundaries, between our inner parent and child, as well as boundaries with the parent and child of others. We saw earlier that if there is too much child evident in a person then there can be situations where they have little or no morality or thought of consequences of their actions. They are irresponsible and are forever letting others down or living excessively or even dangerously. Conversely our internal boundaries can be so strict that the child is never seen or heard: in this case the person is likely to lack warmth, and have difficulty exhibiting any sense of fun, spontaneity or spirit.

When it comes to boundaries, the first ones we really need to deal with are the internal boundaries of balance, moderation and finding safe ways to get our needs met. Without good internal boundaries, life is a roller coaster of inappropriate behaviour either by us, or others. Without good internal boundaries, it is very hard to find a way to have good boundaries with anyone else.

Why Don't You Respect Me?

Sometimes when we seek to put a boundary in place, no one respects it. The reason for this is usually that we in fact do not really respect ourselves. In life, it can look like our fate rests with other people. We might tell them what we need, but they ignore us and do whatever they like. So what do we do then? We can yell or scream, make a scene, or just give up. Alternatively we can look within and do some work on re-empowerment.

When we move inwards from the physical dimension and look in the etheric and astral dimensions, as well as in our soul selves, we will be able to find many ways to create good boundaries, and have them respected by others.

In the etheric dimension, it is possible that our solar plexus chakra is not as strong as it needs to be, and that we are incapable of coming from a place of courage and certitude, because the necessary etheric hardware (chakra) to do that needs work. Also there may be many cords of energy hanging out of us which plug us into situations of disempowerment and disrespect from habit and expectation. These can be cleaned up.

In our astral body, we may have beliefs that we are not worthy or loveable. We may believe "men never respect me" or "women are ruthless" and these beliefs will undermine our relationships, even with a Saint. We get what we believe in. Refer back to the section on the mind, and also look at our 'Yoga of the Mind' and 'Dimensions of Wealth' programs for more ways to deal with the very common problem of self-defeating thought forms.

It is also possible that we are stuck in a paradigm of blame and shame, and that our vibration is pulling negativity from the people with whom we have relationships. This is a soul dimension problem, which we can heal as we work on self-purification and self-love.

Boundaries with Others

One of the complications about boundaries is that we really do not inhabit a black and white world, even though old paradigms of 'good' and 'bad' would have us believe that we do. How do you do the 'right thing' when you are not sure which of several competing priorities ought be given precedence?

Because of all the differences in priorities, values and assumptions of the people in our lives, we can find that we have to put in place personal boundaries in circumstances that can be complex, challenging and confusing. Many of us are not good at this.

Louis

I was once informed by a student that he had purchased an expensive gift worth several thousand dollars that he thought our organisation should give to another spiritual organisation. While this is all very nice, it was done without consultation and when I tuned in I felt that the gift was not going to be understood or really valued. It seemed to me to be a misconceived notion. However Louis, wanting to be helpful and operating with good intention, had already spent the money. The old me would have just forked out money as a contribution to the gift, and rounded up others to get on board as well. However it seemed clear to me that this was a boundary issue. It is not OK for someone to commit me, or our organisation, to a financial outlay when we have never discussed it. So, I told him we would not contribute and gently asked Louis to consider this in light of what we teach about boundaries. He had never thought of this. He was shocked at first and a bit angry, but later wrote to me and thanked me for having put a boundary in place, which helped him to learn where and how to put boundaries in place as well.

To have a boundary it helps to be clear about what is OK and what is not OK given the circumstances in which we find ourselves. For this to work optimally, we need to have situational intelligence.

Situational intelligence is something that includes not just an analytical or logical data-based input, it also includes how we are feeling, what our intuition tells us, and what our spiritual and cultural norms might be. The clearer we are internally and the more balanced we are as people, the more our situational intelligence is likely to be good and wholesome. If we are still grappling with deep core wounds and trying to hide our inadequacies from the world, if we are still in co-dependent relationships because we cannot meet our own needs, then our situational intelligence is likely to be compromised by our neediness.

Where do you put it?

Some people have boundaries that are held close around them, are always on the front foot, insisting that everyone do things their way, and they can be controlling and directive in ensuring that this is so. These people can be overbearing, rigid, and may become aggressive if someone challenges them. Some people have behaviours that are over the top, needy, controlling, overbearing, abusive and demanding. In this case their boundaries are squashing others, and this will not be sustainable in the long term. Living with such a person is like living with a petty tyrant.

Sooner or later, it will be their downfall.

Another scenario is that we have tall strong impenetrable boundaries that cut us completely off from other people and negate any possibility of a relationship. In extreme cases, the person can become a recluse.

Then there are those with no discernible boundaries who put up with just about anything. These people are fearful of conflict and are not secure in their inner parent/child relationship. Often, they need a lot of coaching on self-respect.

Our boundaries might be placed entirely in someone else's hands. Our expectations of others might be so high, that they can never meet them for very long. Eventually our demands will cause at best an argument or at worst the demise of the relationship.

Our internal guidance system as far as boundaries are concerned, really emanates from what we were taught as kids from our parents. Even more significant than what our parents *tried* to teach us, is what we actually 'caught' from living with them. Their habits and unspoken contracts and expectations seep into us in a subconscious way.

If we had parents that were really strict, a bit scary and very demanding, chances are that we became over-socialised and terrified of doing or saying the wrong thing. Conversely, we may have developed into a rebel, or someone who mimics this behaviour, becoming overbearing and dictatorial in our own adult relationships.

If we had parents who were obsessive/compulsive when it came to cleanliness, perhaps our own boundary as to what constitutes being clean enough may be far from balanced. If our parents were very tight with money, or free with it, this might also affect where and how we would put our boundaries in day-to-day living in respect of our finances.

In some areas our boundaries might be quite healthy, but in others they might be repressive, or absent altogether. Sometimes when we think we are putting in place a boundary, all we are really doing is trying to force someone else to meet our needs. We are in fact being controlling and even manipulative and failing to take responsibility for our own needs.

As we get better at situational intelligence, we may find that we desire to change some of our boundaries. This may require some work, and we might experience a bit of pushback sometimes when we call our spirit back and reclaim our power. Nevertheless, we can do this, we can create healthy habits to improve and enhance our relationships using combinations of tools set out in this book.

Where Did I Go In That Relationship?

Lack of boundaries can make relationships seem more like a prison, as we continually give our power away, relinquish our own preferences, style, priorities and objectives, and fit in with everyone else.

When we have a pathological need to please others, this is coming from a state of disempowered consciousness in which we have inadequate boundaries. As a former people-pleaser, I used to do whatever I could to avoid being rejected by others. I couldn't stand for anyone to think I was anything other than a nice person and a good girl, and so I gave my power away continually. Little did I realise then that I was living in fear of being rejected. Pleasing everyone was my inner child's way of getting her need for approval met. Big Kim didn't have a clue how to do this herself. This caused me to put up with lots of unsatisfactory relationships and games within those relationships, because I didn't know what I could do about it. The end result was a kind of disappearing act, where the real authentic me was gobbled up in the façade of who I thought someone else wanted me to be. My boundaries were paper thin, and someone only had to sneeze or look at me the wrong way and I would allow the boundary to be broken.

In my relationship past, I tended to take on the interests and habits of my partner. At one stage I went to football matches every weekend and I don't have the foggiest idea why anyone would do that. At another time I found myself going sailing regularly and hanging out on boats, something that I find either boring or terrifying and either way I can't wait to get off them. My own interests would be snuffed out as my time seemed to be sucked into what my partner's interests might be. It is as though I was a chameleon, fitting in to what I felt was expected of me. This is an example of an over-socialised child.

If you feel that your individuality is being lost and swallowed up in a relationship that you are in, then you may have a problem like I did. When we cannot assert ourselves, no-one else knows who we are. Even worse, we probably do not know who we are ourselves. The lustrous interesting person we were when our partner was attracted to us, disappears under loads of expectations, conditions, responsibilities and habits. This slowly raises bars around us and we end up feeling like we are in a relationship prison. Sooner or later we will break out and leave.

People-pleasers

A people-pleaser lets their boundaries be trampled on regularly. They abandon their routines when others need things, even when to do so is highly inconvenient. A people-pleaser is terrified of doing something that the beloved would not approve of, lest they be abandoned. If the beloved has a problem, the people-pleaser energetically takes it on, feeling anxious and responsible for the situation even if it has nothing at all to do with them. So keen are they for the beloved not to have any problems, that the people-pleaser anticipates the needs of the beloved, juggling all kinds of things to be in the right place, have the right thing on hand and say the right thing so that the beloved is not displeased.

The people-pleaser takes on a great deal of responsibility for the entire relationship and keeping everything on an even keel. In a healthier relationship, both parties would be aware of nurturing the relationship that they have with each other. Each would take responsibility for the happiness and success of themselves, and the relationship. Each would be very interested and helpful in nurturing the success of the other. Their cups would be full from self-nurturing and this would brim over into 'plenty' and from that both parties would be fulfilled.

In a relationship that has good boundaries, the responsibility for the relationship is mutual but in a pleaser relationship one person's needs are habitually secondary to the other.

The people-pleaser is often narcissistic, assuming that everything that the beloved says or does somehow relates to them, and so if they are upset, they automatically assume that they are upset with **me**.

In advanced cases of people-pleasing, the person actually has no life other than the beloved's life, and feels empty, unfulfilled or bored unless the beloved is around for them to focus on. Their entire social identity can become tied to their partner, negating the development of their own life's journey.

In a healthy relationship people can have a good time even if they are apart, and they feel secure in the love and regard they have for each other. In a disempowered relationship, time apart is intolerable because our security rests in being with the beloved, with whom we feel safe, accepted or whose approval we are desperate to have. Without them there is no one and nothing, we think "I am nothing without the beloved".

When one is a people-pleaser, saying no is really hard if not impossible. Half the time the people-pleaser has no idea what they actually want, because they are so unused to thinking about their own life, needs and objectives. When asked what they want, the people-pleaser often says "Oh I don't know, you decide". Even if they want to say no, they cannot. They are addicted to saying yes, although they then may feel resentful later.

In a loving, empowered relationship there is trust. In a co-dependent pleaser relationship there is so much fear of being left or abandoned that the parties are possessive and jealous of any time that the beloved spends with another.

In a loving relationship each party is free to grow and that growth is encouraged. Where co-dependence is at play, there is a focus on maintaining the status quo so that nothing changes. Each may try to control the other so as to prevent change. This is because of a terror of the beloved not meeting their needs. Who knows what will happen if there is change?

In an empowered relationship there is a feeling of spaciousness, whereby it is OK for unexpected things to happen, for a friend to drop by or for plans to change. In a people-pleasing relationship this is hugely distressing because this might interfere with my many expectations of you. You might focus on something else than me, and that will make for anger or resentment.

A people-pleaser never says what they feel, they just say what they think the beloved wants to hear. They are inauthentic from fear of rejection, they fear hurting the beloved's feelings, because then they might leave.

In a healthy relationship love is freely given. In co-dependence or people-pleasing there is always a price for anything, everything comes with strings attached. Perhaps gifts are used as bribes to placate the beloved. Instead of love there is need. You need to be needed.

In a healthy relationship, each party is free to maintain their own identity, to act for themselves even though the other person is in your mind. In a pleaser relationship the primary mechanism is reaction to the other person.

Too much pleasing causes us to feel highly resentful. This resentment seeps in and becomes entrenched within the energy field of the relationship. Pleasing is really only done out of fear. This fear can be anything from fear of making a bad decision to fear of being abandoned if they make a suggestion that does not create approval in their partner. The most common reason for pleasing behaviour is low self-esteem, requiring constant approval. Lack of approval is the worst nightmare for a pleaser. A people-pleaser has never learned to provide their inner child's need for approval and so has to indulge in a range of dysfunctional behaviours to get it from others.

Being supportive and being of service both come from love. The pleaser and the supporter may do the same worldly action, but the 'yin' element, which is motivation for that action, differs 180 degrees. In the first case it is about 'what I will get in return', in the second case it is about giving.

Pleasing is actually dishonest. Pleasing gives your partner the impression that you want to do what you are doing. It may never occur to them that you are just doing whatever it is that you are doing simply to please them. This gives a false impression of your interests, drives, and distorts the potential of the relationship away from co-creation of happiness and peace. It builds instability that sooner or later will come back to bite you – somewhere unpleasant!

Pleasing generally ends in a mess. We allow our life to get so off track that we lose ourselves. All of our time and energy is spent on someone else's agenda. One day we wake up and wonder: '*Who am I and what has happened to my life?*' Depression can set in. Anger can be internalised and seep out in inappropriate, passive-aggressive ways with a range of family members or friends who might happen to be in the firing line.

Susan and Tim

Susan came to us for a healing (actually several) because her marriage was going downhill fast. She and her husband Tim had been married for ten years and had a daughter. Susan was in shock because in recent marriage counselling she had found out that all of the major decisions she thought had been made by both her and Tim, had in-fact been things that Tim had not wanted to do. He had never voiced his doubts, fears or feelings that he was uncomfortable with these decisions, and she felt betrayed, shocked and angry. He was now blaming her for all of their problems, because she made all of the decisions. She felt trust had been undermined because in her head the decisions had been jointly made, and that they were both happy with these choices. To find out that Tim had just gone along with it to keep her happy was actually really painful and disappointing. She felt that any real relationship had been a sham. If he could not speak his truth on these matters she wondered if he had spoken his truth about anything at all. Furthermore Tim in anger during the counselling kept saying that the whole marriage had been a sham. Susan had no idea what he was talking about until she realised that all of Tim's pleasing behaviour had taken him out of his truth and personal integrity. He thought he was doing it for her, whereas she just wanted him to say how he felt and what he actually wanted. She was even more incensed because now a major decision was looming about whether or not they would move interstate. Tim wanted to move, and was now telling her that after all he had done for her, the least she could do on this occasion, was do this one thing for him. So far as her own consciousness was concerned, she felt robbed of her ability to make a decision in the present circumstances because she now felt pressured, guilty and blackmailed.

These issues had been rattling around inside Susan for weeks since Tim had dropped the bombshell that he was in fact unhappy about the way the marriage was unfolding in terms of the choices that had been made as a couple. Susan tried to be rational but found that she became enraged, confused and irrational. It put in doubt all that Tim said. She didn't know, when he agreed to something, if it was what he really wanted or if he was just saying that. This put all of the responsibility upon Susan of constantly having to pander to Tim to encourage him to tell her how he really felt, which was exhausting. It also raised the question as to why he did not feel safe enough to just be honest, which was an issue of his fear of abandonment.

Both Tim and Susan benefited greatly from a crash course in parenting their inner child and assertiveness training. Tim needed to forgive himself as well as Susan for allowing her to make all of the decisions up to that point. Susan needed to forgive Tim for being inauthentic. As they started to see the patterns and began to employ better communication strategies, as well as work upon self-respect, they developed better decision-making ability together.

The most important thing was not whether or not they went interstate, but whether they were both honest with their feelings with each other, and the quality of the vibration of the relationship as a whole. They started to ask that the highest outcome prevail, and worked on themselves. Tim went and worked interstate for a while and Susan stayed in their home. It turned out that Tim had projected all of his dissatisfaction and anger about having been a people-pleaser into the decision to move interstate, which in-fact did not solve anything and he didn't enjoy it. Instead they made several changes to the way they were living and organising their lives, so that both of them were accommodated, their daughter stayed in the same school and they did not have to sell their house at a time when there was a depressed market for homes.

The Boundary Test

I was so bad at developing boundaries when I was younger, that I could not say no to my partner, or for that matter most other people, even when what they wanted was demanding and impossible to live up to.

To combat this I invented a mythical sister who I loved a lot. When I was asked to do things and contribute my time and energy, I would mentally give advice to my 'sister' and tell her whether or not it seemed rational for her to take this on. Many times when I would have said 'yes' from habit, I would advise my mythical sister that she would be crazy to say yes.

When we can objectify the situation and detach from it in this way, it becomes much clearer whether the request was one where my boundary is fine if I say yes, or whether actually I need to say no so as to properly and lovingly parent my inner child.

For example, you are thinking about a seminar you are interested in attending tonight. You have just arrived home from work and the dog is clearly sick. The kids have to go to their sport, your partner is in the middle of a big project and is not due home till late. You take the dog to the Vet and in between ferrying children around, the dog is treated, and you pick up supplies for dinner. Your aunt rings and says she would love to come over tonight and can she stay a few days? And the call after that is your partner, wondering if he could have a colleague over for dinner tonight. Sometimes when we are in the middle of it all, we cannot think what to say no and what to say yes to. When we objectify the situation and consider what we would say to our friend, we are more likely to put the boundary in the right place.

If you are well rested and don't have to work the next day, perhaps your boundary is in the right place by saying yes to all of the above. If you do have to work and you are already tired, then you owe it to your inner child to prune these potential commitments and ensure that you have time to attend to one of your needs: rest. It really cannot wait until your annual vacation! The next thing you know you will be down with a cold, or have headaches, eczema or a whole range of other situations to deal with.

I'll Think About It

Another device that I used, to turn around the habit of people-pleasing was to say "I'll think about it". I was so unused to making my own decisions that I often needed a bit of time and could not answer on the spot. However I would make sure that I actually got back to the other person in a timely fashion, as it would not be fair to say that and then do nothing. Within 24 hours I would be able to make a decision, and then it got faster, and now I can often decide things immediately. However even now there are times when I cannot decide, as I can see both sides, reasons why and reasons why not, so I parent my inner child, tell her she is safe with whatever decision we make, and then just do my best. Because I have learned to love and respect myself, I am no longer terrified of making mistakes and looking foolish. The freedom that this brings is tremendous, even though it has taken a lot of work to get to this point.

Relationship Entity

From an etheric point of view, these kinds of dysfunctional patterns become stuck inside of us and cause all kinds of issues. It seems that no matter what we do it is hard to change. This is because the problem is pervasive throughout our entire energy system. What is more, when two people get together, a 'relationship entity' forms, which is a bubble of energy filled with the vibration of everything that the couple think, do and say. This can get very stale and stuck. Later, in the section on relationship healing, we will show you a way to clean that out. Releasing old energetic patterns combined with parenting our own inner child will transform your experience of relationship.

Daniel and Alison

I met a wonderful man Daniel who was an actor in his 40's. He was very sensitive, and had been practicing yoga for many years. He was in amazing physical shape, and highly attractive to women. He had a string of girlfriends, and eventually found himself in a relationship with a very powerful, older woman, Alison. She was crazy about him, and between running her business empire, the two of them spent a lot of time together. Both were on a spiritual path, and they both loved yoga. Alison was 13 years his senior, and had come from a remarkably different background to Daniel.

Daniel came from a migrant family who ran a fancy restaurant. A lot of Daniel's apparent style had been learnt while he had been pressed into service as head waiter at his Dad's restaurant, which catered to people like Alison's family. Alison came from old money, and she had the assurance and worldliness that her upbringing had afforded her.

As in most relationships, initially there were wonderful, heady times as the two of them grew in love and friendship. They moved in together, and enjoyed exploring each other in all respects. Eventually Daniel found himself falling through small holes of doubt about whether or not this relationship was really right for him. He felt a bit out of his depth at times with Alison, and she brushed this off as ridiculous. Her love for him was very strong, and she thought nothing of whisking him off on luxurious holidays and financing their very gracious lifestyle.

Daniel started to feel more and more uncomfortable, and started to become a bit withdrawn. He felt like his independence and personality were being usurped. In the end he left the relationship.

When I met Daniel, the relationship with Alison had been over for nearly 18 months. However Alison was still hopelessly in love with him, and called him often. He tried to be nice, and she wanted to reconcile and sort out whatever the differences were. Daniel was much less verbally skilled at describing how he felt (despite his professional excellence at the very same thing) and usually ended up feeling like she had won again at the end of any discussion. He found himself reluctantly reconciling with her, then feeling angry and trapped, and expressing himself in an uncharacteristically aggressive fashion. Then he would leave again, then he would feel guilty and apologise, then she would talk him into coming back, and the cycle would start again. Both of these beautiful people were thoroughly miserable.

When I looked at Daniel's energy body, there was a huge, twelve inch diameter black cord going from his navel chakra to Alison. The navel chakra is a lot to do with personal power. When it goes awry, our bowels can become upset. This can manifest either as constipation or the runs.

If it goes on too long more serious bowel conditions can result. Daniel, who was usually healthy as a horse, had started to have tummy problems. He found that he was tired a lot of the time, despite being rigorous about healthy, balanced diet and daily exercise and yoga. There was no physical reason why he should be low in vitality. There was a huge etheric reason.

Unconsciously, Daniel was feeding the relationship with Alison, even though consciously he was trying to get out of it. His navel chakra was haemorrhaging energy to Allison. Unconsciously she could feel all of the energy coming from him, so of course she still felt attached to him and without knowing it, she was pulling from Daniel a feast of powerful, healthy chi.

Daniel told me that he wanted to be friends with Alison and feel normal again, and to get off the see-saw of emotions and to-ing and fro-ing that had been occurring. He really wanted a clean end to the relationship.

I treated Daniel firstly by explaining to him what I had found out about his navel chakra, and then by getting him to cut the cord and call back his spirit from her. We broke all promises they had made to stay together, not only in this life but in any other life as well. The last bit was very, very potent for Daniel, who had obviously needed to deal with unresolved issues with the soul of Alison from a time long past, when he was a different personality and so was she.

You can do the processes we did on your own using a Harmony Centre CD, though it is far more powerful when done in a group setting in our workshops, when high vibrational energy is anchored for your benefit.

The reason for this is that you can only harness as much energy as you are capable of holding in your etheric body. If you are a bit bent out of shape, that might not be very much. A spiritual teacher who is developed energetically (you can tell this by scanning them, see *Ignite Your Spirit* or *Miracles Through Pranic Healing* by Master Choa Kok Sui) can reach well beyond where you can while you are in the grip of the problem, and can anchor huge energy to assist your release and healing.

Like most people who receive this treatment, Daniel felt relief, he felt himself flooded with energy, and his stomach calmed down. He was a very receptive patient, and followed the instructions he was given about meditating and cutting, every day for a month.

The situation calmed right down for him. Unaccountably, Alison stopped calling him, and he no longer felt trapped by her. He really got it, that the problem had been **his** energy body belching out energy to **her**, and that only happened because he had unconsciously allowed it to happen.

No-one can take our power or our energy, but often we are giving it away without even realising. Do you ever feel like your ex is sucking your energy dry? Do you get tired having to deal with him or her? Chances are that you are in the category of people that have not actually energetically separated, even though you may have been divorced for a long, long time. Find yourself a quiet place where you will not be disturbed for an hour and do the cord cutting exercise from Chapter 17 of *Soul Connection* and my relationship healing meditation CD.

Navel Chakra

Of all the chakras the one that seems to give people the most difficulty in terms of becoming empowered in relationships is the navel chakra. People who do not have a comfortable relationship with their own personal power will develop problems in this chakra quite often.

Very often these people had overbearing parents, or spouses who were very controlling. Finding the balance between power and vulnerability, between knowing when to be strong and when to give in, are issues that often have to be faced for the good health of this chakra.

Giving our power away can happen in the blink of an eye, half the time we do not even notice that we are doing it. We agree to things that, if we thought about it for a minute, we really wouldn't want to agree to at all. More and more requests are made of us to do this and that, until our time and energy are not our own. All our energy is spent fulfilling the agendas of others. We gave our power away by agreeing to the things we do not really want to do because we find it so difficult to say no.

No one can take power from us. It is we who unintentionally give it away. With a bit of insight, we can start to notice when we are giving away our power. It happens with small things, and with people who are close to us.

Learning to develop the navel chakra helps us to have the energy to support our growing boundaries. It helps us be balanced and practice moderation and harmony in decision making. We get more conscious of what we are doing with our energy, and better at using it wisely.

Boundaries around Money

When we are in relationships we may find that money or its management becomes a bone of contention. That is because the power and energy of wealth is being fought over and is perceived to be in short supply. In order to change this, one or both parties can start to create different beliefs about money and work on their own relationship to the powerful energy that money entails.

In relationships, one party can assume control of the money. This is a parenting function. This can only be done to the extent we give away our will and power over this issue. Even if we have in the past given our power away, there is no reason we cannot take it back again.

It is important to do the inner work around your relationship with money. Matters to do with money are generally associated with the base chakra. Really, it is about the need for security. Call your spirit back and reclaim your power over matters of the base chakra. As you change, the whole world changes. Decide what you want!

There may be a need to have a discussion about this topic, and you might need to clearly put your view or express your fears or reasons for wanting to change things. Keep the conversation to an "I feel" level and use the empowered styles of communication set out in later chapters.

Boundaries around Sex

Every couple will develop their own habits around sexuality, and so long as both of them are happy this is fine. When issues develop around sexuality, it is often to do with the frequency or kind of sex that each party deems 'normal' and appropriate. Sometimes there are also issues that arise when third parties come into the equation such as when there are affairs.

Cultivating boundaries around sexuality is no different to cultivating healthy boundaries in any other area of life. Learning not to be passive, learning to be assertive without being aggressive about it, using appropriate communication strategies and parenting your inner child go a long way to sort things out.

An additional tool that we have when faced with partners having differing libidos is energy healing and tantric practices. Through purifying and directing energy in the sex chakras of each person and healing the relationship entity, sometimes blockages to sexual energies can be cleared. Certainly it is possible to speed up or slow down the libido using energetic healing. The partner with the higher libido can learn to give sexual energy to their less amorous mate to stimulate their slower libido. This helps to normalise the patterns of lovemaking and helps to create harmony.

Sexual matters may also mask underlying emotional issues, and often a low libido in one party may be on account of the repression of emotions, being passive when they are really quite unhappy about things because they don't know what to say or do to make things better.

You could refer back to the chapter on intimacy to review the stages of intimacy. You might find your relationship is stuck at individual differences or the conflict phase. It may be that you might both need some help from a counsellor in moving through conflict and unspoken issues so that this energy can be cleared. With a renewed sense of emotional closeness it is often the case that sexual matters resolve and a healthy and enjoyable sex life returns.

I once knew a couple who had been married for many years. She came to me for healings, and in one of them told me that she was worried about her marriage. She said they had not had sex for months. I asked her why she thought that might be. She told me tearfully that she had rebuked all efforts on the part of her husband to instigate sex because she didn't like the fact that he had dirty fingernails. He worked as a gardener and grime was part of his daily life. I asked her if she had talked to him about it and she said no, because she was worried about hurting his feelings. I told her that I thought his feelings might be hurting more because she didn't want to have sex with him, than if she told him that he needed to get busy with the scrubbing brush on his fingernails. She decided to talk to him and a couple of weeks later she came by and let me know how things were. He had been utterly relieved by her confession that she felt a bit insulted and somewhat disrespected when he touched her with dirty fingernails. He had no idea and now that he knew, he was scrupulously cleaning his fingernails every day!

If your partner is doing something that you find unpleasant or uncomfortable, then tell them. You can do it nicely, and it is better than the resentment and coldness that will come in if things are not communicated and are left unattended for long periods of time. Try not to make your partner wrong: just share how you feel. It is not a good idea to assume that your partner "should know". This is ascribing to them advanced telepathic powers, which frankly they may not have!

PART

5

COMMUNICATION AND RELATIONSHIP

Chapter

16

THE DEAL WITH COMMUNICATION

If there is any skill that we need to master in order
to have good relationships, it is how to communicate.

How to say things can be more important than what we are actually trying to convey in terms of facts. Much of our communication is non-verbal. The tone in which we speak is also of importance in maintaining healthy relationships.

I knew a man, Dennis, who spoke in a monotone and never displayed any emotional reaction. Even when announcing his wife's first pregnancy, he was unable to muster any sense of interest or excitement in the forthcoming event. His wife was really upset and felt marginalised and hurt by his seeming indifference to the situation. He was actually delighted with the news but was unable to express how he was feeling. He was only capable of speaking through the emotionless adult self.

Unintentionally, what Dennis actually communicated was indifference and rudeness in the face of something his wife regarded as wondrous and sacred. He was an introverted, sensing, thinking, judging type of person. His introversion made it difficult to speak about this deep subject, and his preference for fact and concrete objects made it difficult to anticipate the joy of a child. His wife was an extroverted, intuitive, feeling and perceiving kind of person. To her, feelings and nuances were an important and normal part of life. If he had learned to put even a little warmth or feeling into his communication, he would have more accurately communicated what he wanted to, and would not have caused disharmony in his marriage by mistake.

Sarah was a passionate and talented entertainer. She was great on stage, hilarious, had a very free spirited inner child, and not much parent. When she got angry, she let fly with all kinds of insults, decimating whoever she was talking to and causing them to feel ashamed or embarrassed by her incredibly uncontrolled mouth. She was actually a very sensitive person who had experienced a lot of abuse during her childhood. She was now accidentally dishing out the same kind of abusive language that she had grown up with. Needless to say, her relationships with men were very short lived. She wanted to have a stable relationship and have a child, as her biological clock was ticking. Her lack of skill in communication made this impossible.

Michael was a dentist, and a very detail focused 'adult' person. He kept himself under strict control, and expected that others should as well. He never raised his voice, but his mannerisms and facial expressions made it very obvious that he felt others were not coming up to the standard he expected. He was always polite, but his conversations were peppered with statements like "I think you should..." and "If I were you

I would…" which caused the people around him a fair degree of annoyance. He did not have many friends on account of his superior attitude, and even though he actually had a very warm heart and would have liked to be in a relationship, he could never communicate with any warmth or understanding. His one attempt at marriage had ended after only 2 years and his 12-year-old daughter was a complete mystery to him.

Molly was 76 years old and had been married to Tim for 53 years. She had always been conflict adverse and had relied on Tim to make all of the major decisions in the family. She was a great conversationalist, could always be relied on for small talk and had been a great hostess. She could talk about anything and everything, so long as it never involved expressing an actual opinion, or as long as it never touched anything that might be sensitive, controversial or create friction. After he died she found it really difficult to communicate what needed to happen, because she was so unpractised at expressing any emotion, any sense of what she needed, or dealing with any difficult issue. The truth was, no one ever really got close to her, nor did she get close to others, because everything was kept superficial. Her relationships were skin deep, and without Tim there to be the father to her inner child, she found it really hard to cope. Her spirit wilted and she went downhill health wise, and within 12 months she too had left her body.

We might not be brilliant at it now, but we can learn different kinds of communication strategies. Some will be suitable for certain relationships, for instance with work colleagues. Others will be more suited to conversations with our beloved. Some will be great for cocktail parties and others for giving sensitive advice to our teenage children.

I Don't Want to Make it Worse

Sometimes people fail to communicate altogether about important things. They fear they might somehow botch the communication and end up making things worse. However the energy will start to stagnate in your relationship if you leave big things unsaid.

Even whopping big things like the fact that someone has come to the realisation that they are gay sometimes doesn't get communicated. So badly do people *not* want to hurt each other that they lead miserable lives that are a complete lie. Chances are they will end up depressed, and their partner will wonder what is being kept from them, because in an intimate relationship it will be obvious that something is wrong.

Sometimes people do not communicate about the small things that annoy them because they don't want to hurt their beloved's feelings. The trouble is, when we ignore little annoying things for a long time and don't say anything about them, sooner or later we will become a volcano of unreasonable fury, and let rip on our poor unsuspecting beloved, who never knew that we can't stand it when they hang the towel over the shower railing: which they have done for the past 15 years. If we had just told them how we felt about it, chances are that the beloved would have hung the towel somewhere else.

Not speaking to the beloved is sometimes done because we think "If he/she loves me he/she should know how I feel and what I want". This is a bad relationship mistake. Apart from anything else, we are ascribing advanced telepathic powers to our beloved, who may never have done any study in metaphysics whatsoever and who genuinely has no idea what you feel unless you tell them.

Sometimes we do not communicate how we feel because we fear that we will be rejected and not loved if we do. When we have learned how to parent our inner child, we are confident in the knowledge that even if this person rejects you, you the inner parent will never abandon you the inner child. You always have you, no matter what happens out there in the world. This internal steadfastness will help you to have the courage to say what you need to say.

While reading this part of the book, think about how you communicate, and how those close to you communicate as well. Becoming more skilful in this field is likely to transform your life and open the door to enabling and empowering you to become much more accomplished and happy in relationships.

Chapter

17

LISTENING

Listening is an art-form, a skill for life, and one that is surprisingly lacking a lot of the time. We are all so busy thinking about what we are going to say next, and wanting to pursue our own agendas, that sometimes we forget to be present and receptive to the people that we love. In order to get better at relationships, we need to get better at listening.

If speaking is yang, then listening is yin. On a spiritual level, prayer is yang (something I am doing) and meditation is yin (something I am being). In meditation we are creating a space into which spiritual communication can fall. Meditation is the spiritual equivalent of listening.

Listening involves being receptive to stimuli, ideas and really hearing what your beloveds are saying. It is also an attitude of receptivity. Listening can be done through the heart chakra, and this then gives us access not only to what is physically said but to the energy and vibration sitting behind it. When we really listen this way, we 'hear' what is not said as well as what is.

When people feel heard, they feel valued and appreciated. When people feel that you are *not* listening to them, automatically what is set up is a frustrating dynamic, which encourages people to become more bombastic with their statements and claims. Then we might wonder why they are yelling or thumping the table.

When people are speaking to you it is important to acknowledge what they have said. Here is where verbal and non-verbal cues can make the difference between a frustrating interaction where the beloved feels aggrieved by your attitude, and a pleasant interaction where the beloved feels respected. Failing to give any indication that you have heard what the beloved said, or changing the subject and speaking of something else before you have acknowledged their statement, is a relationship slayer. Often this can be a habit, even something that has seeped into you from other people around you who might do the same thing. It is most definitely a habit worth changing, and one that a little awareness and a desire to build your relationship will help you to change.

Petra and Jim

I knew a couple that had been on a spiritual path for quite a while and they were both evolved souls. Jim managed a large organisation and Petra was a healer. They basically had a good relationship but Petra came to me distressed, wondering what she was doing wrong and how her spiritual practices needed to change in order to solve a vexing problem. She said that when she spoke to Jim he quite often did not respond or even acknowledge that he had heard anything she had said, and just started talking about something else. It was happening so frequently that she felt unvalued, as though she bored him and she wondered if the fundamentals of the relationship were sound.

When I tuned in I felt that the energy field of the relationship was very strong. There was lots of love, lots of strength in the heart chakra and lots of security energy in the base chakra. It looked mainly like a physical world problem which awareness would heal. I gave Petra a healing, and we removed any thought forms and beliefs that she was not valuable, and not worth listening to. Energy certainly moved, and she felt lighter as a result. I was clear with her that changing the energy was great, but she needed to actually communicate to Jim about what her needs were, which in this situation, was to be acknowledged when she spoke.

She went home and cooked a nice meal and over dinner got Jim to look at her. She told him that she had experienced recently on a number of occasions that when she had spoken to him he had not responded, and had begun to speak of a totally unconnected topic as though she was not even there, and she told him that when he did this she felt unloved. He was quite surprised by this, and asked her to give him an example. We had anticipated this, and Petra was able to give a recent and very clear example to him, so that he could understand the problem. She did not judge him, but simply gave him the information. She told him that she loved him and wanted their relationship to be as fabulous as possible, and that she felt that his habit could be a bit undermining of that.

Jim apologised, feeling the sincerity and the lack of blame or judgment coming from Petra. He could feel how much she loved him. He asked her to say something next time he did it, and agreed to be more conscious of acknowledging what she had said. He said that often he did not know what to say in response to her conversation, and so said nothing or changed the topic. She told him that she did not expect answers or for him to help her with the making of her own decisions, she just wanted to be heard, because quite often just speaking of things to someone who cares about you helps you to get clear in your own mind about what you need to do.

Petra had to remind Jim a number of times to respond. She did this by saying "Jim did you hear what I said?" She was careful to keep judgment or criticism out of her voice and to inject love into the statement. She parented her inner child each time it happened, by telling her inner child that "I am listening to you beloved!" Within a few months the problem was gone.

One might hear what a person said as an anatomical reality, but have you really listened to what the meaning of the communication might be? One of the issues with listening is that we hear things through the lens of our own set of expectations. There are times that what one person says is construed different ways by the 5 different people who are hearing it. Like the game of Chinese Whispers, what leaves our lips is not necessarily that which is heard by those who we would like to listen to us, and the same happens when we are doing the listening.

Listening well will make a huge difference to your level of perception in life as well as to the depth and intimacy that you can experience in relationships.

Blockages to Effective Listening

When we are in relationship, things can appear even more complicated than they do in a class exercise such as this. Some of those reasons that people fail to listen are as follows:

- I feel time pressure, you are holding me up.
- Lack of interest, you are boring / irrelevant.
- I am focussed on what I am going to say next and don't even hear you. My mind is made up and nothing you say will change it: rigidity
- I just want to make a good impression and am pre-occupied with myself.
- I assume I know what you are going to say.
- My paradigm is different to you – you are wrong, there is only one way.
- What I am saying is more important.
- That is not what you said before (focus is all about a remembered conversation and not open to what is happening now).

These behaviours and attitudes teach your partner not to speak with you in a meaningful way and create barriers to intimacy. They stop the flow of energy between people and are destructive of relating.

Do's and Don'ts of Communicating

If we want to have wonderful relationships, it is good to understand that how we say something is as important, if not more important, than what we say. Truly, communication skills ought be taught in primary school, and be reinforced throughout our education. So many unfortunate incidents and interactions would be avoided if we were skilful with how to deliver our messages to others, particularly when it is to do with something that we have found frustrating or hurtful.

Imagine that there are choirs of Karmic Angels who assemble all of the data about our lives for review. Imagine being in the middle of a heated argument with another person, where there might be a lack of skill, provocation, even name calling, where both people say things that they might regret later. Imagine if the Karmic Angels only record what you said, not the context in which it was said? Imagine if they were not even slightly interested in "Well he said something horrible to me first!" Imagine if the whole universe took our own contribution to the discussion as a statement of how evolved we are. Would they have files on us that were crazy and filled with vitriol, or would they be OK? How many times are we going to need to be thrust into confronting situations either in this life or the next one, before we learn to stop behaving like a child throwing a tantrum just because someone else is?

Some people can take a small disagreement and turn it into a major conflict. It is as though they know just how to throw petrol on the fire of a conflict. Other people can take a small disagreement or even a large one and turn it into something constructive from which flows real peace and progress.

If you have never experienced conflict then you will not know whether or not you are a peacemaker, and the chances are that either you, or the people around you, are not practicing authenticity. As a peacemaker we learn how to be empowered and able to bring peace into an ever-evolving set of situations. Knowing how to communicate is a key to this.

The energy of communication can be either passive or aggressive, both of which will cause us problems, or assertive which brings forth truth and an avenue for progress. We will look into that more below. First, we are going to look at the actual things we say, in order to bring forth a better communication style. We will see that there are some styles that are better than others, some which are applicable in close, personal relationships and some are better for work, and some which ought be deleted from our repertoire all together.

Heavy Control Communication Style

The first communication style we are going to look at is a very unskilful one through which its users seek to exert heavy and bombastic control over the people around them. This style is aggressive and creates tension as well as hurt to others. It is very accusatory and because of that, it contains many 'you' statements. The speaker wants you to conform to his or her world view, communicated by his or her critical parent and tantrum child. Use of this kind of communication should be weeded entirely out of our repertoire as it is destructive and has no upside. Use of this kind of communication is a pretty good indication that the speaker has done little effective work on their emotional body and most likely suffers from low self-esteem and its flipside, arrogance.

The people who use heavy control style are bullies. Their intention is to win, to dominate, and to escalate things beyond where you will feel comfortable in a show of strength that might make you back down and let them have their way. "Don't mess with me" is one of their key messages. They are looking for submission, not a win-win outcome. They are saying "I will let you know who is boss around here!"

The kinds of thing that you will hear in heavy control style include examples like these:

"It's your fault...", "I told you so." Blame. The object here is to cause you to feel that you are to blame, and the problem is nothing to do with the speaker who is superior to an idiot like you.

"Why did you do that?" You will feel attacked. You are being accused.

"Just you wait you will pay for this" or "I am warning you!" Threats. This is meant to frighten and intimidate the listener.

"Tell me now." "Get home early." Demanding. This is meant to remove any sense of having a choice in what might happen.

"You are a joke." "You fool why did you do that?" Ridicule, belittling. Tear you down before you can tear me down.

"Everybody thinks you are..." Distorting to suit the argument. Seeking to add weight to their claims by causing you to think that your alleged inadequacy is known to all and sundry when possibly one other person may share their view.

"You are so stupid." "You are clumsy." Criticism. Reinforcing your mistakes.

"You never help me." Complaining. Focus upon the negative, instead of rewarding every try.

"I'm not going to tell you." Withholding what might be important and relevant information so that you can be blackmailed into doing what I want, at which stage I may or may not tell you what I know (which may be nothing at all).

"What would you know?" Disqualifying and debasing any wisdom that the beloved may have concerning the situation.

"Poor me, you never say you love me." Whining is a way of controlling people through guilt. The person is saying "I am a victim and it is your fault". This is a very disempowered style of relating.

"Let's not worry about that it's not important." Placating. This belittles the person to whom we are speaking because it trivialises their concerns and stops us from listening to them. They feel unheard and devalued.

"I will force you." Overbearing. This communicator is so scared and filled with fear that they would remove your free will. They will do anything to get their own way.

"Just like your father." Criticising by comparison to someone you have issues with.

"You always..." "You never..." Exaggeration.

Heavy control style communication is aggressive and shows no respect. It creates extremely negative feelings in the person who is subjected to it. It seems positively designed to hinder if not to destroy any chance of deeper communication.

Heavy control style is widely practiced however it has the consequence of destroying relationships and has no place in building understanding.

Heavy control style of communication also has a price in terms of the health and wellbeing of our etheric body. When we speak to someone in these kinds of terms, the aura of the person to whom we are speaking will usually collapse and shrink. This is energetically very negative and will produce bad karma. Not only does it shrink the energy field of the recipient of this kind of talk, but it also shrinks the energy field of the speaker. It is a lose/lose strategy when looked at from a spiritual and energetic point of view.

It is wise to eliminate this style of communication from your relationships altogether if you wish to develop clarity, empathy and joy with your partner.

Light Control Style

We use light control style when we are taking on a position of authority. Our attitude is that we want in some way to control things. Sometimes this is because we think we have superior ideas. Sometimes it is just that this style of communication has become habitual. Light control style relating gives the impression of "I know best". It creates some tension because it interferes with people doing it their own way. It assumes that there is only one way to do things, and lacks respect for someone else's journey.

Lawyers and accountants and other professional people use light control style when speaking to their clients, so that they sound authoritative. This puts them in a situation of superiority when it comes to the relative level of knowledge of their clients. Light control style talks down to people and assumes that they do not have the same ability and insight. Examples of light control style are:

Selling: "I have just been to the best seminar, it would suit you down to the ground and help you in so many ways."

Directing: "You should..."

Advising: "The lid of the toilet seat should be kept down."

Superior: "If I were you I would..."

Teaching: "The best way to do that is to..."

Lecturing: "When you cook it is best to have all the ingredients at room temperature. Make sure you have..." (when all you wanted was for them to tell you where the salt is kept).

Extreme example: Whether you ask Kevin about Chinese politics, how to cull rabbits, what is happening on Wall Street or how to spice a casserole, he always knows best, and wants to instruct you on all the things you should know about. Kevin is the kind of guy that everyone hides from at a party, lest they be cornered by him and given a dissertation on his latest pet idea. He could be completely ignorant of all things to do with the subject at hand, but that will never stop him from having an opinion that he will encourage you to adopt. He doesn't yell or scream, there are no threats, just endless lectures and sales pitches about things.

Another expression of light control style is the rescue, when we do things for people that they could do for themselves, but we are worried that they will not do it as well as we would. Most of the communication in and around rescue situations tends to be light control style, such as "Let me do that for you..." (Sometimes degenerating into heavy control style as in "You idiot, let me do it!")

The positive purpose of light control style is a desire to help. The negative purpose is a sense that 'I should be in control because I know best'. Whilst it is sometimes useful to employ this style when teaching or when professionally engaged in a field of expertise, there are generally better methods.

This style is an intimacy destroyer as it often appears when there is a power struggle. It means that one person is taking a position of authority and superiority and thus implying that the other person is not an equal. It can be very frustrating and annoying. It also can occur where false self-esteem is being built, and the person claims to know everything in order to bolster his or her self-image.

The person who speaks this way may notice a certain coolness in his or her personal relationships and people tend to avoid them, and show very little gratitude for the advice and instruction that is so selflessly being given!

High Stress Communication[7]

The following list of high stress communication strategies is like a list of *don'ts* from a healthy relationship point of view. Have a read, and circle your own pet hates. Try to get rid of these from your own repertoire.

- Monopolising the conversation
- Interrupting
- Showing obvious lack of interest
- Sour facial expressions
- Withholding social cues, e.g. non-verbal responses
- Throwing verbal barbs
- Using non verbal put downs
- Verbal abuse

---

[7] (From paper by Professor Trevor Waring AM, Chancellor of Newcastle University, given to a law firm in November 04)

- Speaking dogmatically, not respecting others opinions
- Complaining excessively
- Criticising excessively, finding fault
- Refusal to negotiate
- Ridiculing others
- Patronising or talking down to others
- Trying to make others feel guilty
- Excessive seeking of approval
- Being short tempered
- Over using 'why' questions
- Breaking confidences
- Failing to keep promises
- Joking at inappropriate times
- Bragging, showing off, talking only about the self
- Throwing gotchas and embarrassing people
- Over-using *should* language
- Making threatening demands
- Diverting conversation to other topics
- Disagreeing routinely
- Asking loaded or accusing questions.

Low Stress Communication

The following list contains some things that you can do to instantly improve your communication with others. Circle the ones that you think you could implement straight away so as to make a real difference to your communication and relationships.

- Giving others a chance to express views and opinions
- Listening attentively and hearing a person out

- Sharing one's self by smiling, greeting and so on
- Giving positive non-verbal messages of respect
- Praising and complimenting sincerely
- Expressing respect for the values and opinions of others
- Giving suggestions constructively
- Compromising, negotiating, helping
- Affirming the feelings and needs of others
- Treating others as equals when possible
- Stating one's needs and desires honestly
- Delaying automatic reactions, not flying off the handle
- Levelling with others
- Confronting others constructively on difficult issues
- Staying on the conversational topic until others have been heard
- Stating agreements with others when possible
- Asking straightforward and non-loaded questions
- Keeping the confidences of others
- Giving one's word sparingly and keeping it
- Joking constructively and in good humour.

Conversational Relating

This is a widely used and wonderful way of relating in many circumstances. It is the oiling of the wheels of society and allows us to communicate with each other in a pleasant and non-threatening way.

It seeks to report what has happened, describing events, joking, storytelling, and involves general chit-chat and pleasantries. It is sociable, friendly, does not create tension, in fact the opposite. It is really safe.

The intention of conversational style is to avoid conflict. It puts people at ease and is a way to start discussions and open the doors of communication again after there has been an argument "Would you like a cup of tea?"

It prevents awkward silences and puts people at ease. It is friendly and comfortable. It can allow us to speak to people with whom there have been problems in the past, in a non-confronting, bland and uncontroversial way.

It always sticks to safe topics like the weather or what is happening in the garden. It is a means by which we can protect ourselves from getting caught up in potential conflicts with difficult people, and also is a bid to be liked or accepted.

We can share the minutiae of the day in a comfortable way whereby we keep in touch with our lives and share our history. It is good for handling transitions, which are the times when two people end up spending time apart and then get back together again, perhaps after a week away working, and they want a place to start a conversation.

It doesn't ever involve revealing our own thoughts and feelings and revolves around things that happen 'out there'.

By itself, relationships would not grow if this were the only kind of communication that took place. You would never really get to know the other person, their hopes and dreams, or their inner landscape. Intimacy could not develop past a certain point, and over time, would diminish as there is no depth or inner disclosure of self.

Some examples of conversational relating would include:

"And then she said..."

"The dog fell into the lake and then shook all over us."

"Sue is going to bridge..."

Explore Style

This is good in work relationships or with acquaintances or people with whom it might not be prudent to share emotions, feelings and intuitions. It is a form of communication in which you can share your thoughts together so as to have a good exchange of ideas. The intention is non-controlling, leading to an outcome that hopefully will be beneficial or acceptable to both parties.

- It speculates about what the possibilities might be.
- It reflects how your mind is dealing with this issue at this point.
- It is exploratory and non-judgmental.
- It does not assume to have all the answers, and genuinely wants to hear your view.
- It does not set up win/lose situations, but wants to work towards in/win.
- It focuses on how you think and does not involve **any** feelings.
- It says let's get together and see what we both think.
- There is an absence of body sensation or feeling statements.
- It is highly effective where issues need to be resolved or problems solved.
- It is calm.

"I would like to know what you think about..."

"I imagine..."

"Perhaps it might be good..."

"I think..."

"My thoughts on this are..."

"There appear to be several options which I would like to discuss with you..."

When we open agendas, rather than trying to control them, we invite people to bring their creativity to the table. The old saying "two heads are better than one" applies here. With explore style we are not seeking to own ideas, or insist that our way is the best way. We put ideas on the table and after looking at them all, we select the ideas that seem most likely to benefit us both and we put them into practice.

Empowered Communication

In terms of coming to deep, intimate, long-lasting and empowering relationships, there is nothing better than being able to share all parts of who you are. Empowered communication is very similar to explore style but it adds in two important ingredients. These are feelings and intuitions. This would include sharing our gut feelings about things, perhaps sharing our clairsentient, dream or meditative experiences when relevant, and speaking freely about our emotions.

When we speak from an empowered place we are sharing ourselves and wanting a form of deep intimacy and oneness.

We are not seeking to blame others when things go wrong. As a multi-dimensional and spiritually aware person, we realise that absolutely anything that occurs in our lives must, at some level, have something to do with us. Therefore, instead of pointing the finger at the beloved, we speak of our own experience. We do the inner work to change our experience through the tools of the Path of Ease and Grace or other authentic spiritual training. Then, we communicate what feels true for us on a personal level.

This kind of communication builds trust and sincerity. We are able to be vulnerable with each other, knowing that the other will not take advantage of us. We aim to be caring and at the same time clear about how things are for us. Instead of adding to tensions, it serves to release tension through skilful sharing of our predicament. It is real and honest, and invites the other person into my world.

Unlike other kinds of communication, which remain more detached or objective, with empowered communication we share our subjective experience as well. Our subjective experience includes our personal reactions to things, how things impact us, and the feelings that arise. We do not hold back but seek to have a genuine communication, reaching into each other's soul.

"Intuitively I feel that we can trust Peter, he has a big heart chakra and so long as we keep talking to him and doing the inner work I am sure that the arrangement will work fine."

"I think that we have become a little distant and I am upset because I care so much about you – can we discuss this?"

"I would like to know how you feel about this..."

"I had a dream last night that really frightened me, and I felt upset knowing that you are going away for a while. Can you give me a hug?" "I feel a bit scared when you..."

"I realise this might be my stuff, but I feel angry and a bit uncared for right now. Can we please talk about this?"

"My inner child is pissed off, and I am parenting her and am OK, but thought you ought to know – just give me a bit of space until I am ready to talk about what is going on for me."

You are saying "It is about me not you and so I am entitled to my own feelings and thoughts. You cannot say I am wrong because I am not talking about you (as I would be in heavy or light-control style). I am trusting you with how I feel from my heart." This style of communication invites a similar level of reply.

If the person responds in a manner that you do not want, for instance, they do not agree with you, it can be tempting to revert to controlling communication. Try and resist, and if you do, say you are sorry! Instead do inner work on self-respect and self-love. Do some relationship healing. You might need to drop back to conversational relating for a while as you sort yourself out, and then when you are ready, have done some inner work, meditated on the situation and want to communicate, try empowered communicating again.

FAMILY

I ran into a stranger as he passed by,

"Oh excuse me please" was my reply.

He said, "Please excuse me too; I wasn't watching for you."
We were very polite, this stranger and I.

We went on our way and we said goodbye. But at home a different story is told, How we treat our loved ones, Young and old.

Later that day, cooking the evening meal,
My son stood beside me very still.

When I turned, I nearly knocked him down.
"Move out of the way," I said with a frown.

He walked away, his little heart broken.

I didn't realise how harshly I'd spoken.

While I lay awake in bed,

God's still small voice came to me and said,

"While dealing with a stranger, Common courtesy you use,
But the family you love, you seem to abuse. Go and look on the kitchen
floor, You'll find some flowers there by the door.

Those are the flowers he brought for you.

He picked them himself: pink, yellow and blue.

He stood very quietly not to spoil the surprise,

You never saw the tears

That filled his little eyes."

By this time, I felt very small,

And now my tears began to fall.

I quietly went and knelt by his bed;

"Wake up, little one, wake up," I said. "Are these the flowers you picked for
me?" He smiled, "I found them, out by the tree.

I picked them because they're pretty like you.

I knew you'd like them, especially the blue."

I said, "Son, I'm very sorry for the way I acted today; I shouldn't have
yelled at you that way." He said, "Oh, Mom, that's okay.

I love you anyway."

I said, "Son, I love you too, And I do like the flowers, especially the blue."

Author Unknown.

PART

6

EMPOWERMENT

Chapter

18

What is Empowerment?

We could hardly have a book about empowering relationships without looking in depth at what we mean by 'empowered'. An empowered person is someone who holds power. So, what is power?

Power is a spiritual phenomena, a function of our level of consciousness, and which is cultivated through the practice of virtue, ethical behaviour and striving to maintain a high vibrational life. It involves connecting with the vast source of Divine energy that is already inside us, usually in a dormant or semi-dormant state. Real power is Divine grace personified.

In the introduction to this book there is a reference to two kinds of power: external and internal. External power relies upon one's position, wealth or class, whereas internal power just is, irrespective of any external factors. Internal power is a real and lasting spiritual quality that we can learn to hold.

Many of us are, or have been, inherently afraid of power, powerful people and most importantly, our own power. We worry about misusing it, or hurting ourselves or others through it. Often we abdicate our power in relationships, so as not to be the responsible one if things go wrong. We engage in people-pleasing, ignoring our own truth so as to 'keep the peace' with someone else. We do not listen to our own truth, and do not stand up for our inner child. We let someone else do the parenting.

If we are in a situation where others do what we want them to because they are afraid of us, we are not using power, we are using force. This is only as good as your positional or external authority, and will evaporate if the external circumstances change. Force breeds resentment, anger, and all kinds of other negative reactions that undermine relationships. There is a short term 'win' for us, and a 'lose' for them. The longer-term relationship prospects are weakened by the use of force.

Power is often mixed up with force. Force means that I will make you do what I want you to do. It is egoic and has a 'one up one down' feel to it. One has to submit or there will be negative consequences. Free will and respect for the personal sovereignty of the other person is missing.

Power is born of love and caring and is most potent when we recognise that it is a feminine energy. This means, we access it through being yin, or receptive, not by being yang or active in the world. It is the Holy Spirit, Shakti, something that we are here to learn about and utilise. Relationships are a perfect vehicle in which to learn about power in conjunction with an authentic spiritual path. Spiritual guides, both in the physical world and in the inner world, can help us come into our power with as much ease and grace as possible.

Power is not just handed out by the Universal Intelligence. It is something we need to work for, and the work will transform us. Whatever our motivation might be to want to hold more power, it will end up changing. Personal and selfish motivations melt in the fire of Divine power and cannot be sustained.

The journey into self-empowerment is the journey of a lifetime, and involves adventure, tenacity, courage, insight, the capacity to transform and the will to do so. Empowerment is really a spiritual concept with great practical application. It helps us to become one with the Christ Consciousness and allows us to live our birthright as Children of God. At the same time, it gives us the capacity to be authentic, respected, loving and loved in a very wide range of relationships.

Internal power is cultivated through coming into oneness with other human beings and with the Divine. We leave behind our Egoic separateness and fears, and enter a world where we are more conscious, and where our agenda is broader than the instant gratification of our sensory desires. When things go wrong, instead of thumping the table and demanding answers we are capable of speaking in a normal voice and asking questions, working towards another solution. We are able to be flexible and accommodating, while not letting go of our vision or ultimate direction. Instead of fluctuating wildly, our vibration becomes steadier, and creates an attractor field of possibility around us that is wholesome, positive and conducive of happiness. Holding a high vibration changes the range of possible futures that we could inhabit.

Chapter

19

SOUL POWER: FINDING THE VAST SELF

Your own soul is nourished
when you are kind; It is
destroyed when you are cruel.

Proverbs 11:17

When we incarnate there are two parts of us that vie for our attention and fight for resources. These are the soul and the ego.

When we are coming from our soul self, we are coming from a place of purity and we have opened the door to authentic power, which is Divine, and which at the end of the day is love.

When we are coming from the ego we are out to obtain something. That something might be the feeling of being in control. It might be territory, or money, or prestige, a partner, or a circumstance. Our

227

attachments to how we thought things should be are all caught up in that part of ourselves. By comparison, our soul is light and free.

The agenda of the ego is to live on the Earth with as much security as possible. The agenda of the soul is to live on the Earth and experience as much growth in virtue and wisdom as possible. These two agendas do not always meet up, and from time to time we all experience an inner dilemma. Do we do the noble, pure and selfless thing, or do we do what to the ego, feels safe?

The two parts of us can be illustrated by reference to the diagram below. In the top is the soul and Divine self. This is endless, and so the hourglass has no upper limit. It is connected to the infinite energy and power of the Universe.

The bottom of the hourglass is the world of the ego. This has definite boundaries. Here we live our lives in a finite world, drawing comfort from controlling our environment for optimal security. Here the ends justify the means.

To the person living in the bottom of the hourglass the world of the soul and the vastness of choice and creation that exists in that landscape are invisible. To the ego, it is just delusion.

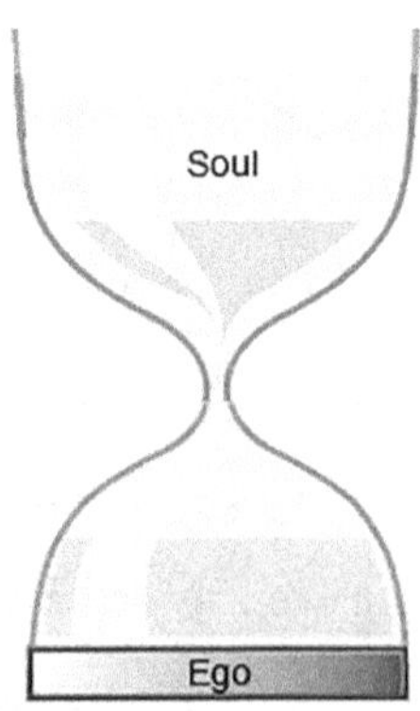

However when we are on a spiritual path, we float upwards from the bottom of the hourglass and eventually come to the vortex or 'eye of the needle' through which we have to pass if we want to get to the top.

By definition the ego never wants to go there. A big band of fear lives high up near the opening from the bottom chamber of the hourglass to the top. This darkness, or ignorance, obscures the door to love. The door to love is guarded by fear. It always was and it always will be. We have to go through our fears to get to the place beyond them, where a more Divine and wonderful life awaits us.

The way to get from the bottom to the top involves getting past fear. It also involves a kind of surrender. This is the surrender of the ego, to enable the soul to pull us up into a world where we do not know what will happen.

Think of an hourglass. The sand naturally drifts to the bottom. Turn it upside down, and the process starts again. Through our many lives, the purpose is to become stable in the top half of the hourglass. Up there, life is different. The miraculous can occur, the reality of the Divine, angelic beings, spiritual energy and the potency of the virtues is real and tangible.

To the soul, the ego's agenda is upside down. To the ego, the soul's agenda is the one that is upside down. The tarot card the Hanged Man signifies how, to a spiritual aspirant, what is down is up and what is up is down. The ego in the bottom of the hourglass wants to take. It has expectations of "what is in it for me?" It wants to control and be territorial with its things and its beloveds. The soul on the other hand wants to give. It has expectations of what it can contribute. It wants to learn and grow and be light and free. The agenda of the soul is upside down and inside out from the demands of the ego.

In Christianity there is a teaching that the meek shall inherit the Earth. Personally, I think that 'meek' really means surrendered. There is nothing meek about surrender. To do it properly means to move through a valley of fear. It is not about giving up, being a door mat or allowing another to determine your own future. Surrender is a conscious choice to live a Divinely informed life, to move through a place of fear and grow into a place of love and freedom. It is a sublime thing once we have done it, and feels like hell just before we do. Generally every impulse inside of us, and much which is mirrored back to us from the world, is to the effect that we are mad. But when we follow real guidance, our lives might turn inside out and upside down, but the result will be a deep sense of peace and rightness that was worth it. What we surrendered is replaced by something infinitely better. Even the relationships that we had before can be transformed when we surrender them and then learn to hold them from a different place.

Relationships are a valid and very amazing pathway to self-realisation if we allow them to be. Getting up close and personal with another human being will put us in positions of conflict or disagreement, different values at times, different priorities and expectations. Working through things, we will discover all of our Egoic tendencies. We will also discover those of the beloved. Quite often we project our tendencies onto them and blame the beloved for our issues. This is spiritually disempowering.

Every time we give in to the Egoic demands such as being in control, being right, being in charge, holding a grudge, being judgmental or arrogant, we effectively pull energy out of our own etheric bodies as well as causing damage to the relationship energy too. If we do this often enough, the entire relationship may end up crumbling. In the bottom of the hourglass, if someone does something wrong the ego wants to attack and blame them, criticise and judge. It wants to make them pay for what they did, and extract an eye for an eye and a tooth for a tooth. The way of vengeance is only found in the Egoic part of who we are.

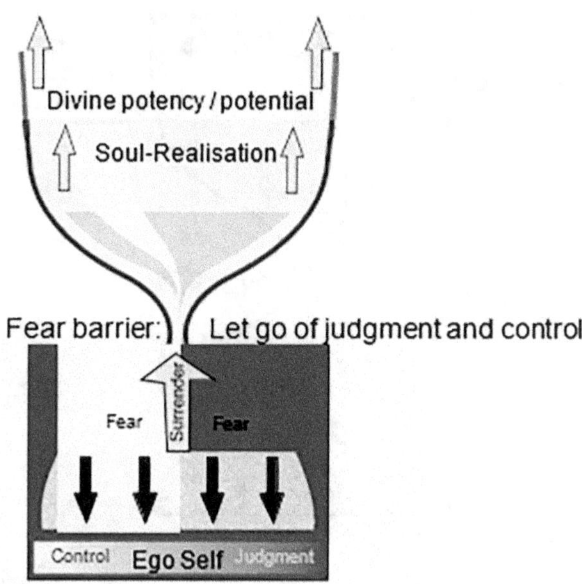

Through relationships we have many opportunities to experience surrender. It is not so much surrender to the beloved as it is surrender to the will of the Higher soul instead of the will of the ego. Every time we surrender to the will of our Higher Soul we will gain access to more love and Divine grace than ever before. This will actually have a beneficial effect on our relationships and in the end, we will experience more love and happiness.

Compassion or Judgment?

In the top of the hourglass, the soul does not dance to the rhythm of judgment. Here it is all about compassion. One cannot have compassion and judgment at the same time. One is of a high vibration, one is of a low vibration.

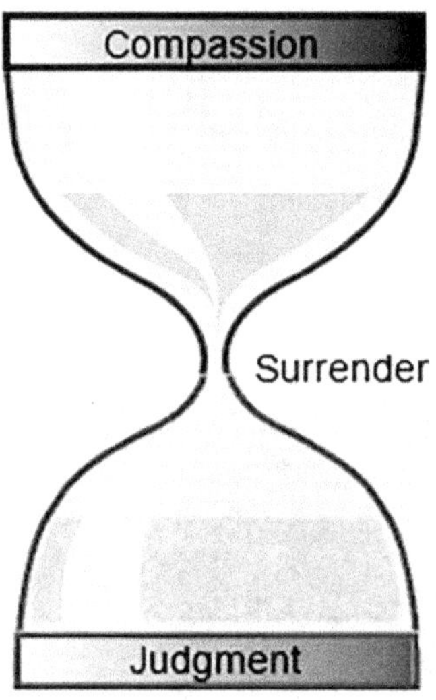

When we judge others, we cut off the energy flow with them and we move into a place of separation. We move deeper into our Egoic vehicles. When we have compassion, we start to see more of what is really going on. We get to understand things from a deeper and richer perspective. It might be that we still have to put some pretty strong boundaries in place and take certain actions which are much the same as would be taken if we were in judgment, but the energetic effect is very different. Compassion helps us to float up into the top of the hourglass.

Surrender is required in order to move from judgment to compassion. This will take us to the eye of the needle, and in that place, (the doorway to love) we will encounter fear. The fear we go through is around the cessation of judgment, which to the ego feels a bit like a small death. Letting it go results in us feeling light and free, whereas being stuck in judgment will cause us to continually experience anger, frustration and a raft of other negative things.

Judgment is an energy which puts people off side. If we ask someone to do something or try to instil a new boundary and our communication contains the energy of judgment, there is likely to be a reaction. If we deal with our judgment and come from our hearts, being compassionate and loving while we say what we have to say, it is likely that the reaction that we get is very different. Learning not to judge and yet to have discernment and compassion is a way to grow in our ability to have unconditional love.

The Power of Forgiveness

Another example where we go through the eye of the needle from the bottom to the top of the hourglass is with forgiveness. Spiritual paths the world over exhort us to be forgiving. Generally, I am sure we all think that is a good thing. However, *doing* it in circumstances where we have been hurt badly is very hard. Letting go of the story of being a victim to the other person, and allowing love to flow again can be very scary. It is challenging and causes us to think about whether or not this is actually what we really want to do. The ego would much rather hold grudges.

To the soul however, the heaviness of a grudge is a weight that it definitely does not want to carry. A grudge or feeling of blame and vengeance is held in the heart chakra and interferes with our capacity to love. It diminishes our energy levels generally.

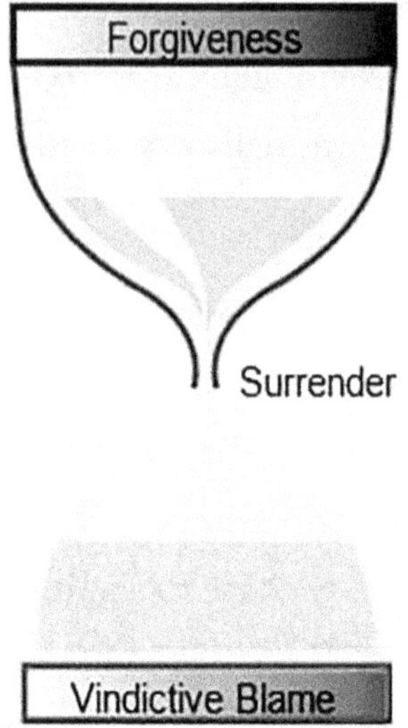

Forgiveness is something that tends to happen in layers. We just do the best we can at any given time to practice forgiveness. We know that we have truly forgiven someone when we feel a lot of love for them again. When we really surrender the pain, the blame and the negative experiences, we float up into the top of the hourglass. It feels amazing.

Conflict and Making Up

Any time that we have had an argument with our beloved, there is some kind of surrender involved when we kiss and make up. We talk about what was in our heart and move forward. But to do it effectively, we have to release the hurt. That hurt is held onto by the ego in the bottom of the hourglass, and enough little hurts all joined together create a big impenetrable shield behind which some people live. Getting rid of our defenses and shields, becoming genuinely authentic and spiritually empowered is a formula for better relationships.

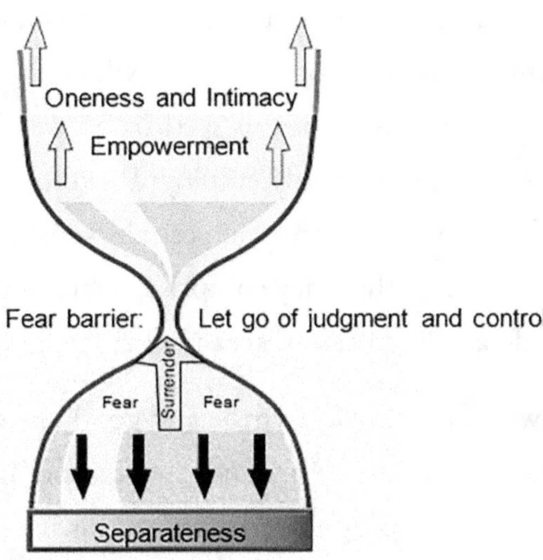

The more we can move into oneness and intimacy by letting go of judgment and control, the better our relationships will be. We access Divine grace, more love and unity than ever before.

Fear keeps us stuck in a small paradigm. If we don't deal with it constructively, it causes us to have thought forms that are very disempowering. We end up in a spiral of judgment and control that ends up causing us to feel very alone. By letting it go and learning to flow more, we float upwards and before we know it we are experiencing new life in our spirit and our relationships.

Wisdom is the embodiment

Of the right virtue at the right time.

Shakti Durga

What are the Virtues?

One of the best 'anti-gravitational' strategies for moving up from the bottom of the hourglass to the top is to cultivate and live the virtues.

The ancient Vedic tradition regards consciousness as masculine, and creation as feminine. Feminine or yin power, which includes the power to create, is Shakti. The nature of this spiritual power is the combined might of all of the virtues, perfectly employed and realised. The virtues are the fabric of creation. They are, energetically speaking, one with the essence of all matter. Together they comprise a state of ecstasy and love. Relationships held at this vibration are unbelievably good.

Every time we behave *without* virtue and goodness we diminish the energy in our energy field. It shrinks and energetically and spiritually so do we. We move more into Egoic separation. This is not going to help our relationships.

Every time we behave with virtue and goodness, we add sparks of light to our soul. It grows and so do we. Our relationship prospects improve as we start to pull from others a vibration that matches our own.

When we behave in a non-virtuous way, we are like a drop of spray becoming separated from the power of the entire ocean. We might make a momentary splash, but the amount of energy behind us is limited. Sooner or later we are going to crash, and the energy of our action will be dissipated. When we behave virtuously, we are acting in oneness with creation and all of its power is with us.

The power of virtue is slower acting than the force we can exert by doing the wrong thing. Doing the wrong thing (stealing the washing machine we want from someone else) or even doing a mediocre thing (it is legally OK but still quite a long way from virtuous) takes a short cut to attain an objective. However, these seemingly quick solutions will be inherently flawed and will quickly disintegrate into even bigger problems. If we lie to avoid taking responsibility for something, we just create a bigger problem later, even though we seem to have 'got out of trouble' in the now. In fact, we just got into deeper and more diabolical trouble that we don't know about yet. This must occur, on account of the law of karma. This might not even strike in the same incarnation! If we steal, something even more valuable may be stolen from us, whereas the power of doing something with virtue just keeps on keeping on. It is relatively timeless. That which is built upon solid virtue is difficult to destroy.

Looked at from the perspective of the soul, the development of the virtues are the real classrooms that we have on Earth. When we develop virtues, they blaze like beacons within our light body. The quality of the light that shines forth tells all beings in all dimensions about us.

A realised soul has embodied the virtues, turning life experience into wisdom and empowerment. This person is liberated from many of the restraints of normal 'earth school' classrooms and is empowered in ways beyond the imagination of most people. Virtuous souls are capable of many miraculous things. They are generally humble and do not exhibit their power so much as they use it behind the scenes to create better life circumstances for millions of people. Without these advanced souls, humanity would have destroyed itself long ago.

Behaving virtuously in the tasks and objectives that we are seeking to attain on Earth has the added bonus that it *builds us.* When we think, speak or behave virtuously, we grow our energy field. Conversely when we are lacking in appropriate virtue in any situation, we may win the day but we lose our 'yin power' and we fall down the snakes and ladders of our life experience. Overall, we lose. Embodying the virtues is one of the main reasons that we incarnate.

Our conscience (a function of our consciousness) is our best guide to knowing how to become virtuous. Through repetition of virtuous thought, word and action, we grow in vibration and become empowered. The virtues may not be fashionable, and are often overlooked, but they are the essence of being powerfully yin. They form the basis of ethics and in a Golden Age they form the philosophical foundation beneath all of our enterprises, laws, and institutions of society. Relationships are the perfect container or classroom for us to practice truly embedding the virtues into realised action.

There is a thought form in the Matrix that to be virtuous means giving up many things that might be deliciously fun. However, we are wearing blinkers which prevent us from seeing the tremendous joy, love, happiness, peace and prosperity that awaits us when we break through to ever higher levels of vibration and energy. When we get to that point, the things that we used to find fun seem boring, because a new world of Divine majesty is open to us and nothing compares to it!

Some researchers in the 1990s created the Virtues Project.[8] The point of it was to teach children about virtues in a societal matrix in which most children nowadays do not get a religious education. To define the virtues, they searched the world's sacred texts to discover the virtues that each one held sacred.

The virtues that they found were common to all faiths are listed on the next page.

---

[8] Linda Kavelin-Popov, a psychotherapist, organisational consultant, and community healer; her husband Dr. Dan Popov, a clinical pediatric psychologist and senior computer scientist; and her brother, John Kavelin, an art director with Walt Disney Imagineering founded the Virtues Project to assist young people and families learn and practice the virtues.

Virtues

acceptance, accountability, appreciation, assertiveness, awe,

beauty, caring, certitude, charity, cheerfulness, cleanliness,

commitment, compassion, confidence, consideration, contentment,

cooperation, courage, courtesy, creativity, decisiveness, detachment,

determination, devotion, dignity, diligence, discernment, empathy, endurance, enthusiasm, excellence, fairness, faith, faithfulness,

fidelity, flexibility, forbearance, forgiveness, fortitude, friendliness,

generosity, gentleness, grace, gratitude, helpfulness, honesty, honour,

hope, humanity, humility, idealism, independence, initiative, integrity, joyfulness, justice, kindness, love, loyalty, mercy, mindfulness,

moderation, modesty, nobility, openness, optimism, orderliness,

patience, peacefulness, perceptiveness, perseverance, prayerfulness, purity, purposefulness, reliability, resilience, respect, responsibility,

reverence, righteousness, sacrifice, self discipline, serenity, service, simplicity, sincerity, steadfastness, strength, tact, thankfulness, thoughtfulness, tolerance, trust, trustworthiness, truthfulness, understanding, unity, wisdom, wonder and zeal.

We recommend the reflection cards produced by the Virtues Project for further contemplation and as practical tools in this area[9].

---

[9] The Virtues Project, www.virtuesproject.com and the virtues cards produced by the virtues project are highly recommended by the author.

Tricks of the Trade

Virtues as life tools are not always easy to use, and it is beneficial for us to practice them. A way of looking at wisdom is that it is the embodiment of the right virtue at the right time. When should we practice moderation, and when should we employ zeal? When should we practice truthfulness rather than tact, or vice versa? When should we be flexible, and when should we be reliable? When should we be disciplined and when should we show mercy? Many interesting ethical questions come up every day when we try to be virtuous.

Meditation or Dinner?

I remember a retreat that I facilitated years ago. It was a small retreat of about 30 people. We had agreed on cooking rosters and some real 'foodies' were on the first evening shift preparing dinner for all of us. The problem was that the Divine program went overtime, seriously over time. We were in an ecstatic state of Divine oneness in which time does not really have much meaning: everyone was receiving big blessings. There was tremendous downpouring of Divine energy and a lot of devotion. Meanwhile the foodies were fuming that the meditators were late for dinner. Their elaborate and amazing kitchen creations were over heated, the greens had turned grey and when we turned up to the dining room we were not very popular.

The next day we had a discussion about the virtues, and how each group had done 'the right thing' from their own perspective, and yet this had caused anguish for others.

The foodies felt aggrieved that the others had not had the courtesy to be on time for dinner and had not been accountable when there had been a decision that dinner would be served at 7pm.

The people who had continued with their meditation felt aggrieved by the inference that the Divine program should have been interrupted just for food. They felt that this showed a lack of flexibility, and a lack of commitment to the reason that we had been on retreat in the first place, which was not to eat, but to be with the Divine.

Both sides of the dispute felt that they were right. Both sides sited virtues which proved their point. What we needed to do was to surrender our stances and go into a state of meditation, with everyone expressing a willingness to expand our consciousness to a new place of understanding where we could reconcile these issues.

Part of the success of this spiritual exercise was that, despite their adherence to their own preferred virtue, both parties were more interested in arriving at a place of peace and continued practicality over being right and controlling what the others did. We therefore lifted the dispute out of the bottom of the hourglass and into the top of the hourglass.

We ended up coming to an agreement, which has stood us in good stead at every retreat since. We came to the conclusion that the Divine program came first in priority, and that food was a secondary consideration. Knowing this, each person could then prepare food that would be OK if it was not eaten for several hours after we thought it would be eaten. The meditators apologised to the foodies for not being accountable for time, and the foodies apologised to the meditators for judging them.

In all, it was a perfect Divine classroom for us all to see how even when we seek to use the virtues, we can come unstuck if we do not agree which virtues or circumstances have priority.

By the end of the retreat we were all laughing about this Divine Leela (a play that the Divine puts on in order to teach us something) and we had cemented our friendships much more deeply than ever before. We had gone through the conflict phase cleanly, and popped back through the Golden After Glow, into the Honeymoon phase again.

Since this time we have been careful to establish which virtues are our primary consideration when embarking on various different kinds of undertakings. Then, the virtues can be utilised as reference points for the resolution of disputes.

Cultivating virtue creates a set of high vibrational values with which to live. If we just pay lip service to them but actually behave in a manner that is incongruent, we create a split in the personality through which fear slips in and can distort our thinking. We are drawn through our fear into an, as yet invisible, downward spiral leading to failure and misery. We might bag the result that we wanted short term, but we lose peace of mind, security, health, happiness and self worth. Our 'yin power' and the light of our soul are disintegrated. Thus, how we live and embody virtues-based values is really important.

Virtues are not astral. It does not matter whether we believe in them or not, and our belief will not affect the timeless truth of their very nature. They are the 'non-stuff' of creation itself. The power of virtues is real whatever we might think.

Applying Virtues in Relationships

Virtues can be left on the sidelines as the lure of achievement and the perceived importance of the outcome we want is so great that we will do almost anything to get there. How far will we go for what we want? Good people doing things in the world pursuing worthy goals can become unhinged when they make bizarre and harmful decisions in order to protect the 'good' outcomes they seek. They can even interfere with the freedoms and rights of others. When we fail to behave in accordance with the virtues such as honesty, reliability, service, compassion and so on, we shrink our yin energy. This is the same as shrinking the amount of Holy Spirit or Shakti that we have inside of ourselves.

Not so Sweet

I once knew an amazing woman who travelled the world giving spiritual teaching, which she did with zeal and selfless dedication. She attracted many people who assisted her with a great deal of gratitude and devotion, and she beneficially affected many lives. She was a truly wonderful person, until you disagreed with her. So long as her followers did what she told them to, she was happy to foster their development and teach them many things, but if they deviated from her path she would drop them like a stone. Not only that, she would then engage in character assassination so as to remove any desire of those that stayed within her organisation from following suit, or siding with the now expelled member.

This kind of treatment of dissenters can be seen in fundamentalist religious sects as well as new age movements, and shows us the values that underlie the movement. You are either with us or you are against us. This leaves no room for peaceful coexistence and holds a vibration of separation and fear. This will eventually take the organisation backwards on the spiral path rather than forwards, and sows the seed of destruction at the very same time as it is being built. When values are not being lived and applied, negative karma starts to gather and sooner or later this will create a downfall.

Strength and Longevity

When starting a new enterprise or relationship of any kind, the higher the vibration at which it was founded the stronger it will be.

If something is begun with a motive of pure self-interest, this is a mediocre value and will result in an enterprise or relationship of mediocre or poor longevity. If the motive for starting something is pure love, then this gives an entirely different vibration to the enterprise or relationship and will have a different effect upon those who started it.

There will also be a longer natural lifespan of an organisation if it is given virtuous foundations. Christianity was founded on the vibration of love. The vibration of the *foundations*, which is the part that Jesus himself played, gave tremendous *shakti* or yin spiritual power to it. I do not know of any business that has lasted 2,000 years. Businesses are generally not started with the same intention or vibration as an Avatar begins a mission.

The Divine creates at a massively high vibration of ecstatic joy. Anything that the Divine creates has a natural tendency to evolve and grow. Think of nature, which is so abundant, beautiful and restorative of our sense of calm and inner peace.

If we want to access our Divine inheritance including all kinds of wealth, then we need to 'meet it' somewhere. Imagine that everything that we ever wanted is already created, we just are not yet in a state of vibration at which we can access it. Because we are Divinely created, and each of us has the Divine dimension already inside us, we and everything in our life are perfect already. A reason we may wish to raise our vibration, learn the virtues and embody more life skills is to have a different set of life experiences.

If your relationship is not optimal, think of it from the point of view of the virtue you are putting into it. Do you tell white lies to get round things? Are you respectful to the people you live with? Do you display warmth and consideration or are you always waiting for others to be nice to you so you can then be nice to them? By working with the virtues, you may be surprised at how much 'they' seem to change!

To assist people with understanding how to apply virtues, which are strengths of the soul, I recommend my Strength of the Soul inspiration cards. By shuffling the cards, considering your relationship situation and asking for Divine guidance, you will pick the card that is perfect for you. Then, imagine that the situation in your life is there to help you to cultivate this virtue or soul strength. As you put your awareness onto that assignment, it will automatically shift your focus from the problem to a potential solution. Try it yourself and see. It has helped change countless relationships for the better.

Chapter

20

VIBRATION
AND RELATIONSHIP

Energy and Vibration

Whenever we think, speak or act, we are sending out powerful vibrational signals that are picked up on a subconscious level by those around us. These vibrations are also picked up unconsciously by the people about whom we speak. You might as well assume that everyone hears everything you think and say because, on an energetic level, that is true. If we believe we are a 'loser', so will everyone else. If we believe in our own ability and have the right vibration, we can succeed beyond our wildest dreams. If we have an inner dialogue in our heads that another person is selfish and untrustworthy, that is the kind of behaviour that we will automatically draw forth from them. This is the essence of the Law of Attraction.

You can, through your own negativity, call forth low vibrational behaviour from someone who is normally a Saint. Similarly, you can call forth noble behaviour from someone who is normally not very reliable or considerate. Our attitude and the vibration that it creates is actually very important. This information can be read in conjunction with the *Child of God* book, which gives a lot of detail about the power of our thoughts.

Every thought, word, deed or objective we have has a vibration. In every moment, we are drawing nearer to some experiences and further away from others. Choices filled with love inevitably lead us away from dangers and pitfalls. Judgments and choices filled with fear or negative intention take us closer to problems and experiences we will not enjoy very much. We move away from peace and happiness.

Our vibration is integral to our real empowerment. When we are in relationship with people our vibration is constantly tested. Many situations arise in daily life where we have differences of opinion or different priorities to others, and there are opportunities for conflict. It is easy to maintain a high vibration when everything is going right and people are being relaxed and friendly. But what about if someone misunderstands a situation and behaves in an unexpected or fearful way? What if they say something that hurts us? What if someone makes a mistake, or is unskilful in their communication? Are we able to meet that with a high vibration or do we instantly get reactive and let our vibration crumble?

When faced with not getting our own way, the temptation is to achieve the result we want in the short term by asserting situational or positional power (force) over the other person. We can become either actively or passively aggressive, become a victim and complain, or bully the other person into agreeing with us, forcing them to put up with our decision even if we both know that it is not consensual. Low vibrational responses to daily life situations include coercion, lack of respect, manipulation, arrogantly ignoring the stated opinions or needs of the other person, failure to take the time to find a win/win situation, being sneaky, taking control, white-anting, head butting, angry insistence and so on. These are all poor relationship strategies which will cause our vibration to free-fall and our relationships to be undermined.

An empowered person does not adopt any of these strategies. The empowered person feels any feelings related to a situation or conflict. He or she then reflects upon it, and avoids becoming attached to prior conceptions.

Following contemplation there will be a clearer understanding of the situation, the type of multi-dimensional classroom this represents, our part in this creation, and the inner motivation of others. The empowered person holds a vision of what they wish to occur and waits while the universe delivers it. They are assertive and clear in communication without being aggressive or passive. Meanwhile the empowered person gets on with feeling peace, happiness, acceptance, bliss and love.

A mutually satisfying arrangement can always be found if we are prepared to lift our vibration so as to attract it into our lives. If this does not seem to be your reality, all I can say is that you need to raise your vibration. Then, it will be.

Vibrational Scale of Consciousness

Dr. David R Hawkins, who is a psychiatrist as well as a spiritual teacher in the USA did some ground breaking work on human consciousness, experimenting and collecting data for over 20 years. His objective was to see if there was a way that human consciousness could be calibrated. He developed what he calls the vibrational scale of consciousness, which ranks human awareness on a scale of 1 to 1000. This scale can be seen in his books including Power versus Force.[10]

Dr. Hawkins' research into vibration was done using muscle testing. We can easily learn how to do this and then validate Dr. Hawkins findings for ourselves. We can also check the results by scanning energy with our hands, which is taught in *Ignite your Spirit*.[11]

Dr Hawkins says that the scale is logarithmic, that 300 on the scale is not twice the power of 150 but is 300 to the tenth power (10 to the power of 300). A small movement on the scale translates as a very large advance in consciousness, which he says directly correlates to a large advance in empowerment.

At the lowest end of the vibrational scale are very unpleasant states of consciousness that we would call 'negative', which include states of consciousness such as shame, blame, vindictiveness, misery, despair, hopelessness and humiliation. These all have a vibrational rating of less than 50 on the scale. These kinds of consciousness disempower us. They render us incapable of recognising real truth. We get caught up in a web

---

[10] *Power versus Force* by Dr David R Hawkins, Veritas publishing Arizona USA 2001. I have also written more about this in my previous book Spiritual Mastery, in which there is a chapter on the Law of Vibration.

[11] From my own experience, I don't think you can scan or accurately test for the future.

of delusion, because of the lens through which we are looking. If we are feeling shame, we cannot believe in ourselves. If someone gives us a compliment, we don't know how to receive it.

Vindictiveness is always destructive and productive of tragedy. Through the law of karma we are creating hellish conditions for our future when we get caught in these states of consciousness and act it out.

The scale goes up from there, through various kinds of consciousness standpoints. Pride and indifference are in the 100s on the scale, and both of these states of consciousness according to Hawkins are also disempowering.

At the lower end of the scale we have to use force (not personal empowerment), which may include underhanded tactics, deceit, betrayal, slavery, misery or destructiveness to get things done.

At the highest end of the scale are the most potent forms of vibrational consciousness that a human body is capable of withstanding[12]. These include love, joy, happiness and peace, bliss and ecstasy. Dr. Hawkins says that at the highest end of the scale, the vibration of 1,000, we find empowered people who can co-create wonderful things; he cites luminaries such as Jesus, Buddha and Krishna.

According to Dr. Hawkins' analysis, there is a crucial vibrational benchmark for the development of human consciousness. This is the level of 200 on the vibrational scale. This is the basic vibrational level of consciousness where we move from disempowerment to empowerment.

---

[12] You may ask "How can it be that a human body is only capable of withstanding a certain voltage of vibration?" Refer to Dr Hawkin's work and also my book *Child of God* for more information about this.

We are no longer stuck in an achingly painful tragedy, enslaved to others, filled with anger, shame, blame, hatred, revenge, scorn or fear. With consciousness moving above 200, we find courage, trust, release and hope. From there as we develop ourselves vibrationally, things just get better.

Dr. Hawkins claims that the average human vibration over the past 2,000 years has been *less than 200*, thus most people are easily led and manipulated by ruthless authority figures and relatives, and by fear-based and coercive political doctrines and religious beliefs. He says that in 1986, for the first time, the average level of human vibration rose above 200, and that this accounts for the plethora of new ideas, personal empowerment and progress that has been made over the past twenty five years.

In the 300s, capability and willingness emerge, and in the mid-three hundreds there is the capacity to take personal responsibility for situations that emerge in life. However, in the 300s, political solutions, ideologies, wars and slogans still sway consciousness away from pure logic and reason or higher vibrations of love, joy and bliss, higher realms of consciousness and concomitant behaviour.

In the 400s, logic and reasoning prevail. This is the realm of the great thinkers of scientific history. Huge advances in our way of life and understanding of science have occurred with the help of great individuals within this band of consciousness. Yet in the 400s the inner world is not revealed, and there can be an over-intellectualisation of issues. Science is revered as God. It is considered that everything can be dissected and discovered using increasingly sophisticated scientific tools.

Dr. Hawkins says the heart (chakra) opens only when the vibration hits 500, revealing the inner world of love. It is here that the ability to transcend the world of opposites begins. Vibration then climbs through the 540s, where there is unconditional love (you can hurt me and I will still love you), then peace at 600 (peace is a higher vibration than love: you can love people and still want to kill them!). He says that less than one person in ten million has a consciousness above 600[13]. At 700, we enter the radiant world of Gurus and Saints, who have enlightened consciousness, no judgment and radiant energy that is capable of assisting others to attain peace and unconditional love. Here, the experience of Divine bliss can be imparted to others with the touch of a hand. Dr. Hawkins says there are only a few such people in the world.

We are a mixture of vibrations. Some days we are more loving and peaceful than others. Some days we revert to being victimised by others and some days we are very stressed. The analysis assumes that each of us is moving vibrationally all of the time, but that we could be said to have an average vibration or resting place for our consciousness. Our habits of thinking, reacting, judging, blaming and resisting in a myriad of situations, determines our vibrational rate.

Can you feel for a moment what it would be like to be in a relationship where the average vibration within it is hopelessness? Where each party is condemning the other, where there is a lot of fear and anxiety and a sense of despair?

Can you feel now, instead, what it would be like to be in a relationship with a lot of acceptance, where people were forgiving and loving,

---

[13] *Power versus Force,* page 74

inspiring and understanding? Imagine having a loving relationship, filled with joy and deep harmony.

It is obvious which of these we would prefer. The problem is we so often point the finger at our partner, falling into the trap of thinking that "if only you would change...". Trying to change another person is a recipe for disaster and will be frustrating for you both.

The most successful strategy to lift your relationships from doom and gloom to love and joy is to *work on yourself*. You will become more empowered. Your consciousness will change. The kinds of thoughts you think will be different. Your responses to challenges and difficult people will mellow and become more authentic, more enlightened, more empowered. You will get more in touch with your spirit and start to attract the miraculous.

The journey will take some time and application, and will probably be lumpy, by which I mean, the trajectory of progress is usually up and down. If you stand back and look over time however, you will see that you spend more time enjoying your relationships, and less time in process about them. You get better at it. The people around you will seem to spontaneously change for the better. Actually what is changing is you. That is the secret, the key and the only way to self empowerment and happiness in relationships. Become the change you want to see in the world.

Multi Dimensional Chess

Imagine that you are actually inside a giant chess board, which not only goes two dimensionally on top of a table, but has depth as well, and you can go up, down, forwards, backwards and sideways. This goes on endlessly in every direction. When you move upwards, you move into a higher vibration and when you move downwards, you move into a lower vibration.

The trouble is that you are not moving by choosing the moves, you are moving by living out your normal life as best you can. Moves occur every time you react, think, interact, or relate, depending upon the vibration of your choice. As moves happen a doorway appears to either side, or the top or bottom of the box you are currently in. You go through the door, because there is nowhere else to go, and you don't have a choice. You will probably not notice as this happens.

Every time you scream at the kids or beat yourself up, the doors on the lower sides of the square open, and down you go. Every time you nurture yourself or help someone else, or exhibit patience, one of the doors at the top open, and you float upwards. This is happening every minute of every day.

It is the small things that count. Through the minutia of life, you move a long way either upwards or downwards in the big game of life, and your own personal energy vibration as well as your life choices are affected. This draws you in a natural kind of way, either closer to your greatness and your highest destiny as your vibration becomes lighter or, alternatively, you move closer to pain, loss, ill health, poverty and failure if the small things in life are done with low vibrational consciousness of shame blame guilt, dishonesty and so on. Omnipotence is going on all around us, and no action, no decision and no thought, no matter how small, escapes its notice.

Every thought, word, action and reaction either raises or lowers our vibration based on its inherent quality. If our thoughts, words, actions and reactions lower our vibration we energetically shrink, and move away from our goals. We have to use more effort and struggle harder to get anywhere. We have moved out of the flow. Relationships get really tough. If it raises our vibration it makes us energetically bigger. Our etheric body can hold more energy. This moves us more towards positive goals. We are in the flow.

Bodhi Festival

Bodhi Festival is a multi-faith celebration of spirituality and consciousness through music, yoga and inspirational speaking, held each year in Newcastle, Australia. In the first year of the operation of Bodhi Festival the team working on it, which included over 400 Shanti Mission volunteers organised into 42 teams, had a lot of challenges to work through. We were all learning and growing and for nearly all of us it was the first time we had been involved with a project of this scale, involving so many teachers, musicians, yogis and performing artists as well as thousands of members of the public.

Every morning, in the week leading up to the event, the volunteers would come together for meditation. We would all commit to doing everything that we did that day from the vibration of love. As we put it: we committed to being love on legs, being of service in every way possible, using healthy communication and parenting our inner children. We were determined to practice empowered relationship skills and the festival became a 'laboratory' of learning for us in which we did so.

The result was astonishing. This team of students, initiates and disciples actually created a field of love in which the whole of Bodhi Festival, held over 3 days, took place. They remained united and were able to sort out all kinds of issues and problems without treading on each other's toes or getting cross with each other. Everyone stayed calm and had a great time. The feedback from the volunteers was that they not only had a tremendous time, they experienced real empowerment. The feedback from the public was that they had never before felt the warmth, love, vibration and bliss of the field of consciousness that had been co-created. To me it was a miracle of grace, brought to Earth by a committed and devoted group of people who really wanted to experience the Divine through love in action (karma yoga).

One of my beloved disciples Bhavani Ma, is the managing director of Bodhi Festival. At the 11th hour, when we were due to open the Festival in 2 hours, we received a visit from a local council official who informed us that instead of being able to have 7,000 people in the building we could only have around 1,200 on account of fire regulations. It turns out that while we had been in long and wonderful discussions with the council about the event, no one had realised that a particular form had not been submitted and that there could have been an issue. Several of the directors came to the meeting and we were shocked, and of course our inner children wanted to panic, and perhaps kick someone. We all instantly parented our inner child and invoked for Divine help. We were cordial and friendly with the council official and with the fire department officer who had attended the meeting. I started sending them love and asking Parameshwari, my Guru, to fix this as we had all worked so hard and with such devotion to create this event, it seemed odd that this test would come in the form that it did.

I released attachment to the outcome, and invoked that the highest outcome prevail. Bhavani Ma kept up an open, respectful and clear dialogue with the two gentlemen concerned. Soon after, the fire officer said that he would go and get the regional fire chief, and also the big boss from Sydney to come and see if there were any other ways to fix the problem. Late on a Friday afternoon it would seem to be a miracle if these two 'top brass' would be able to come all the way to Newcastle, however that is precisely what they did. They were friendly and helpful and we soon had a solution in place that was workable and effective, and we had orders from the fire department that allowed the festival to continue in a fulsome way.

After it was all over, the original fire officer said to Bhavani Ma "I don't know what it is about you people, but you would have to be the nicest people I have ever encountered. Most people faced with the news you got just hours before the festival opened, would have been swearing and cursing, shouting and yelling and thumping the table, but you were all so nice, and so I really wanted to help you. I am glad everything turned out OK, and let us know if you need more help with anything in the future."

Through being steadfast in our vibration in a situation that would normally produce stress and even panic, we opened doors to the miraculous, which would not have opened if we had let our vibration drop. This impacted upon some important relationships and was of inestimable value.

Making Decisions

Often we find ourselves in situations where we wonder what is the correct choice to make here? Should we stay in this relationship or should we leave? These large decisions can be quite stressful and bring up a lot of fear.

Rather than worrying about the big decisions that we have to make in our lives, it is more effective to concentrate on the moment. In each moment, try to be the highest thought, the highest speech and the highest actions in a vibrational sense. This means: think, do and say that which is loving and respectful of all concerned. We may know someone is unreliable or even dishonest, but does it help to dwell upon it? Our angry and judgmental thoughts about dishonesty will sink our own vibration and have nothing to do with the dishonest person. We could instead think "Ah interesting, that person has just displayed dishonesty", and we could focus on their good points instead. (We may also choose not to trust that person with our life savings.)

As we use each moment as a spiritual exercise in high vibrational consciousness, we actually pull a different future reality towards us. This has to be done in a sustained way. There is no doubt that this works, and that we can change the direction our life is taking for the better, through awareness of vibrational reality.

Try to embody loving kindness and non-injury at least most of the time, and you will magnetise more luck, good fortune and a better life to yourself. You will grow and progress and so will your relationships.

Chapter

21

POWER GAMES AND HOW TO STOP THEM

Disempowered people tend to engage in all kinds of behaviour which is dysfunctional, negative, underhanded, abusive, manipulative, controlling and generally unpleasant in order to get their needs met. While this may achieve an immediate result of the need being satisfied, each of these non-virtuous acts is a nail in the coffin of a great relationship with the person or persons concerned. While they might get what they want through force, they are not empowered at all. Empowerment stems from unconditional love, and this is the exact opposite of what is going on when needs are met in this way. What is more, sometimes people who do not live in the world in an empowered way resent and fear those who do. The empowered must be mindful of this and send love and reassurance to others. If the empowered are arrogant, the disempowered may even attack them. This is the basis of the tall poppy syndrome.

People do not destroy their relationships deliberately. It is just that they are unable to meet their own needs for security, approval, acceptance, attention, love, hope, rest and fun. Putting it another way, they are unable to parent themselves. If they could, they would be able to meet the needs of their inner child without resorting to intrigue, game playing and the negative habits that they learned from their early relationship experiences.

Energy in Merging

When two people turn their attention to each other, they literally merge energy fields, pooling their energy. The issue quickly becomes, who is going to control this accumulated energy? If one can dominate, managing to get the other to defer to his point of view, to look at the world through his eyes then this individual has captured both energies as his own. He feels an immediate rush of power, security, self-worth and euphoria. This is at the other's expense. The beloved usually feels off-centre, anxious, disappointed or drained of energy.

Two separate energy fields   Two merged in relationship

When we are forced to defer to someone who has manipulated us into confusion, intimidated us, ignored us, thrown us off balance or made us feel guilty, we suddenly feel deflated. This is because energy is literally pouring out of us to that other person. We are giving our power away. They cannot actually take it without us colluding in the game. We might not know we are doing it, but we are actually *letting* them do these things on an energetic level.

People manipulate each other in ingenious and often unconscious ways in order to get energy they need. Really, all they need to do is learn to connect with the ever present and infinite Divine supply of energy that is all around us. Many people are so spiritually disconnected that they have no idea how to do this.

Taking energy from another through a relationship power game is like theft in a circumstance where the person being stolen from lets it be taken and then regrets it. Why would a person allow someone else to take their power? Generally, it is because they feel that the other person is necessary to them for a need to be met. This is why learning to meet our own needs is so important. When we can love and approve of ourselves, accept and honour ourselves, we are not beholden to others to do it, when the cost in them doing so might be quite high.

Without meaning to, from time to time, all of us engage in disempowering strategies to meet the needs that we have. The thing is to get more conscious about it. When we have more of an idea of what these games are, we can then try to avoid playing them.

We are going to look at four kinds of manipulation, all of which are destructive to relationships. As you read, consider which of these dramas is your favourite. It seems that we all do at least one of these things, and starting to notice it is the first step in changing our responses to tricky situations, so that we can be more healthy and wholesome in our dealings with people.

Control Dramas

In his book *Celestine Prophesy,* James Radfield[14] asserts that there are 4 main ways that humans try to control each other. He named them control dramas. They are:

1. We become a Victim.
2. We become Aloof, withdrawn, withholding and unapproachable.
3. We become an Interrogator: a Nag.
4. We become an Intimidator.

These control dramas range from very passive to very aggressive. Radfield says (and through experience I agree) that everyone has a dominant drama from these four.

These disempowering relationship strategies can be seen in all parts of our life. Sometimes we may favour one of them when at work, another at home, and yet another with certain people. Think of those around you: what patterns of control do they exhibit?

As you reflect on this information and the exercise we did earlier about our families of origin, you may see patterns that are helpful in identifying the problem. Become aware of when you are going into an old pattern, and see if you can stop yourself. Awareness is the first step in changing, realising a healthier and more positive way of handling life and ensuring that we meet our own needs.

---

[14] The information on 4 types of control dramas came from James Radfields book, *The Celestine Prophesy*, and I have found it to be very handy when working with people in relationships (including my own).

Control Drama 1: The Victim: Poor Me!

The most passive control drama is that of the victim, who seeks to win attention and get what it wants through the manipulation of sympathy or guilt. A victim is someone who feels that they have no power in a given situation. They see power as sitting with other people, with circumstances, governments, parents, teachers, employers, and all kinds of external factors, but not within themselves.

Victims try and avoid confrontation because they fear that they will come off second best. Instead they can be undermining, talking behind the back of the person with whom they have an issue, getting others onside so as to feel safer if they eventually have a situation where they cannot avoid speaking to the person. Victims can be passive aggressive, saying yes to something even when they have no intention of ever doing what they just agreed to. They are reacting to what they construe to be someone pressuring them or forcing them to do something. They never venture an opinion until later when they say "I knew that wouldn't work out", at which time they feel smug and superior to the person who has just experienced a difficulty. The victim never wants to be wrong, and so would not communicate their doubts at the beginning.

Victims generally engage in people-pleasing so as to avoid the possibility of disharmony. They fear that they will come off second best in any interaction and so they avoid difficult subjects. Victims bottle up their emotions, putting up with more and more from others until they snap and go from passive, right past assertive and into an aggressive response.

Whenever we think like a victim, we are not in empowered consciousness and thus are not in a position to change anything about the situation.

Victims like to be rescued. They insinuate their needs and invite someone else to save them, and are happy when this happens. However if the rescuer does not fulfil some criteria that the victim was expecting, then the victim will turn on the rescuer, criticising them to anyone who will listen, and in effect, the victim turns into their persecutor.

"I expected you to call yesterday and you didn't!" It is your fault. The victim is too passive to call you, they just complain when you don't call them.

The victim is focused on how rotten life is in general, how overwhelming their situation is, how much they have to do, and they lose themselves to all of this. This control drama is almost completely unconscious as the person often believes that they are without fault or failing. The victim thinks that the other person is responsible for their situation and that if only the other person was not so insensitive, bullying, controlling or dominant, then their life would be better.

Often the victim shirks responsibility for their life. When it gets hard, they just abdicate, allowing someone else to run the agenda.

A specialty of the victim is to create a feeling of guilt in others. This is an effort to attain or retain the moral high ground.

The victim can also exhibit the characteristics of the martyr. They selflessly serve others, but not from a 'cup full' position. It is from the position of wanting approval, or to be thanked for what they do.

The victim is often tired, and lets others know how exhausted they are. Really they are saying that they do so much more than anyone else does, and no one appreciates them.

If they are asked to step up, or to adopt a different strategy, the victim is likely to retort "I'm doing the best I can, it's how I am!" and be affronted that you dared to suggest that they change. The victim is terrified of change, because it fears even greater loss of empowerment than it already suffers.

When asked how they are, the victim will answer "I'm fine", in a voice that clearly indicates that they are anything but fine. You might ask them what is the matter, and they will say "Nothing!" as they stomp around the house. Clearly they are upset, the inference is "It is your fault, you should know what you have done to upset me, and you should feel guilty". The victim asserts that you really don't care about them "Poor me!"

Another strategy of the victim is to selflessly do things because clearly you can't do it, and "I have to do everything around here anyway". Because the victim is basically insecure and feels worthless, they have to become indispensable so that you need them. They remind you how much they do for you and how much you need them, just in case you have forgotten.

The victim creates dramas and actually energetically (and unconsciously) calls into its life people to abuse them so that they get to be on the moral high horse, decrying how dreadful these people are and all the while getting lots of energy out of other people who sympathise with them "Yes, it must be horrible for you, I don't know how you put up with it".

Because they feel so disempowered, you cannot rely on what a victim says. They will say whatever they think you want to hear, and then do whatever they want to when you are not there, and this will be justified on the basis that you wouldn't have listened to them anyway, and why should they do what you want them to.

The martyr part of the victim says "Don't worry about me" in a voice that says "You bastard! Why are you not worrying about me!" Basically, they need external recognition because they are incapable of giving themselves any approval or attention by themselves.

The victim can be identified by the tales of woe and large stories of injustice that fill their conversations. Instead of doing something about it they just whine. They feel powerless, and just want to get lots of people on their side, so that others will be 'white knights' and fight their battles for them.

If someone shouts at a victim, they go into a huff. They nobly say nothing, cry, and may eventually listen to an apology, so long as it is served with large lashings of guilt. The victim wants you to know that they are a much better person than you are.

Dental Dramas

My beloved and I at one stage shared a dentist, a very expensive and well-regarded Macquarie Street specialist in Sydney. I am basically frightened of dental work, I have to almost carry myself bodily into a dental chair and I have to practice meditation so as not to give into a primordial panic. I can't stand it. I would rather do almost anything than go to the dentist. My experience of this dentist was that he would hold me up, being constantly late for appointments, he bruised my lip, made a crown that didn't fit resulting in a painful double process and delay, and created fillings that later fell out. I thought he was the worst dentist in the world, hopeless, even dangerous!

Every other person that has ever seen this man, to my knowledge, swears by him as the best dentist God ever put breath into. He is a professor at the Dental College, and a really nice man but my experience was dreadful. You know why? Because I *believed* that going to the dentist will be horrible. Because of my belief, (which I am working on) I pulled forward the worst treatment from even the most eminent dentist in Sydney. I was complaining about him to Shiva who laughed at me and told me to clean up my thought forms and stop being a victim. I looked at him gobsmacked, felt angry, thought "You uncaring bastard", and then went away and thought about it. Much to my annoyance, I realised he was right. I had allowed a virtual stranger to become a persecutor because I was holding tightly onto the energy of the victim in this particular situation.

Similarly, we all from time to time may have a tendency to find others victimising us. Because we unconsciously expect to be disrespected by others, then this is the experience that is created by a beneficent universe which listens to out beliefs and grants them.

I actually think everything that happens to us is perfect. When I reflect back on difficult periods of learning where I thought I was being victimised, I now look back with gratitude.

As a victim (I have a PhD in being a victim as I was one for so long) one can expect to be picked on, overlooked, cheated, lied to, harmed, have people tread on our rights and our personal boundaries. We do everything for others and they don't appreciate it or reciprocate. People will judge us and criticise us, and we can even draw to us serious problems such as bankruptcy, rape, burglary, motor accidents, trees falling on our heads and any number of calamities.

As we awaken, we do not want to continue with victim consciousness. Instead we know we are multi-dimensional beings who draw things to us in a number of different ways. The most prevalent method is our conscious thoughts and unconscious beliefs. Here it is good to change our thinking from "I am not worthy" or "I will be victimised" to "I am empowered, I am an amazing human being".

Some of the characteristics and behaviours of the victim control drama are:

Victim

- Blaming
- Shaming
- Sour facial expressions
- Withholding social cues, e.g. non-verbal responses
- Patronising or talking down to others
- Trying to make others feel guilty
- Excessive seeking of approval
- Breaking confidences
- Lacking discretion, on your soapbox

Control Drama 2: Aloof and Unattainable

The aloof control drama is about having you energy pulled from you by having to chase them. They lure you into courting them. You feed them energetically because they make it so hard to communicate with them.

The aloof is a little less passive than the victim, but is still passive by comparison to the other two control dramas.

Someone who is in the habit of aloof control drama finds it difficult to give a straight answer to a question, because they hate disclosing anything about themselves. Because of this, they can come across as being **sneaky.**

An aloof person can be distant, detached, cryptic in their responses, and vague in their summaries of what happened. They converse in such a way that you have to ask follow-up questions even for the simplest of inquiries;

Q: "Where did you go for your holiday?"

A: "I travelled around a bit"

Q: "Well, where have you travelled?"

A: "Many places"

This forces us to use energy in digging information out of them. In this process, energy flows from the beloved into the aloof. This builds the energy field of the aloof and exhausts the other person.

It is not that the aloof necessarily wants us to disappear out of their life. They just want to speak with us on their terms. They are using a manipulation to lure us in but at the same time, keep us at a distance.

The aloof person feels that the world is full of people who can't be trusted with intimate information. The aloof person is often unsure of what to say, may lack confidence in communication and may be unused to conversing in ways that bring feelings or emotions into the discussion.

They are possibly out of touch with how they feel and so give indefinite answers or grunt when you ask them for information.

Aloof is often seen in teenage children, who come home from school to Mum who asks "How was your day at school?" to which the response is "Good", as they keep their eyes glued to their Gameboy. It doesn't matter what you ask, the response will be one word, will tell you virtually nothing and will sometimes feel frustrating to the person who is asking. The more you ask, the more they clam up. Getting information is like extracting teeth.

Sometimes the aloof wants to protect his own world, to keep you out so that you do not bombard them with your ideas, your preferences and your judgments about them or their projects, friends and interests. Often there is insecurity.

Aloofs sometimes control others by withholding affection, praise, approval or love. This hooks the beloved into doing more and more to show them how good they are, to prove themselves again and again, all the while feeding the aloof with their energy.

When dealing with an aloof it is better to back off when your questions are getting one word answers or grunts, or being ignored. Give them space. Also, see if you can create a space and time in which they can come to you and initiate a discussion if they want to. It will not be helpful to be aloof yourself in response to an aloof, when they are ready to open up to you.

An aloof is telling you that they would appreciate a bit of freedom, a bit of privacy, and so trying to micro-manage or nag an aloof is usually just playing into their control drama and will send them deeper into their shell. Basically, aloofs get hooked on wanting to cover up fear, self doubt and confusion.

Some of the characteristics and behaviours of the aloof control drama are:

Aloof

- Showing obvious lack of interest
- Refusal to negotiate
- Turn their back, leave the room mid-conversation
- Grunt
- Diverting conversation to other topics
- Failure to communicate
- Failure to keep promises
- Disagreeing routinely
- Keeping their head in a book, or TV to avoid people

Control Drama 3: Nag

Have you ever experienced catching up with someone and they just talk at you non-stop? This is the advanced version of the nag. They suck your energy by incessant talking. They are people who want to share every detail and think that everyone else is interested in every miro-point.

Another version of the nag is the critic. This person pulls energy from others by criticising anyone and everything. This makes them feel superior and hides any lack of skill or accomplishment of their own. It is more aggressive than the victim or the aloof, but not as aggressive as the intimidator.

When we are in the presence of a nag we feel like we are being monitored. It is as though we are inadequate or unable to handle our own lives, they may say "You are making a huge mistake". The nag loves to tell you that he 'told you so', "I know more about that than you do". This is so that they feel needed.

The nag sometimes aims to become the dominant judge of other people's lives so that as soon as interaction begins, others defer to his or her worldview, providing a steady flow of energy.

The nag believes he is the hero and the only one paying attention and making sure things are done carefully and perfectly. Often, the nag comes from a family where the parents were either **absent** or not attentive to his needs.

The nag always wants to know where you are, because they are terrified that you might leave them or get hurt in some way if they are not with you or don't know where you have gone.

The nag also loves to know everything, and gets hooked on being a know-it-all. They feel more confident when they are in possession of every conceivable fact or piece of information, no matter how seemingly insignificant. They have no difficulty prying into other people's feelings, emotions or personal information and very often the nag loves to gossip. Unlike the gossipy victim, the motivation is not currying support. It is sharing something no-one else knows about.

Some of the characteristics and behaviours of the nag control drama are:

Nag

- Monopolising the conversation
- Interrupting
- Complaining excessively
- Criticising excessively
- Finding fault
- Over using *why* questions
- Breaking confidences
- Joking at inappropriate times
- Over-using '*should*' language
- Endlessly asking questions
- Wanting to know every detail
- Wanting to tell you every single detail
- Bragging, showing off, talking only about the self

Control Drama 4: Intimidators

An intimidator is someone who uses their energy, intellectual or physical superiority to make other people feel unsafe, and therefore people around them tend to agree with them. They are too scared not to. This is the most aggressive control drama, and causes people around them to feel helpless, fearful, drained, exhausted, affronted, uncomfortable, unsafe, or endangered.

Around a really advanced case of 'intimidator' the joy is sucked out of things. The world turns ominous, threatening, and out of control. People pussy-foot around them desperately trying not to upset them. The intimidator wants to get our attention and our energy by creating an environment in which we feel so threatened that we are totally focused on him/her. Everything has to revolve around them.

The intimidator says and does things that suggest s/he might erupt in rage or violence at any moment, break furniture or throw things across the room. There is very little feeling of safety or ability to relax and be yourself around an intimidator.

Usually the intimidator has been intimidated and severely deprived of energy, and has been involved in relationships with other intimidators who are dominating and abusive. Usually they were intimidated by one or both parents as a child. None of the other dramas worked for these people and so they resorted to this one to force others to meet their needs every time.

Intimidators sometimes believe that they are unloved, no one understands them, and that they would not be intimidating if people around them were more in accordance with what they expect them to be. The list of things the intimidator gets upset about is long and sometimes random. Because they are so aggressive, they actually manifest the very thing that they are terrified of: abandonment and rejection. The game can go on for a long time however, as the intimidator generally stalks its prey by successive cycles of intimidation followed by heart felt apology and promises never to do it/say things like that again. This lasts until next time one of their needs seems not to be met.

Intimidators get hooked on the adrenaline rush of overpowering and winning fights. They pick fights about ridiculous things and of all the control dramas the intimidator is the one most likely to resort to actual violence.

If you live with a very intimidating, violent person then the first thing to do is to know that you deserve to be safe, that you are a worthwhile human being no matter what they may have told you to the contrary, and you do not need to put up with their behaviour. It is possible to get away from these people, even though they may have made threats that if you leave they will find you. One can obtain the help of various community service organisations to get free, and also one can do a lot of inner work to clear old thought forms of lack of self worth. Taking charge of their own safety helps pull the victim back into balance and is an enabling thing to do. Relationship healings will also help to clear the energy and get some perspective and empowerment back again.

Remember, if we will not be a victim, they cannot be a persecutor. Moving out of these roles is possible; I know, I used to be a very advanced victim!

In many instances the intimidator is not violent at all, but they shout a lot and are aggressive in their delivery of their point of view. They intimidate people on account of the speed and energy with which they verbally lash out. They dump their anger onto people around them, which makes them feel better temporarily but then later they feel worse. Guilt can set in, which the victim then plays on to restore their own energy and the game goes on.

The intimidator displays lots of anger. Sometimes they seem incapable of other emotions. They are actually terrified of not having any power, control or love in their life and they fear being controlled and hurt as they have been at some previous point in their lives. Because the intimidator is actually feeling an inner disempowerment, they resort to forcefulness to get what they want any way they can. They feel justified in behaving this way and have an intense fear of losing.

The intimidator can assume that no one cares about them or notices them unless they act out. So, they put themselves first, and may often seem arrogant in their demeanour. Arrogance is always the hallmark of a person with poor self-esteem who has learned to cover it up through assuming an air of superiority. People with real inner self confidence are able to be humble and gracious in their dealings with others.

Some characteristics and behaviours of the intimidator include:

Intimidator

- Throwing verbal barbs
- Using non-verbal put downs
- Verbal, emotional or physical abuse
- Speaking dogmatically, not respecting others opinions
- Ridiculing others
- Being short tempered
- Bragging, showing off, talking only about the self
- Throwing gotchas and embarrassing people
- Making threatening demands
- Asking loaded or accusing questions

Matching Dramas

Each of the control dramas has an opposite that it attracts. Aloofs are opposite to and attract nags, nags are opposite to and attract aloofs. Victims attract persecutors and you cannot be a persecutor unless you can find a victim. If we do not want to attract the opposite, we can become empowered instead. This means we don't do control dramas in the first place.

When raising children, victims tend to create children who are intimidators, aloof people tend to create children who are nags, nags create children who are aloof, and intimidators create children who are victims. With intimidated children, they may flip into becoming intimidators themselves, as this is learned behaviour.

Power Games

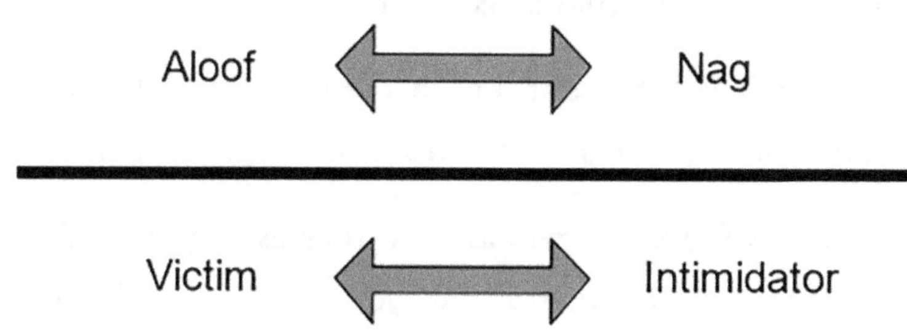

Dealing with Control Dramas

Using a control drama does not make you a bad person, it just makes you not very skilful in this aspect of relationships. The idea is to try to break free of your drama, without going into the opposing drama!

If you have been a victim for a long time, you may find that you become a bit of a persecutor for a little while as you try to break out of the old mould. Don't despair, and don't give up! Persevere with the work on parenting the inner child, and practicing better communication strategies. Before you know it, you will be empowered and assertive, as well as loving and compassionate. When this happens, you will pull a matching response from others.

When dealing with control dramas in others, the best thing to do is to persevere calmly, not getting sucked into the control drama that would usually be the opposite of the one being exhibited. This takes some practice, and I have found that meditation and the daily reflection technique (taught in *Child of God*) are invaluable in making changes to how I respond to others.

Another healthy strategy is to name the game. If you notice someone is playing a game with you, don't judge them, just call it as you see it. In a normal (non-judgmental) voice you can say "You know, right now I feel as though you think I should feel guilty".

When dealing with an aloof, give them some space. They will come back towards you, wondering why you are not nagging them.

With a nag, you may have to ask that they listen to you. Set limits upon the time that you have to spend listening to nags, without being aloof. Being aloof will make them nag more. Another strategy is to talk more to a nag, as it stops the game.

What is your main control drama?

My control drama is: . . . .

Be aware and learn to avoid this pattern in future. You are disempowering yourself.

If you are a Nag you can practice:

- Giving others a chance to express views and opinions.
- Listening attentively and hearing a person out.
- Not taking up more than half the available conversation time and space.

- Understanding that not everyone likes to share everything that is going on in their life.
- Understand that when you talk all the time it makes others tired even if what you are saying is fascinating; it becomes a wall of words and drains energy.
- Not being offended if others do not wish to talk right now. Perhaps you can make a time when you will both be fresh and available to discuss something.

If you are Aloof you can practice:

- Sharing yourself by smiling, greeting and so on.
- Giving positive non-verbal messages of respect.
- Negotiating.
- Finding a few friends with whom you can have conversations about things you enjoy.
- Helping and serving: it gives you something to talk about.
- Affirming the feelings and needs of others.
- Levelling with others.
- Stating and keeping agreements with others.
- Making an effort to share something about yourself in a safe way.

If you are a Victim you can practice:

- Making sure you are safe.
- Finding how you personally have something to do with an interaction that seems to be persecutory to you. How did you co-create that?
- Not giving your power away by blaming others.
- Not making others feel guilty.

- Avoidance of people-pleasing; it creates an atmosphere of unauthenticity.
- Not judging others as morally inferior.
- Stating your needs and desires honestly.
- Asking straightforward and non-loaded questions.
- Raising difficult issues in a constructive and safe way.
- Keeping confidences.
- Not assuming that others know how you feel.
- Cultivating self-respect.

If you are an Intimidator you can practice:

- Not taking your anger out on others, learning anger management techniques.
- Speak in a normal voice when you have something to say, not a threatening voice.
- Delaying automatic reactions, not flying off the handle.
- Speaking up before you get to the boiling over phase.
- Parenting your inner child and not letting the child do the talking.
- Getting more exercise, particularly when angry, move the energy by doing something physical such as running, chopping wood, cleaning out cupboards, scrubbing, vacuuming. Once the charge of energy has gone then discuss what needs to be discussed in a normal voice.
- Expressing respect for the values and opinions of others.
- Giving suggestions constructively.
- Ask, "What would love do now?"
- Not having to be right.

All of the control drama types can practice:

- Learning to be assertive (see next chapters) rather than aggressive or passive.
- Keeping the confidences of others.
- Keeping your word.
- Obeying the rules that have been established to deal with conflict.
- Joking constructively and in good humour.
- Conversational communication style, to get things back on track.
- Empowered communication style with loved ones.
- Search and explore with work colleagues.
- Being willing to learn a new strategy for communication.
- Being open to feedback.
- Speaking in a normal voice when discussing something tricky.
- Getting healings and doing relationship healing meditations regularly to keep the energy clean and clear. It is amazing how well it works to normalise and improve relationships.
- Working on self-esteem and self-love.

Power?

Once, while I was at Hong Kong airport I saw a little red book called Power. Naturally, I opened it, and was appalled to see that it was actually a manual for how to betray, out-manoeuvre, undermine, control and subdue other people. It was the opposite of power, and I found it incredible to think that people would actually buy it. (Well actually, I bought it, because I thought it was a great description of what power is NOT).

The matters that are listed in the table below in the 'Using Force' column mostly come from the book. In the 'Using Power' column is the approach that an empowered person would take to these things.

Exercise:

Look at the table below and try to identify the control dramas in your life that may employ the negative controlling tactics mentioned. Be mindful that you are not employing any of these force tactics in your own relationships.

Using Force	Using Power
Never trust someone too much	Assume and believe everyone is honest – and be honest yourself
Conceal your intentions	Lead clearly and openly
Always say less than necessary	Explain and get buy-in
Don't make mistakes	Experiment and grow, 'fail forwards'
Worry about what people think and behave accordingly	Watch what you think, act don't react
Court attention at all costs	Give and receive attention from 'cup full'
Get others to do the work but take the credit	Be generous in giving recognition & support your team
Make other people come to you, use bait if necessary	Stand for something, give freely

Win, don't worry about argument	The journey is more important than the destination
Avoid the unhappy and the unlucky	Develop compassion & service
Keep people dependent on you	Encourage intra-dependence, be an enabler
Use selective honesty and generosity to disarm your victim	Be honest and generous with no strings attached
Crush your opponent totally	Give something to another in every circumstance, never shame
Keep others in suspended terror, cultivate an air of unpredictability	Create a safe environment
Do not commit to anyone	Engage and commit to wholesomeness
Seem dumber than your mark	Listen carefully
If you can't win, surrender and regroup	Find another way to reach agreement
Play to people's fantasies	Live your own
Find a person's strengths and criticise them for not having them	Applaud their strengths

Chapter

22

THE DRAMA TRIAD

Drama Triad

A model that has been useful in helping to get clear about relationships is the Drama triad[15], something that has been looked at by psychologists and counsellors since the 1960s. It is derived from transactional analysis, the same derivation as the inner child/parent/adult work. It uses a triangular model to describe three roles played by people at times in relationship. These roles are: the victim, persecutor and rescuer. We looked at victim and persecutor in the control dramas in the last chapter. Here we are going to meet the rescuer as well. This model has nothing to do with actual rescuers like firemen who might be rescuing actual victims of car accidents or fire. This is a psychological model, which can be seen in both subtle and more obvious situations in human relationships.

---

[15] First described by Stephen Karpman.

We saw before that the victim is someone who is passive, and who is treated in an aggressive manner by a persecutor. The Persecutor uses threats and intimidation to get their needs met by the victim. The victim uses guilt and the moral high ground to get their needs met by the persecutor or others. From time to time the victim becomes the persecutor and vice versa as circumstances change.

The rescuer is someone who is trying to help the victim. However, the rescuer persona can have a subtle desire to seem superior, to be acknowledged as the white knight in shining armor, and to make it all good so that everyone will appreciate them.

The rescuer's hidden motives might include control, or wanting their own world order to be accepted by others as correct. The husband who feels protective of his wife can become a persecutor towards anyone who she has an issue with, rather than letting her sort it out herself. His intervention then causes the person who was hassling his wife (formerly seen as a persecutor) to become the victim.

Why are they all in this game? The inner child of the husband fears that any harm to his wife might take her away from him and he needs her for the love she gives to him. The inner child of the wife does not like conflict and is not very assertive and so she prefers her 'daddy' (husband) to sort out a difficult situation. Understanding the hidden inner child dynamics can often help us to know how and why a control drama is being played out. We can learn to meet the need in a healthy way and when we do that we can stop the game.

Even though these are three distinct roles, they are not always played by three different people, although they can be. The roles can also be played by two people who are moving around the triangle as circumstances play out in a co-dependent way. The victim can turn on the resented rescuer and in fact become a persecutor. Even victim and persecutor can change roles.

Sometimes the victim does not actually want to be rescued and gets resentful of the interference. The rescuer then says she was "only trying to help". The rescuer at times, can become controlling and even persecute the victim if they do not do what the rescuer thinks that they ought to do. The rescuer's self-esteem may be tied up in rescuing. They may take on a moral sense of superiority. They may be very insistent, becoming patriarchal and using heavy control style language to protect someone, thereby becoming persecutors in the drama. Using heavy intervention in order to 'help' someone who is perceived to be a victim, just changes which hat each party is wearing, but does nothing to stop the game.

Sam, Maggie and Rick

Sam, over time, had developed a habit of getting drunk after work. He was a pretty heavy drinker, even though he did not drink every single day. He would come home and behave inappropriately, keeping everyone awake with loud carry on, or getting violent, usually verbally, but occasionally in a more physical way. Maggie, his wife, was terrified for a number of reasons, not least of which was her own safety and ability to get a good night sleep without a drunk careering around the house making a racket for hours on end before he fell into a stupor. She felt victimised by Sam, who was normally a gentle and nice person. Several nights in a month she would experience being mentally, emotionally or physically frightened. The next morning Maggie was furious about what had happened and berated Sam over the drinking, persecuting him and causing him then to feel like a victim. After a few months of this, Maggie insisted they see a counsellor for help. Sam promised that he would no longer drink, and Maggie threatened that if he did, she will leave. Rick the counsellor tried to get each person to have more insight into why there is a drinking issue in the first place.

After several weeks of being sober the former drunk told everyone else how they should be giving up drinking, and started rescuing his friends.

Then he went to a work party and 'just one drink' led to 20, where upon he came home being loud and obnoxious again.

A distraught Maggie rang Rick the therapist in the middle of the night in light of once again having a drunk and obnoxious husband on her hands, and thus she victimised the rescuer, who was then unable to get back to sleep and was exhausted at work the next day.

The next morning a furious Maggie threatened to leave, and Sam felt victimised, and ashamed as well. A persecutor, such as the wife in this instance (who the night before was the victim) can be convinced that they have a valid complaint and that their anger or indignation and reactive abuse is justified.

In this situation no one is getting their needs met and therefore each has to try to control everyone around them to do so. It just gets worse, until at some stage the marriage breaks down, someone has an affair, **or** they learn to parent their inner children. In a situation like this, safety is a number one need of the child, and Maggie will need to take swift action to ensure that she is safe.

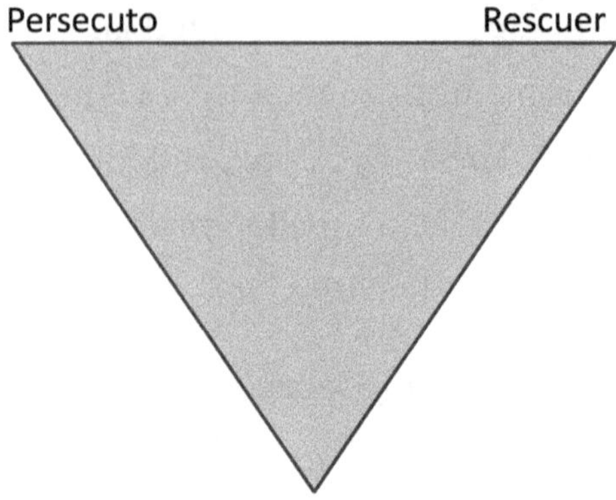

Victim

When dealing with these problems it is important to see what the payoff for each person playing the game might be. For instance, the victim is feeling helpless. The real way forward for a victim is to undergo some internal changes, and to learn to be responsible for the meeting of its own needs through the cultivation of better self-esteem, expectations and so on. But often it can seem better to just get someone else to come and rescue us and take us away from our drudgery, a bit like Cinderella getting rescued by the charming Prince. Who knows what he turned out like? Unless Cinderella did some inner work, it is most likely that he turned out to be much like her stepsisters and stepmother. Cinderella needs to change her energy in order to change the patterns of behaviour that she experiences in her life. Even if the Prince is OK, she will be victimised by other people at the new Court, or even by the servants unless she develops her own inner landscape in such a way that she can be respected.

Various kinds of games play out in the drama triad. One game is "If it weren't for you…". This is a blame game: the speaker gets to be a victim and the person spoken to becomes the persecutor, even if before he was the rescuer.

Another game is "It's all your fault" which is never actually true. If we look beneath the surface of events we will see dimension upon dimension of our own being that called forth the situation in which we find ourselves.

"See what you made me do" is another game. This one is where the speaker totally abdicates any semblance of self-empowerment, and gives all of his power to the beloved. "You got me into this" is a variant of "See what you made me do".

"Look how hard I've tried" is a cry the for approval that has not been given internally. This person needs to give themselves approval.

Another game is "Let's take sides together against a common enemy", also called "I'll let you and him fight'. This is another way that people get their needs met. Becoming an ally against a common foe makes people feel secure. It is also dysfunctional.

In any situation someone who is a victim actually has many options. They are not as helpless as they feel that they are, there is a wealth of potential within just waiting to be tapped, but it will mean some change, and some people are very resistant to change.

The rescuer, when motivated by getting his own needs met (such as to be loved, approved of and so forth), is not really all that helpful, and it would be better if the rescuer could instead speak to the victim about what they themselves might be able to do in this situation and empower them instead of fighting their battles for them.

Persecutors often want to blame everyone else for their behaviour, expecting that if people were perfect they would have no need to be angry, violent or critical. However, perfection does not exist in this universe, and so if we are waiting for other people to be perfect before we can behave appropriately, it is never going to happen.

"Yes But" as a Means of Control

Candice and Beatrice are business partners. Candice poses a problem with which she would like some help, and Beatrice comes up with a stack of ideas. Candice points out the flaws in all of those ideas, with a "yes but..." response and nothing gets decided, nothing gets done. The project goes no-where.

Another range of issues that "Yes but" can cause also happens with

Candice and Beatrice. After they finally come up with a decision as to what should occur, when Candice is meant to be implementing the plan, she will find some fault with it and not do it. She does this unilaterally without reference to Beatrice, who assumes that things are going ahead as per their agreement. When Beatrice finds out, she is angry, feels victimised, frustrated, a bit let down and somewhat the martyr to Candice. She speaks to Candice who says "Yes I know that is what we agreed but...".

Candice continues to pursue her own unconscious agenda, which in both of these examples is a search for perfection born from fear of being criticised or not good enough. This incapacitates her, stalls the project and will continue to cause ructions in the business life of this partnership until Candice learns to take a risk, let it be OK not to be perfect, and parent herself while things happen.

So, dramas are created because the victim feels powerless, the rescuer needs to be needed, and the controller or persecutor is terrified of being criticised for making a mistake and so wants to control everything and will make threats if necessary to ensure compliance by others.

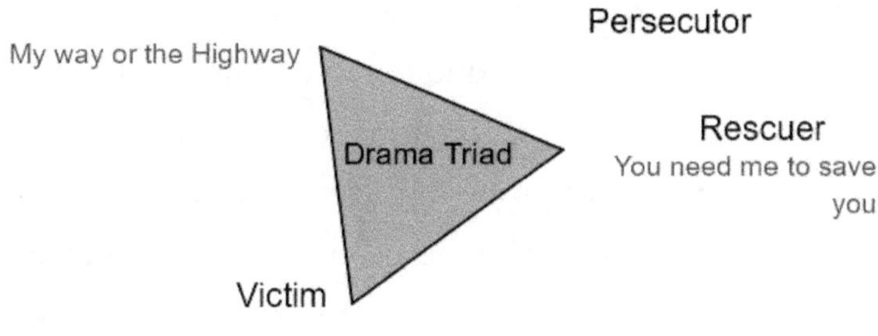

Another Way of Seeing Things

John Harradine[16] is a brilliant business mentor, strategist and change leader who has helped us to create Shanti Mission as a high vibrational organisation for social enterprise. One of his helpful strategies is to lift the Persecutor, Rescuer Victim, model into a Create, Promote, Allow model, which he learned with his spiritual teacher John Roger.

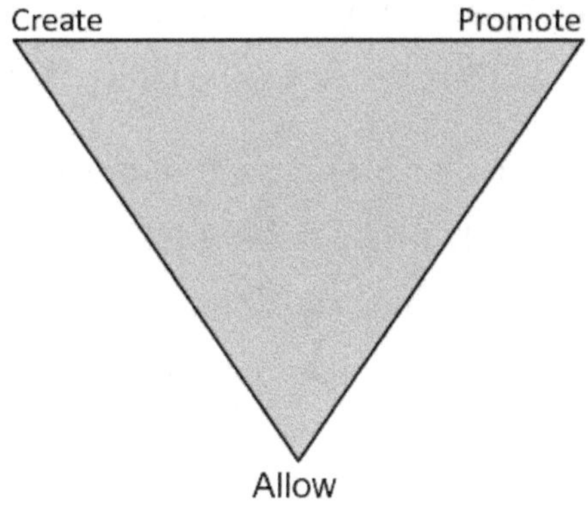

---

[16] www.aspirall.com.au

The persecutor of old becomes the person who is trying to 'Create' a new thing. The 'Promoter' replaces the rescuer and the 'Allow' position replaces victim.

The secret to moving from persecutor to creator is to have a very clear intention, get free of our internal game playing and secret agendas, take responsibility for our actions and to respond instead of reacting to what is going on around us. Reaction often contains a fear element. The fear creates the impetus to be pushy and controlling. John says "be hard on issues but soft on people". This means, ensure that our decisions are based on ethics and principles, and be clear that we expect that people will adhere to those ethics and principles. If people fall short however, be moderate and respectful, encouraging and clear with them about how adopting a different methodology/behaviour/set of choices will assist their part in contributing to whatever is going on. Say what needs to be said, but say it from your heart, not from your critical parent.

Sometimes it is better to agree to part in a respectful way, than allow a situation to continue where promises are broken, principles are ignored and the inner drives and motivations are not congruent with the task at hand. It is much better, however, to do the inner work and sort it out, or we will only co-create the very same kind of thing in the future.

Moving from rescuer to promoter is about enabling the former victim to do something that they did not know they could do. Thus, instead of jumping in and doing the doing, the promoter mentors the victim in moving out of their disempowerment and allows them to handle the situation themselves. An example here is that in our Centres we have many teachers and therapists providing spiritual direction and guidance to thousands of people. From time to time I am asked to intervene in a difference of opinion or a breach of boundaries that has occurred, and sort it out. As a rescuer, that is exactly what I would do. As a promoter, I counsel the teacher or therapist about the strategies that they might adopt in their role of leaders showing their clients how to get through the issue in accordance with our principles. I will use questions to help them reflect, before I offer a perspective. I will check to see if they are ready to receive some feedback. If they can't find an alternative solution, I'll point out the outcomes that may result from their choice, not in a threatening way, but simply what will, or will not match what they want. If our mission is negatively affected by the choice they make I will simply be more directive about the solution. This may seem like 'persecutor' to the receiver, so I need to find *neutrality* inside me as I deliver the message. If there is a charge behind it, they will be right about my persecutor being present and the process will recommence.

Notwithstanding how neutral I am there is no guarantee the other will respond from 'create, promote, and allow'. In fact if they are upset there is a good chance they may not. In these circumstances John suggests we first ask "What can I create, promote and/or allow right here right now?" or "How did I create, promote and allow this right here right now?" This question alone will give us space to take ourselves out of the 'Power Triangle' (the name John and his business Aspirall Pty Ltd have applied to 'persecutor, victim, and rescuer' and into the 'Accountability Triangle' ('create, promote, allow').

Another interesting facet of the rescuer is that they often put the needs of other people before meeting their own needs and end up feeling exhausted and wrung out. By focusing on enabling and promoting the victim to sort out their issues themselves, the rescuer then has more time to focus upon his own needs. Often, someone who is a chronic rescuer knows deep down that the person who really needs rescuing is them! As a promoter rather than a rescuer, we will ensure that our own needs are met first. This is modelling right-action and sends out energy that is conducive to a functional way to interact. When we *be* the change we wish to see, we empower others.

The journey from victim to person who 'allows' is a profound shift from perceived powerlessness and dead ends, to a person who can perceive options and strategies to achieve them. The important thing is for the victim to shift from a person who feels that they cannot meet their own needs, to someone who can. For the victim it is important not to write off someone who has persecuted them as 'a bad person'. This sours any chance of mending things. Instead, the victim can contemplate how they called this person into their life (how did they create, promote and/or allow this?) and what the lesson might be. Victims need to learn not to be black and white with their thinking, instead understanding that good people can exhibit a poor relationship style, and that this can be resolved through communication and good-will most of the time. This flip in attitude is a great way to make real and lasting progress in very tricky relationships.

The Empowered Empower Others

Those who have authentic spiritual or inner power are beacons of empowerment for others. People find that they become enlivened, empowered and uplifted through contact with them. As a flame is lit, it is then ready to pass the light on. Talking about it is not enough. Real power gets digested by the energy field and soul of the individual and oozes out around them in a way that affects the reality of others for the better. This is the basis of the Guru/Disciple relationship. This is such a sublime kind of relationship that I am writing a separate book about it.

Power is not exercised just for personal achievement, that would be a misunderstanding of the concept. Power creates a wave of grace that will take many other people to better places as well. At the end of the day, power is a capacity to influence and create beneficial change that is good for all concerned.

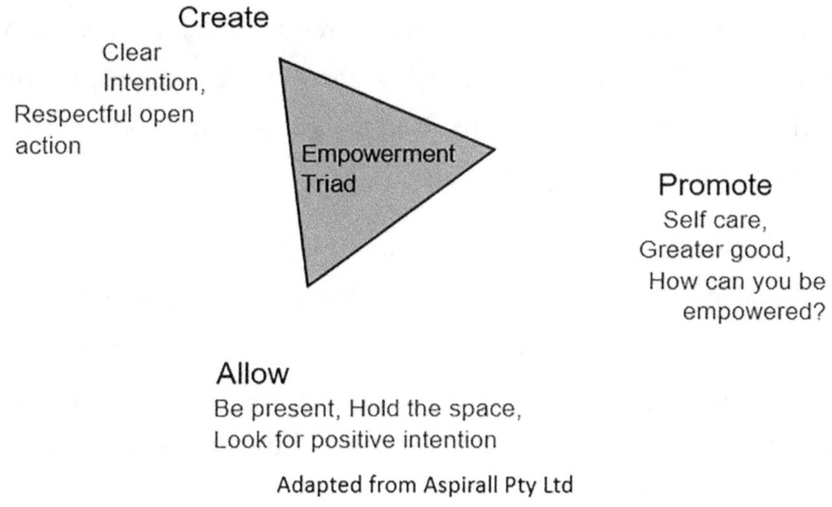

Effect of the Failure to State what we Need

We are responsible for meeting our own needs, but we also have a responsibility to state what our needs might be, in a situation where we are having problems meeting our own needs.

When we do not ask others for what we need, we rob them of the opportunity of entering the law of flow with us. When we do not state what our requirements are then we push away from ourselves the ideal of a dance between giving and receiving.

Reward every Try

What we are trying to do when we are dealing with issues in our relationships is to bring constructive changes. Moving out of victim/persecutor/rescuer and into create/promote/allow is a process. There are some tricks to this that can help. This entire book is a manual for how to do it.

I learned from a horse whisperer many years ago that one of the secrets to empowered relationships was to reward every try. Instead of waiting for the beloved to be perfect, give them credit and praise for any tiny thing that they might do that is in the general direction of where you would like to see things moving.

In the olden days, breaking in a horse was just that. You controlled the animal, often through fear, and there were times when the spirit of the horse was completely broken. If they 'did the wrong thing', like kicking or bucking for instance, they were subjected to dreadful beatings and poor treatment. Eventually they submitted and did what the trainer wanted them to out of sheer intimidation.

Discipline in human affairs has often been dealt with in a similar manner, with those in authority feeling that they have the right to subdue and control other people through force. Even people in relationships can take a dictatorial attitude with each other, which gets very uncomfortable. In very dysfunctional situations, both parties can feel victimised and afraid of the other party who is trying to get their needs met by force and control.

In a more enlightened age, we are now learning that there is another way to do things. This is to form real and respectful partnerships. In many of the systems of natural horsemanship that have emerged, horse and rider develop incredible capacities to do things together, with both feeling free and working together. In the images below you will see a horse going over jumps and being ridden without a bridle or headstall controlling it. The horse is moving in accordance with what it understands to be the right thing, of its own free will. The method used by the horseman is rewarding every try, even if what eventuates is not actually perfect.

Marianne

I once knew a woman who we will call Marianne, who had 2 teenage boys aged 17 and 19 who were living with her. She was a single mum. She came with us on a week-long retreat and while we were on the retreat we did a lot of work on relationships. She told me that she had a dreadful struggle with her boys, who were not supportive of her, would not help around the house, and she had a very difficult time going to work then coming home and having to cope with all of the household duties. They were messy and would not clean up after themselves and their attitude left quite a bit to be desired.

We talked about her level of self-esteem and self-respect and did some healing on that. We discussed the need for a 'game changer' in how she was dealing with the boys. We also talked about the need to hold a vision of the beloveds, her sons, as she would like them to be and not allow her mind to constantly ruminate on their shortcomings. What we focus on grows!

For years she had been victimised by the boys' behaviour. To try to get some help she generally ended up shouting at them, thereby moving from the position of victim to the position in the force triad of persecutor. I told her about rewarding every try. My advice was that when she got home from the retreat, even if the place was a complete mess, find something that they had done right and comment on that. Each time they did absolutely anything at all that was helpful, thank them and let them know that she appreciated it.

When Marianne got home the place was a total mess. There was a week's worth of washing up in the kitchen and it was clear that no laundry or other tasks had been done. She felt disheartened but then remembered to find something they had done well amongst the carnage. She found two coffee cups washed up and draining in the rack. When the boys came in she thanked them for washing up the cups. They were expecting to get the usual kind of negative attention that they got when they had ignored their responsibilities and could not believe that Mum not only seemed happy and content, she was thanking them for doing next to nothing. Without her asking, they cleaned up the kitchen. This was the beginning of a new chapter in the relationship between Marianne and her boys. The physical dimension of it had necessitated a flip in attitude, progress was made when she had the inner resolve and patience to reward every try. By doing so she moved from being a victim to being someone who allowed change to occur. It was empowering for them all.

Chapter

23

ASSERTIVENESS

Passive, Assertive, or Aggressive

Anybody can become angry. That is not difficult,

But to be angry with the right person and to the right degree, And at the right time, and for the right purpose, and in the right way:

That is not within everybody's capability and it is not easy.

Aristotle, 384-322 BC, Greek Philosopher

Assertiveness is the empowered quality of being able to bring the right level of consciousness and energy to our communication with others in any given situation. It is a skill, and if we are not assertive now, we can learn how to be. Assertiveness gives us a huge freedom and ability to engage with others in all kinds of situations, even difficult and unforeseen ones. We can learn to be compassionate, sensitive, clear with our boundaries and position the dialogue in a way that we can co-create an outcome about which both parties feel peace.

An assertive person has a kind of inner strength that others end up feeling they can trust. Assertiveness is a huge asset as a leader and is essential to anyone who wants to be a peacemaker. It is a way of dealing with the powerful emotional energies that are part of life, including anger and frustration.

The opposite to assertiveness is passive/aggression. When we do not know how to be assertive, we resort to the control dramas that we looked at in the last chapters. These alternatives do not ever lead to real peace, but to reactivity, and win-lose outcomes in which someone is always dissatisfied. Lack of assertiveness is always going to have complications and ramifications down the track.

To be assertive one needs to be able to be authentic. Becoming authentic by itself may take some time, as we are so used to being told who we are, what we think, and influenced by family and friends, not to mention media and advertising.

Reasons we are not Assertive

Some people are not assertive because they really don't know what they think about an issue. Therefore, stating their point of view is impossible. Rather than let people know that they don't know, they either get passive and say nothing, allowing another to set the agenda, or they get gruff and defensive, derailing the discussion through aggression.

Some people know what they think, but they are not assertive because they don't know how to *communicate* it. Particularly if the issue is near to their heart they may be forceful with their opinion in an effort to silence any opposing points of view, or they may just be in the habit of poor communication strategies.

Others have fear that if they communicate how they think or feel about an issue they will be vilified, made to look stupid, criticised, rejected or wrong. If they are not able to approve of themselves, then this fear of rejection will be far more powerful as a deterrent to assertiveness than the merits of the situation being discussed, even when it is something very important.

Some fear that people will not love them if they are really authentic, and they are afraid of speaking up, having been shamed or punished for doing so in earlier parts of their life.

Still others fear that they will lose control and get angry, or provoke anger in others if they are assertive. They will go to any lengths to avoid confrontation and consider anger to be inherently bad. There is a real or perceived inability to manage situations that carry the energy of strong emotion. Therefore, they repress it.

Other factors in not being assertive may include lack of confidence, fear of coming off second best, uncertainty about the outcome and fear of rocking the boat.

Assertiveness

- *Assertiveness is empowering*
- *Lack of assertiveness leads to problems*
- *The opposite of assertiveness is passivity or aggression*
- *Learning assertiveness is a critical skill for a peacemaker*

All of these fears can be dealt with as spiritual issues. All of them are helping us to get from the bottom of the hourglass – the egoic level, to the top of the hourglass – the place of wisdom. This is done through meeting our fears and moving through them. Parenting the inner child is one of the big keys to being able to do this. At the end of the day, it is about self-love and respect. This will help us have good boundaries, and assertiveness will help ensure that those boundaries are respected.

Speak In A Friendly Voice

Sometimes we put up with things that upset our boundaries for a long time. When we eventually speak to the person about the issue we are so up-tight about it that we yell at them and come across as sour and bad tempered. Another option is to simply tell the person what your issue is, using a normal friendly voice, so that they actually know that you are wanting something to be changed.

I remember many years ago living in a share house in Sydney with a group of people. Our next door neighbour had a very large van and 2 old cars, one of which did not ever seem to move. He habitually parked them all in front of our house, making it impossible in the busy street to find parking when we got home in the evening, and necessitating that we always had to carry things a long way from the car to the house. As I know that no one actually owns the street outside the house, I knew it would be inappropriate to tell the man that he should park his cars somewhere else as though I owned it. Further, across the road was a very aggressive gentleman who yelled and screamed and threatened anyone who parked their car directly outside his house! He actually threatened some of our visitors that he would slash their tyres if they did it again. He was really full-on.

Not wanting to be construed as being a rat-bag like the man across the road, for many months we all said nothing about these cars. The problem was, we were all getting more and more annoyed by it. While I didn't like his methods, I could see why the old guy across the street was being so territorial.

Then one day I had an epiphany. I realised that having never communicated with this neighbour, he had no idea that having all his cars parked incessantly in front of our house was not OK. I did a relationship healing just to be as clear as possible, which took me half an hour. Then, the next day I popped over to our neighbour and with a smile and a normal, non-angry, non-accusatory voice, I told him that sometimes we experienced that it was a little inconvenient for us when he had his vehicles all parked out the front of our house, and would it be OK for him to move them. I also sent a lot of love from my heart as I was talking to him.

He was amenable and receptive and said "No problem". As of the next day, he rarely ever parked his cars outside our house again. I thought with a laugh about the amount of wasted energy that we had all spent being passive in our relationship with him while at the same time huffing and puffing to each other about these cars, when all we had to do was nicely ask that he move them elsewhere.

Energy in the Interaction

The illustration below shows how passivity, assertiveness and aggression are all relative to each other on a spectrum. The spectrum runs from employing too little energy in the situation on one side and too much energy on the other side. In the middle is the 'sweet spot', where we find ourselves empowered.

What will be enough, too little or too much energy in any given interaction is something that comes with experience. It is not something to be thought about so much as felt. We can review interactions mentally to adjust our energy volume for the next time something like this comes up. Done this way, becoming assertive becomes a spiritual practice.

As our heart chakra becomes clearer, more robust and our intuition becomes more developed, we are able to discern the correct use of energy. Like anything we want to master, it takes practice.

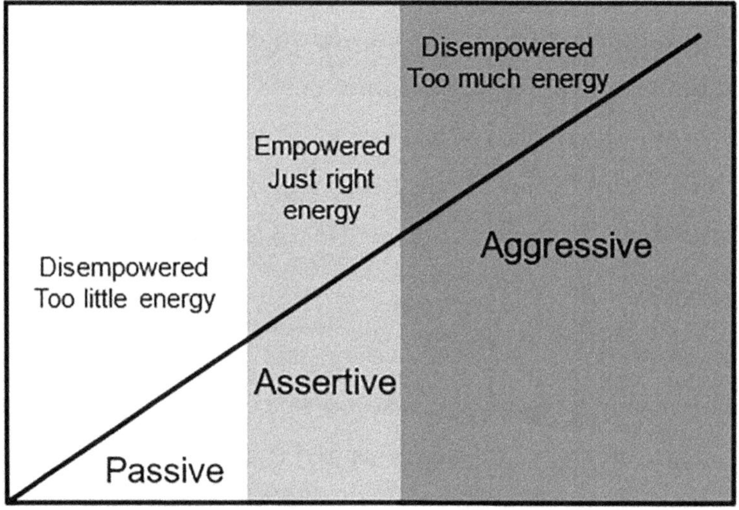

Amount of energy in the interaction relative to what is required

In some cultures, an attribute of communication is that there is very little actual energy in it. Take the British 'stiff upper lip'. This archetype of British communication is restraint, avoidance of emotionally charged or personal topics of communication, suppression of the energy of emotion and taking a minimalist approach to the amount of energy that is put into a communication. To people in this extreme paradigm, some of what is within the assertive range would seem overly aggressive to them.

By contrast, try spending time in the company of Southern Italians. They can say "Pass the salt", and it sounds like a declaration of war. Even "hello" can be accompanied by a lot of arm waving and loud voices.

Listening to them, without being able to speak the language, it sounds like they are fighting, but really they are just a group of friends having lunch. Much of what others would think falls over the line into the area of aggression, to these people would still be in the range of assertiveness.

Depending on who we are with, we can learn to put the right amount of energy into a discussion so as to communicate effectively and authentically, even about difficult subjects.

When we exhibit too much passivity we are failing to put enough energy into expressing our truth such that the other person fails to really appreciate our views. We actually need to say how it is for us with a bit of energy, so that the other person is put in the picture. Lack of assertiveness through passivity leads to lots of misunderstandings, hurt feelings, crossed wires and mixed messages.

Conversing Through the Cold War

I knew a couple Vanessa and Ian, who were living with a flat-mate Sandra, in Brisbane. I stayed with them and felt that the atmosphere in the house was decidedly frosty. I asked Vanessa what was going on and she said that it was tricky living with a third person in the house. She and Ian wanted to put boundaries in place so that they had couple time, instead of it always being a situation where the three of them were hanging out. Truly, the entire time I was there, Sandra didn't go near the two of them. She was quite independent and not at all burdensome, but she did share with me privately that she thought that they were quite grouchy people, which I knew was not normally the case. However, Vanessa and Ian were cold and unwelcoming with her and she was considering moving out on account of their disagreeable natures. She had no idea that they were just afraid of her encroaching on their relationship and didn't know how to discuss it with her as they didn't want to hurt her feelings or seem to be saying that they didn't like her.

I realised that Vanessa and Ian did not have very good assertiveness skills, and had not ever had a discussion with Sandra about when they needed private time, and when they were fine for there to be interaction with her. Instead, they just ignored her all the time. As the couple were students in Shanti Mission, I suggested to them that they may wish to have a discussion and possibly set some flexible but agreeable boundaries in place so that they could enjoy time with Sandra, a person with whom they had much in common, *and* enjoy other time alone with each other. They eventually agreed that most weeks they would try and have dinner all together on Tuesdays and Thursdays, and that otherwise they would do their own thing separately. This took the need for defensiveness out of the equation, they all knew where they stood with each other and things got a lot friendlier in the house.

At the other end of the spectrum, we put too much energy into the communication and it comes out in an aggressive or overbearing way. When we do this, quite often the only thing that people hear is the anger or aggression, and they do not actually take on board what we have said. In fact, they can become immediately defensive. If someone is getting defensive as you are speaking, consider whether or not you are using energy that is somewhat attacking. Perhaps your energy is turned up too loud. We can learn to drop our voice, pull back our energy and speak in a normal way so as to deliver our message in a voice that can be heard.

Bell Curve

We can look at the issue of being passive, assertive or aggressive on a bell curve. The point of this diagram is to show how we find the most positive way to express our selves, and the point at which we start to decline into negativity again.

Buddha and many other great spiritual teachers, including my first living Guru Master Choa Kok Sui (may his Divine soul be eternally blessed), taught that we need to follow the middle path. All things in moderation, non-excessiveness, balance and harmony are seen as the key to right action and enlightenment.

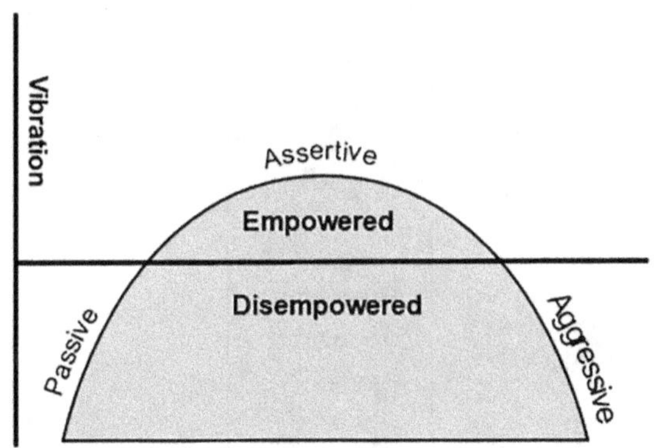

Look at the figure above. Along the vertical line we can see a vibrational cut-off between empowerment above the line, and disempowerment below the line. The bell curve itself shows that there is a place in the middle between the negative state of passivity and the negative state of aggression, in which we can learn to operate. Too little energy, and assertiveness, and we are passive. Too much assertiveness and energy and we become aggressive. Notice that there is a bit of bandwidth in the assertive area. It is not as though there is one absolute place of being 'right' with our assertiveness. It is more that there is a range within which we stay empowered, either a little more or a little less but still doing OK. Then there is an invisible line that gets crossed where we fall out of that band width and into disempowerment.

Characteristics of Assertiveness

On the vertical axis can be plotted the vibrational scale of consciousness. Below the line are the disempowering states of consciousness referred to by Dr. David R Hawkins. Above the line we are successively more empowered as we travel upwards. Things that we might encounter above the line include courage, peacefulness, wisdom, love and compassion. These are all elements of assertiveness.

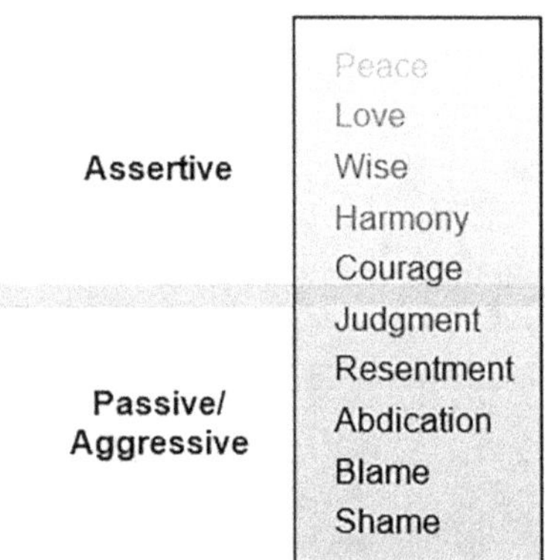

The things that we might encounter below the line might include blame, shame, abdication of our power or resentment. These are all contributory elements in passivity or aggression, in which we behave in a disempowered way.

Assertiveness starts from a place where there is respect for the person with whom we are going to need to interact. In a relationship we might generally respect our partner, but when we are angry with them or feel let down, humiliated or betrayed by them, that respect can fly out the window as we respond with a similar kind of energy. Learning to hold onto respect for our beloved even when they are exhibiting in that moment an energy we do not appreciate, is important. Remember, energy flows. This is not the entire truth of who they are. It is just what they are exhibiting right now. Respect the entire person, and you will be much less likely to be negative in your response to them.

The assertive conversation is not bombastic. It is not laying down the law in terms of absolutes, but rather says how things are for me. With assertiveness we are able to ask questions and search together for a solution, whereas with aggression and even passivity, we are seeking to impose a solution.

Remember, the passive person is often not so sweet when their beloved is not around, and they whinge and whine to many other people about the behaviour of the beloved, rather than speaking directly to them. They can spend days or even weeks stomping around the house saying "I'm Fine" when clearly they are furious, and through this kind of passive behaviour they seek go get their own way.

Both passivity and aggression are controlling in their own ways. Assertiveness on the other hand is an attitude of stating how things are for you with clarity, non-blame, using language that includes how you feel, but without condemnation or rage. The agenda with assertiveness is to find a solution: quite often the passive and aggressive models also include punitive elements: you have done the wrong thing and I am going to punish you. Assertiveness can be attained through patience, skilfulness in action, and empowered communication style. It will lead to progress in your relationship and will bring in grace.

When we are non-assertive we seek to impose solutions aggressively, get impatient, heavy, ego centered and usually want to dump our 'gunny sack' of issues and baggage onto the person concerned. Here we see knee-jerk reactions, table thumping, reactionary behaviour which ends up causing resentment and undermining trust. Passivity also undermines trust as we are not honest with sharing our feelings.

For many people the pull of the ego into passive or aggressive patterns is very strong. There is a fear of releasing the patterns we have used for so long because we can feel that we might not win if we do things another way. The reality is that we are not really winning now either. When we use force on others, sooner or later it will rebound and come back to us. Surrendering the need to control things, and being willing to flex, flow, search and discover a new way of doing things, is the path to assertiveness and a higher vibration.

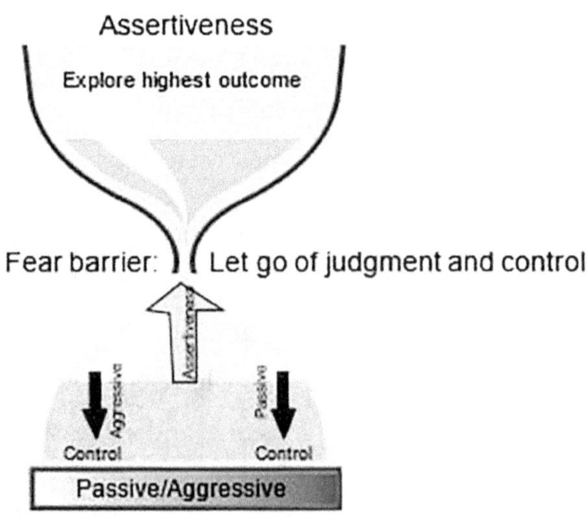

Tool for assertiveness: Om Durga

Sacred chants have a powerful effect upon our energy field and our minds. They are able to transform us with regular use.

Durga chants are highly protective, and help us to infuse our souls with the energy of that facet of the Divine. Durga energy is that of the Divine Mother who loves us unconditionally and protects us fiercely. Durga is fearless and empowered. By chanting the name Durga we are 'cleaving' to the aspect of the Divine that holds the energies of assertiveness, empowerment and protection.

When a Guru infuses a chant with spiritual energy, the chant becomes a very powerful tool for spiritual growth. There is a saying in teaching: more is caught than taught. This is particularly true when you work with real Gurus, whose main method of teaching is energetic transfer and activation.

The chant: *Om Durga, Durga Om* has been infused with the energy of assertiveness, to help people 'catch' energetically how to be more assertive and less passive or aggressive.

If you struggle with assertiveness, then a 40-day spiritual practice of daily chanting of Om Durga, Durga Om may be of tremendous benefit.

Chapter

24

ANGER AND ASSERTIVENESS

A very common reason that people become either passive or aggressive instead of assertive is that they do not have a healthy relationship with anger, and the realisation that anger is like everything, holy and part of the Divine when it is in its right place. Having re-thought anger, here are some things I did that helped me turn from a passive person into an assertive person.

Mental Mastery

This involves continuous wiping out, with electric violet light, the thoughts that come up when I am upset about something, and replace them with neutral thoughts. This skill is taught in 'Yoga of the Mind', and is a constant practice for me, just like weeding the garden or doing the housework. It is a discipline for life. Speaking of discipline, some people tell me that while they know how important this is, they cannot seem to actually do it. If this sounds like you, then find some place in your life where you are disciplined. This might be your work or sporting life. Transfer that skill to be disciplined into not letting your mind be a bolting horse, or creating huge thought forms of disempowerment, rage, blame and frustration.

Validate, Then Manage Your Inner Child

When you feel like hurting someone who has hurt you, or yelling at someone who is being ridiculous, start by letting your inner child know that you have heard her and thank her for telling you these things. Don't judge her for telling you her truth. Remember that it ought not be up to the inner child to decide what to do about it, that is the inner parent's job. An inner parent who fails to listen to the inner child, will end up sooner or later in a situation where the child takes matters into her own hands and creates carnage. If as the parent, you hear the child and then fail to act appropriately to protect and nurture the child, you will not be trusted by your own inner child again. This will lead to distrust in other relationships, and set up many disempowering situations as classrooms in your life.

Gently educating our inner child that even though we know she would like to kick them (maybe several times) that we are going to do something even better: we are going to dissolve the multi-dimensional classroom in which she has this experience, and she just needs to be a bit patient. Give her lots of approval and reassurance and let her know that you are going to practice being empowered and assertive: then follow through.

Stop Judging Anger As Bad

Give yourself permission to have the angry feeling and erase any sense that it is bad, or that you are a failure/bad/(insert negative words of choice here) for feeling angry. Anger is the fire in the belly of the Goddess, telling us that a boundary needs re-aligning. It may be that up till now, anger has been a shadow characteristic, and it is time to bring it into the light. We look at this in the next chapter.

Don't Dump

When we first start to experience anger, we can have an eruption of 20 years of suppressed anger rather than just the anger that is currently there for whatever the current situation might be. Know that what you are doing is really big and important. Use meditation, therapy, counselling, exercise, positive self-talk, healing and such strategies to get support as you go through this stage. It is important not to dump this on anyone. Later on, dealing with anger is not nearly so difficult and becomes even enjoyable. Becoming assertive and dealing with our own frustration or anger is challenging and satisfying when you get to be empowered.

Move The Energy Physically

Get the charge of anger out of your body. For me, this is something that has usually needed a physical release: vigorous vacuuming, cleaning out cupboards, punching bags, walking, stomping while you are walking, these and other things you might think of are harmless ways to release the energy, and it is important to practice so that the energy can actually move. Once you have received the message that anger is delivering to you about your boundaries, you do not need to hold onto it. As an aside, two foods that I have found compound anger are red meat and sugar. If you eat these, it would be good to just take a break from them for a while till the anger is dealt with because they are like putting petrol on the fire. While people may not notice these refinements at first, the more your vibration becomes lighter and more purified, the bigger the effect upon you will seem.

Relationship Healing

Do a relationship healing. Use our Relationship Healing CD or attend a seminar. This will release a lot of the pent up energy and help you to be more skilled when you actually have the conversation you need to have.

Have the Talk

Have the conversation that is necessary. The appropriate time to talk will become evident when the main charge of anger goes through you. At that point, it is about being restrained, keeping your inner child behind you or out of sight, and being really clear before you meet with or phone them about what you need to communicate. Use "I feel..." kinds of statements for getting traction in the situation, avoid dumping judgment on them.

As an alternative to a face-to-face meeting when we are learning about assertiveness, I have benefited in the past from writing to the person when the situation had so much energy that I wasn't sure I could trust myself to say what I needed to say. Doing it in writing is good because you can do the first draft (let it all out but on no account send it) then refine it so that it reflects healthy communication styles and contains no judgment or blame. The thing is to convey the content of the reason you are upset in a factual way, and in as normal a voice as possible, and it is OK to say "and I am feeling angry about it" as part of the message.

PART

7

LOVE

Chapter

25

LOVE

Love is the most powerful and most sublime quality in the world. It is the greatest healer, the eliminator of every kind of sorrow, ignorance, disharmony and mistake. Without love, life is a bit of a wasteland where we have to look for diversions so that we forget how bereft we are without it. People can do all kinds of crazy things in pursuit of love. An inexpressible yearning for love exists in every single person.

Love is like magic, redeeming every human heart that is touched by it. Given enough love, *anything* can be transformed and healed. Love is limitless and infinite. Love is our contact with the Universal Substance. When life presses heavily on us and we need courage and strength, it is amazing what effect true love can have.

Most people think that love is an emotion. Actually, love is God. It is the invisible no-thing of the Divine Void. Tapping into love is actually tapping into the Divine. Learning to love more than ever before is what we are here on Earth for.

The great Spiritual Masters, Gurus, Prophets, Rishis, Sages, Rabbis and Saints who have inspired humanity have in common their uncanny ability to love. Love issues forth from them in such a torrent that often the mind is rendered incapable of thought in the presence of such great souls. I have had the experience of utter stillness, reverence, unbounded love and awe in the presence of several great Gurus in my life.

How does the current of love become so strong in these people? How is it that they can do things that to the average observer appear miraculous? How could Jesus command demons, bring life back to the dead, manifest things and inspire people, and how could others through history do similar kinds of things? The answer is that they cultivated love. Each one at some time started off being able to love the things that he or she was culturally conditioned to love: the God of their religion, their family, and people who shared their world view. Each one embarked and successfully completed an epic, heroic journey that culminated in their ability to love everything in creation. Not only do they love all the nice things that 'normal people' love, but Spiritual Masters love the not-so-nice people, circumstances, beings and parts of creation that none of us could. They can love the unloveable.

First and foremost, Spiritual Masters love God. By whatever name or style they worship the Divine, their love is oceanic. The power of devotion is worthy of an entire book by itself. Through their devotion to the Divine and the love they have, which is without limit, they seem extraordinary to us, yet they are just normal people. Except of course, for their capacity to love.

The door to love is guarded by fear. It always was, and it always will be. Spiritual masters have the courage to be vulnerable, as it is in our 'yin', or vulnerability that we find the greatest treasure on Earth. Because they surround themselves with and emanate love in every circumstance, even loving the unloveable, they walk safely through any valley of fear or darkness.

Is It Love or Not?

Sometimes people mistake love for other strong emotions, such as lust, or attachment through fondness. People fall in love and then they fall out again. Mostly people fall out of love because something happens that either or both parties find unacceptable. The high expectations and hopes of the honeymoon phase of the relationship fail to materialise; the 'negative' (meaning I don't love it) characteristics of the other person are perceived and experienced.

Where love is dependent upon our expectations being met, love is conditional. If we only love people if they stay with us, or tell us the truth, or behave in certain ways, then there is likely to be more manipulation and judgment than actual love. We are going to have to try very hard to control them so that we can safely love them. Where there is Divine or unconditional love, there is no need for control. Love brings with it expanded consciousness, and the knowledge that anything I experience is only a mirror of my own internal landscape. This is a strange concept at first. However it is something that separates Masters from the rest of us, so it is worth trying to grasp it.

Masters love the same way God does. God does not just love us when we are 'good'; God loves us all the time. God loves the weeds as well as the flowers in a garden. In other words, Divine love encompasses people and characteristics that most of us would think were unloveable. In order to emulate our Divine parent, and to help free ourselves from many negative kinds of interactions, it is prudent for us to cultivate love in a growing number of situations and circumstances.

The Courage to Love

Loving in the unconditional way that Masters do takes courage. When we love, we give selflessly. This feels risky to the ego but entirely natural to the soul. There is a very deep satisfaction that comes from really loving selflessly.

In order to have the capacity to love selflessly, the first person that we need to learn to love is ourselves. If we have not yet learned that, all of our attempts to love others in a selfless way are doomed to have problems associated with them. If life is about learning, then love is one of the most consuming classrooms that exist.

Love overrides our analytical thinking power. It propels us into situations that we might find are sometimes painful. Love does not insulate us against pain, it opens our heart, so we can feel all kinds of emotions and living forces pulsing through us. Through love we get in sync with the outpouring of creation, and we can hear the rhythms of life. Love opens doorways into spiritual worlds that are closed to those whose fear overrides their capacity to enter deeply into the intoxicating, transformative and purifying fire that is love.

"Love means to commit oneself without guarantee,
To give oneself completely
In the hope that our love
Will produce love in the beloved.
Love is an act of faith,
And whoever is of little faith is also of little love"
Erich Fromm

Chapter

26

LOVING THE UNLOVEABLE[17]

Know that when all of God's works are each in its place,

they are good in this place of their creation,

as assigned to them and predetermined for them;

but when they rebel and leave their legitimate places,

then they are evil."

Joseph Gitakilla[18]

Loving the unloveable is not just some theoretical idea on how to be good. It is extremely useful and valuable as a spiritual practice. It is a means to see how we create the situations and circumstances that we find emotionally challenging. Armed with that

---

[17] Much of this chapter comes from my book *Spiritual Mastery*. A book on empowering relationships would be very incomplete without this information and so it has been reproduced here with minor alterations, for ease of reference.

[18] Quoted in *Kabbalah Key to your inner Power* by Elizabeth Clare Prophet, Summit University Press 1997

knowledge, we can work on our consciousness, and discover ways through the maze into a more peaceful and enjoyable future.

Not Everything is Warm and Fuzzy

If everyone was polite and kind to everyone else all the time, and always agreed with us, how easy would it be to be constantly calm and loving. Yet if this were so, how could we learn right conduct and extend our capacity to love in more challenging circumstances? Would we have the faintest idea of how we react under the pressure of being picked-on or needled? Everyone can be nice when others around them are being nice. How much harder is it to be nice to someone who is not being nice to us?

If someone makes a rude and nasty remark about us or about our beloved, a common response is to bite back with a similarly nasty remark addressed to the antagonist. The trouble is, this leads to an escalation of hostilities that can get really ugly.

A choice that takes more strength of character is to not respond in kind. Either walk away or change the subject, then think, "Ah, interesting. How did I create that?" Breathe deeply, and let the stab of energy go straight through you. This gets easier with practice, although the Universe is amazingly good at delivering people to provide specific and precise goading that will push our buttons.

Buttons can only be pushed if we have them. At the end of the day we are better off spending our efforts getting rid of our own buttons, rather than trying to stop others from pushing them.

Dealing with ignorant/angry/abusive people gives us practice at becoming loving and strong. We are always going to be tested (helped to become empowered) by challenging situations of one kind or another in our lives. The way we manage even one week of conflict and upset tells us more about ourselves and other people than ten years of good times and happiness. When we are being criticised and when people are behaving badly, there can be a lot of pressure on us to behave just as badly as they do. We can get defensive, angry, distant, passive aggressive, and judgmental.

The spiritually mature can be nice even to those who are disrespectful, offensive or gross. Spiritual Masters go even further. In the most trying of circumstances, the Master can manage not only to be respectful, but can actually hold love in his or her heart for those who mock or taunt him. This is because the Master has learned not only to master love but to master his shadow.

The Shadow

Our shadow contains the characteristics that we might see in others, which we cannot see in ourselves. It is the disowned part of our psyche. Because it is disowned from 'in here' we project it outwards, where it has to be mirrored back to us by others.

The shadow can contain all kinds of riches and wonders as well as things we might not like to look at. Some people disown their beauty, others disown their beast characteristics, and some people disown bits of both.

We create our shadow as a result of our judgments. We might be judging others, or we might be judging ourselves. Everyone has a shadow. The bigger you are the bigger your potential shadow. Think of a tall tree in a field. The bigger the tree gets, the bigger the shadow it casts in the field.

Usually, as light workers, we are focused on light and love, and looking metaphorically speaking, towards the sun. We cannot see our shadow because it is behind us. Ask our enemies however, and they will describe the negative characteristics of our shadow to a tee.

When we have an interaction with another person and we are upset by it, the characteristic that we identify in the other person that we do not like can generally be termed part of our shadow.

Lynda

Lynda was a spiritual aspirant who had been brought up by a controlling and domineering mother. Her mother had used threats and withholding of love to get Lynda, a sensitive and intelligent girl, to do what she wanted her to. After several years of study with her spiritual teacher, Lynda got really upset when another of the spiritual aspirants was given an opportunity that Lynda thought rightfully should have been hers. She felt envy, jealousy, and resentment for the teacher, who in her mind was favoring the other student. Her fear of speaking up held her silent, because she feared that if she spoke her truth the teacher would send her away, just as her mother used to do.

The pressure built up in Lynda who finally was so mad that she wrote a blistering letter to her teacher, accusing him of all the things that she thought were going wrong, how unfair he was being, and so on. The teacher immediately sent her love. He knew that this was Lynda's shadow showing itself so that healing could take place. He calmly emailed back a message of love and encouragement, and asked her to come and speak with him.

Lynda had expected to be yelled at, told she was wrong, and rejected. Her jealousy of the other student was the driving force for her angry outburst. The Master was able to tell her why the other student had been chosen, and to help Lynda see how this situation had been created by her for learning about the shadow characteristics of jealousy and unfairness.

Lynda could not love herself if she was unfair. She therefore sought in this interaction, to project these qualities onto her teacher and the other student. The teacher helped her to understand how fairness varied from person to person. What was fair could be changed according to what parameters one worked within. If we only look at events of the last 2 years, then Lynda's position was fair. If we looked at the last two lifetimes, the Master's position was fair. The Master was promoting a person with whom he had worked intensively for several lifetimes, and it was within his memory that this was so. He knew that the best person for the job was Emily, someone who was relatively new to the school in this life but who had an ancient connection with the teacher.

Lynda went through the exercises you will see below, and identified various characteristics that helped her learn to love things that she used to find unloveable. In doing so she revealed part of her own shadow and pulled it into the light. You are invited to learn to do the same.

Please complete the following exercise as frankly and honestly as possible. If you have done it before, do not just repeat the old exercise. Have a new look, choose a new person to work with (as explained below), and all kinds of wonderful things will be revealed. Every time I do this, and I have done it scores of times, I find out more about myself.

Firstly, choose a person that you like and respect and list 8 of their most wonderful attributes from your perspective. Then choose someone who has been a big challenge for you and put 8 challenging characteristics of that person in the other side. If you can't think of 8 characteristics of one person, it is all right to have an amalgamation of a couple of people. What is it that really delights you or frustrates you about these people?

8 characteristics I admire in....................... are:	8 characteristics that drive me **nuts** about .... are:

Have a look at your list. The things that we like about others are things that we have already learned to value and love. We would love it if we could see those characteristics in ourselves. If we could, they would be part of our radiant light, or our beauty. If we cannot see those things in ourselves, then these characteristics are buried in our shadow.

The things that we do not like about others are the things we would not love in ourselves. We would judge ourselves to be bad people if we displayed these qualities. These characteristics could be termed part of the dark of our existence; things that we have not yet learned to understand, accept or love. This is also part of our shadow.

But Why?

Remember from the V diagram that we have physical, etheric, astral, soul and Divine dimensions to our being. You may also recall that the physical, etheric, astral and soul part of our being is not merged in the Infinite Oneness, but exists as an identifiable thing: the self. When we are in the consciousness of the Egoic part of the self, we see the rest of the world as 'out there' and me as 'in here'. As we start to expand our consciousness and develop even a little Divine consciousness, we start to understand that 'out there' has a lot to do with what we are thinking, feeling, expecting and believing 'in here'. Eventually we learn how to change 'in here' so that 'out there' changes too.

Inside every cell of our being is Divine energy. There is nothing at all that is not of Divine origin, and so therefore when we expand our consciousness far enough, we can see that there is nothing at all that is actually bad. God created all of it, so even if I don't like it or understand it, it must be meant to be there. If it is there, it must have a purpose.

Rather than questioning Divine purpose, it is more fruitful to expand our own consciousness so that more can be understood.

We are all everything or we are not actually Divine. If we are just a *bit* Divine, what then is the rest? Are we going to blame the Devil? Well, who created him? Why is a Devil or a demon tolerated by a beneficent God unless there is a purpose to dark as well as light? At its most basic, how would we recognise light if there was no dark to contrast with it? How would we know kindness if we had never experienced meanness? How would we understand what peace meant if we had never felt rage, anger or resentment? How would we know what love was if we had never suffered its absence?

Everything has its use

Evil is just the wrong thing in the wrong measure

in the wrong place at the wrong time

If the Divine is everything, as I believe it is, the Divine is not everything except the stuff on our list that we don't like. God is everything including all that! The people we have pulled into our life who embody our shadow characteristics are children of God, just like we are, all the time, no matter what they think, say or do.

Murderer

The first murderer I met when I was a barrister was a young man of about 19 years of age. I went to Long Bay prison to interview him and felt the usual dread as the heavy steel doors of the prison clanged shut behind me, and another equally large set of doors opened before me, and in turn clanged shut behind me. Then I was in the legal conference room area, and he was shown in. Simon was concerned for my wellbeing, helped me to push in my chair, and smiled sadly at me as he spoke. His gentleness was obvious, as was his shy warmth. He was a polite and serene person who calmly told me his story. I couldn't put the picture of the person sitting in front of me, with the violent attack that had occurred a week previously. My client was charged with violently stabbing someone to death in a pub.

It turned out that when Simon drank he underwent a complete personality change. He was no longer sweet and considerate, he was violent and dangerous. Despite his sweetness, he was dangerous when he drank, and he couldn't stop himself from drinking. Quite properly, he ended up in prison for several years.

The learning for me was that all of these characteristics; sweetness, good manners, intelligence, warmth, violence, irresponsibility and addiction existed inside the one person.

'Good' People Carry Negative Energy

It would be easy if we could divide people into 'good' people and 'bad' people like they often do in the movies. It is not so simple. 'Bad' people can be capable of great acts of compassion and kindness, and 'good' people can, from time to time, behave atrociously.

A particularly common way in which people trap negative energy inside themselves is by harboring negative thoughts about the people who push their buttons. This causes conflict, and conflict is often not handled very well in our culture. Often the conflict following a disagreement is far more severe than the original disagreement itself. Conflict breeds on itself. Often the inability to forgive those who have caused us to experience pain, creates more hostility and greater conflict. This scenario is very evident during and after marital separations and divorces.

> *The Divine is everything*
>
> *I am one with the Divine*
>
> *I am everything*
>
> *I cannot be everything except anger*
>
> *(or hatred, or whatever is in my shadow)*

A New Way

Every action has consequences, even in practical day-to-day terms. We are all free to decide how we use our time and resources. If we choose to be loving and considerate, people will enjoy our company. If we choose to be selfish and insular, our partner might leave us. We might be a really nice person but if we kill someone we are going to end up in prison. We are no more or less Divine depending on our choices, yet every choice will have an effect upon our future.

Instead of judging the things that we have on our negative shadow list, we can develop new approaches. For me it has been a journey, which usually has a few steps. First is accurate recognition: yes, this characteristic is being displayed. Next comes responsibility: it is happening in my life so it must have something to do with me. If it is upsetting to me, then it is part of my shadow. It is something I have not yet learned to love and so I am holding it in darkness. Here is an opportunity to change that. After that I can choose to view the situation with compassion: none of us are perfect. I have trust in the law of karma: if they act badly, the Universe will ensure that they are sooner or later on the receiving end of what they are dishing out. Finally, I look at my shadow: Ah, interesting. How did I create this? What characteristic do I not love or accept in me that has pulled this difficult situation into my life? I then set about finding a way to accept and love it.

Tin Tacks Time: Look in the Mirror

Look back at the lists of characteristics that you have created, your 8 beauty characteristics and your 8 shadow characteristics. Cross out the name at the top of the list and insert your own name. This is you, even if you can't immediately see it in yourself.

Many people start to feel a little uncomfortable at this stage. However, this exercise is not about beating ourselves up, this is about re-empowerment.

Let's start with our beauty. When I first did these lists, I identified on my beauty list a friend who was funny, witty, intelligent and vivacious. At the time, I knew I was intelligent but the other things didn't sound like me at all. The teacher said that they definitely were a part of me, because I was everything. It took me a while to think of myself as witty, funny or vivacious.

The 'dear friend' list is the reflection of what we already find loveable, and it is also a reflection of our own beauty. Sometimes it is really odd that we don't see our own beauty, but in this exercise you get to do so.

The nemesis (foe) list you have created above, no matter what you might think about it, is a reflection of your shadow. This is what you judge as bad. Looked at through universal eyes, it is what will be chasing you in your life.

None of us thinks of ourselves in shadow terms, because who wants to think of themselves as obnoxious, selfish, angry, dishonest or whatever it is that is written on the list. Our ego works to disown and project this unloved part of self onto others. Having lived and taught this exercise over many years I can assure you that if you work through these lists, find where these things are inside of you, and find the good or useful aspects of them, you will transform your relationships and empower your life.

The things on our shadow list may be the very things that people who do not like you, say about you. How can this be? Because these are the things about yourself that you have not yet learned to love. So, they stick out of your 'wholeness' like a sore thumb. You don't think that they are anything to do with you. The Universe thinks otherwise, and knows you are a Divine Being, one with **everything**. The Universe will keep shoving these characteristics under your nose through person after person until you get it. You can learn to accept and even love people despite them portraying these characteristics. You can even love yourself.

My shadow was very confronting for me when I first did this exercise many years ago. I thought I was such a good girl. Yet on my shadow list I had things like malicious, jealous, dishonest, unfair and angry. Let me explain to you how I made friends with these former enemies.

What To Do

The advice I received was to try and find something good in all of the things on my shadow list. I needed to see all the attributes without judgment as to whether they were good or bad, and to discover how they could be used positively or negatively depending on *context*. I needed to learn to see the things on my beauty list as neutral, 'it just is', rather than judging it as good or bad. I needed to accept that *I* had put a judgment on it.

For example humour, from my beauty list is fine, but not when you are at a solemn funeral. Loyalty is great, but not if you are loyal to a person or cause that is corrupt. Being goal focused is good, but not when you become obsessive about it.

Some people put things on their beauty list that others put on their beast list. One woman complained that her husband was too changeable, and had that characteristic on her beast list, whereas another woman in the class had changeable on her beauty list. Over time I have come to see that many things could be switched around depending on the value and meaning an individual has given them.

Good and Bad?

Emotions and states of consciousness are not actually good or bad, they just are. There are times when it is really appropriate to feel grief. It is natural and normal, not negative. If we feel it without any resistance, it will just flow through us. If we hate feeling grief and we try to avoid it and stuff it down, often what happens is that we freeze a part of ourselves, and suffer from it for years on end.

Think about lazy people. Most of us categorise lazy as 'bad'. However, lazy people make motivated people look really good, so what are they worried about? More to the point, many well motivated people become such workaholics, that they would be better off being a bit more lazy, so as to retain better mental and physical health!

One person's tenacity is another person's pig headedness. There used to be a joke going around about female lawyers and male lawyers:

A male lawyer is assertive; a female lawyer is pushy

He is careful about detail; she is picky

He loses his temper because he cares so much; she is bitchy

He follows through; she doesn't know when to quit

He is firm; she is stubborn

He makes wise judgments; she reveals her prejudices

He is a man of the world; she has been around

He isn't afraid to say what he thinks; she is opinionated

He exercises authority; she's tyrannical

He's discreet; she is secretive

He is a stern taskmaster; she's difficult to work for

He is focused; she is obsessed

He is career minded; she is ambitious.

He is using his initiative; she can't follow instructions.

The point is that depending on the circumstance and point of view, one person's 'good' can actually be another person's 'bad'. It is more useful to see that everything is *relative*, and everything is actually there to help us grow as souls.

Anger

My introduction to the concept of shadow came at a time in my life when I was surrounded by angry people. At the time, I was such a 'good girl' and so incapable of meeting my own need for approval that I tried to be some kind of a saint, and totally rejected the idea that there may be a part of me that was not so saintly: a part which was human, growing and learning.

Back then, I never got angry. I had been brought up to believe that showing anger was bad. Thus, (being very good) I did not display anger, and in fact, I thought that I was a very calm, peaceful person. Because of my judgment of anger I could not express it, and instead I shoved it down inside of myself. As a young child I had a chronic problem with tonsillitis, then bronchitis in my 20s, Usually I could keep the peace at all costs, but at this particular time in my life my partner was angry, my daughter was only a baby and she seemed angry, the judges in the courts in which I was appearing seemed angry, my opposing counsel were angry, my clients were angry. Everyone was angry. I couldn't accept that the anger had anything to do with me because I had judged it as bad. Because it was bad and I was good, it couldn't be part of me. This lead to a situation where the Divine basically had to show me that I was angry.

When I saw my then teacher, Barbara Tebo, and spoke with her about all the angry people in my life, she said to me: "Have you ever thought that you might be angry?" I said to her, "Don't be ridiculous, I am not that kind of person". She was such a kind soul, she even didn't laugh at me! She said that anger was a part of life, and like anything, if we judge it as bad, the Universe has a way of creating classrooms of it until such time as we come to realise that this thing, which we do not like, is inside of us too. I really did think at the time that I was just naturally a very calm, peaceful person and that 'they' had the problem.

'Saint Kim' as I refer to myself back then, was not very happy about being told that the anger might be to do with her. However, considering that the rest of the things this wise woman had taught me had turned out to be true, I later realised that there was much wisdom in what she was saying. Perhaps it did have something to do with me!

At the time I struggled with this, but trusting my teacher I agreed to try and find something good about anger. After a while I realised that anger for me is the fire in the belly in the goddess. It is the motivating force that helps us to break free of restrictive or negative situations, and move on. Anger helps us to redefine our boundaries, as we saw earlier when we looked at the four families of feelings in chapter 8. Anger is the door through which change is activated, fuelled by having reached a stage where we decide we are never, ever going to experience whatever it was again. Motivated by healthy anger, we do whatever we have to in order to effect change.

For me, getting a handle on anger was like being given a new key to the Universe. If people were treating me badly it became the tool, the motivating force through which I learnt to say "Enough, I am not putting up with this any longer. Stop it!" If I couldn't feel my anger, I couldn't get to that place of being empowered enough to put in place healthy boundaries. So then I decided that anger wasn't so bad after all, that there were times when it could be quite beneficial.

When I started to think about anger in that way, I realised that a lot of the problems I had experienced in my past few relationships had been a result of *not* getting angry and ensuring that my boundaries were properly established and clear. It had been my *lack* of anger, not my partner's evident anger that had been the problem. If I had been comfortable with my own anger, my partner would not have had to be the carrier of all of that energy for our relationship. I was able to make a **distinction between feeling anger, and what you do with it.** The anger itself wasn't bad, it was just telling me that something was not right.

Even though I got it intellectually I still didn't get it deep inside. I really could not feel any anger inside of me, but still I had all these angry people around me. Then I did another of Barbara's seminars in the series *Free to be Me*, where releasing anger through beating a tennis racquet on a mattress was part of the agenda. When I started, I just felt ridiculous. Then, this huge wave of energy rose up inside of me, it was hot, and it was big. I started whacking that mattress like there was no tomorrow. My hands became blistered, and still I whacked it, and for quite a long time I felt the anger coming out of my body. At the end I was exhausted, shaky and emotional. But I also knew something really important had happened, and I felt lighter and freer than I had ever remembered feeling.

At first I was not very good at expressing anger skilfully, and felt a bit out of control and volatile when the fiery energy that I had previously suppressed or projected onto others, came out. I learned to apologise for my lack of skilfulness and to have the conversation that I needed to have

- that had been brought to a head by the anger. I persevered, and tentatively began to allow myself to feel angry. I persisted with trying to love it, and found ways to get the angry energy out of my body, through exercise and harmless physical means. I learned techniques for channelling the emotions out of my body in safe and non-harmful ways as is set out in chapter 24. For example, moving furniture, vacuuming or banging pots and pans helped me move the charge of anger when I felt it welling up. Others might prefer chopping wood or running. Now I find Pranayama (yogic breathing) very helpful. Generally some kind of physical movement is required to release the charge.

While the charge of anger was to let me know something was not right, I did not find it particularly helpful to discuss my issue while I was still angry, because all people heard was my anger. After calming down I could have a reasonable discussion with the person, and usually that was enough to have things move. If I met with resistance or more anger, I knew that I had internal washing up to do, and I did purification of my mind and energy field to change myself. After that things tended to flow.

Through all of this, I realised that anger is part of being alive. The more conscious we become, the more we grow in awareness that we are one with everything. We can't be one with everything except anger. The more we think that anger is not who we are, the more the Universe will bring anger to us until we can accept it.

As I realised that anger had a place in the Universe and that it was not bad per se, an amazing miracle occurred. In time I got to be comfortable with my own anger, and comfortable with other people being angry. I started to notice that people were being friendly again. Then the anger seemed to have magically evaporated. I developed better boundaries, and to my great relief, I found that I was no longer surrounded by angry people, particularly by angry men. I came to understand that this improbable sounding explanation of how all those angry people had been in my life, to show me my own shadow, was most likely true.

Malice

When I unpacked this one, it took me some weeks to work out what could be good about malice and where it was in me. How could there be anything good about deliberately setting out to hurt another human being?

After quite a bit of meditation about it I came to a realisation. The legal profession as I experienced it, was a very gossipy profession. I gossiped with the best of them, thought it was great fun, and didn't really notice that it was actually malicious. My use of humour was also a bit on the malicious side. There were people who were the brunt of my jokes. When I thought about that I realised that if you watch comedians, quite a bit of humour that we all laugh at is negative and destructive. Having discovered this I decided that I was not going to do it any more and so I made a big effort to find methods of humour that are not malicious. Changing the vibration of our humour is something we can do to ensure we are not being malicious.

As I focused on this realisation over the coming weeks, magically the malicious people began to melt out of my life. They found someone else to torment.

Jealousy

Jealousy overcomes unconscious denial and lets us know what we truly want and value. Have you ever met a person who is very out of touch with themselves, and out of touch with life in general? People can construct a whole life inside their heads which has little to do with reality. Our emotions (all of them not just the nice ones) are a means of communication from the soul and body that is real to us. Emotional responses can cut through the denial or inertia in our minds.

There can be various reasons why we are in denial about what we actually want. We might think it is not right to want that, or that we don't want to be competitive. Jealousy means 'I really want what they have got'. My body and soul are telling me through the powerful impulse of jealousy, to use my mind to work out how to get something similar to whatever it is that they have. Knowing this allows me to reorient my priorities in the truth of my being, and to know which way I want to head.

Since this discovery, jealousy and jealous people have never really troubled me. I don't care if people are jealous or not, because I know they are only finding out how much they really want something.

When jealousy enters into a relationship, it might be that there are issues of self-esteem that need to be worked on. As we start to feel better about ourselves, it seems more probable that our partner will continue to love us and jealousy can often recede.

One can feel the energy of jealousy without acting inappropriately. The law of karma urges us to be kind in all circumstances. When I learned about energy I discovered that the thing to do when I feel jealous is to bless the person of whom I was jealous. By blessing the person who had what I wanted, I was asking that God grant them even more of whatever it is that they currently have. It works like this. Suppose your friend gets a really fabulous boyfriend and you feel jealous. If you go into a spiral of negativity based on jealousy, or wish ill on the relationship you push a loving relationship further away from yourself, and invite a flawed, low vibrational future. We may even damage our friendship by behaving jealously. Instead, feel the jealousy and understand that it is saying that you are ready for a relationship like that. Bless your friends with the intention that they find love and that they are blissfully happy together. By blessing in this way, some of that happiness is automatically returned to you, making it more probable that you too will find a fabulous boyfriend and are blessed with happiness yourself.

Dishonesty

Dishonesty is a characteristic that emerges often on people's shadow list. We all consider ourselves to be honest, however are we really? We have seen before that there are many levels of truth. Have you ever said to someone "Oh, you look lovely", when they really look like an unmade bed?

For a spiritual aspirant it may be damaging to be completely honest because the primary value on a spiritual path is loving kindness and harmlessness. Being honest when honesty would hurt a person may not be the smartest thing to do. If someone who has been very ill and depressed has made an effort to get dressed up, it may be 'dishonest' to tell them they look great even if you think they look terrible. However, your diplomacy or discretion may be more beneficial than the harsh truth at that point. Therefore, this deception is a *positive* deception.

Consider an old man on his death bed, a family man all his life, whose grandson has just been convicted of being a drug dealer. The old man doesn't know. Is it good to tell him that his beloved grandson is about to go to prison, or do you let him die peacefully in the absence of that particular piece of information?

In everyday situations people ask us how we are, and we say "I'm fine", but really that is not the truth. We may feel crap but don't think it is the right time or place to talk about it. We may not be in the right environment or with the right people to say how we really are. If you have ever done this, then you are someone who has been dishonest. This does not necessarily make you a bad person.

If we have dishonest people all around us, we need to find a way to love dishonesty by finding a useful place for it. We also need to see where we may be blind to our own dishonesty.

Honesty is a two edged sword and can be used as a weapon. You can really harm people with honesty, and similarly dishonesty, which could be called diplomacy, can be positive. The context is always relevant to whether something is good or bad.

Manipulation

Many people would put manipulation on their shadow list. However like anything else, manipulation is neutral. It is our motivation behind the manipulation that could either be positive or negative. If we manipulate people for selfish purposes, this is a problem. However, if we manipulate people for a purpose that they themselves want to achieve, is it so bad?

Hands up all the parents. If you are a parent, you are a manipulator or you are not doing your job properly! We all manipulate our children, trying to help them be better people, make sound choices, become virtuous and so forth. Guiding our children is our responsibility. Manipulation is a tool with which we work, usually unconsciously, in order to help our kids.

Gym instructors, weight loss coaches and personal trainers are hired to help us change and their skilful manipulation of our personalities, competency level and motivations help us to achieve the goals that we might have set together. Chances are that if they didn't manipulate us at least a bit, we would never get there.

Weakness

Weakness is annoying when it is employed in the wrong place in life, but weakness per se is not evil or wrong. Giving in when we are slogging it out and getting nowhere with someone might seem weak, but really it may be a beneficial thing to do.

Weakness is a form of vulnerability. Vulnerability is a state of openness to all that is. Without vulnerability we will never find true authentic power. For instance, it is one thing to have everyone do what you ask when you hold a high office or have heaps of money. It is quite another to get the same people to be motivated to follow you if you hold no office at all and cannot pay them. When we are in a position of high office, people might be respecting the office rather than the individual. Lose the office, and you have lost the power. To the truly powerful, it makes no difference whether they have a job where people have to follow them or not, and whether they have money or not. They will still be followed and respected. Sometimes we have to become weak in order to learn this.

How many times have you heard of a person making significant and beneficial life changes owing to an illness that made them too weak to continue in a lifestyle that was killing them?

Being a Drama Queen

This is something that is on lots of peoples shadow list, but think how entertaining it is. It is fun! Yes they might make a mountain out of a molehill, and be very dramatic in their presentation of what they refer to as facts, but life would be very dull without someone in our life who can be a drama queen. If it annoys you, look into your shadow for where perhaps you can be a bit of a drama queen at times yourself.

Violence

Most of us would put violence on our list of things that we cannot love. However, I once had a person in an Empowering Relationships class put violence on the good list. He said that there are times when violence is necessary. Tyrants, oppressive regimes and criminal behaviour have to be stopped. It sometimes takes a war to do that. There are times when violence is absolutely necessary to right action. If a person attacked your child, you would no doubt unhesitatingly defend him or her, because that is human nature. The Bhagavad Gita, one of the most sacred texts in the world, is a story about spiritual advice being given to a warrior. It sanctions 'right use' of violence, and says that if we do not protect people from negative forces, then we are as much at fault as the wrongdoer, and will suffer a karmic penalty for our omission.

Peace

Peace would be on most people's 'OK' list. However like anything, too much peace can be destructive and bad. This could show up as being a door mat and putting up with things when we really ought to stop them. Peace that is not founded on virtue is the peace of the damned. Through fear of speaking up we end up with tyrannical regimes, religions, family and societal leaders. Like Gandhi, we can hold peace in our hearts while disturbing the peace somewhat to stand up for something that we believe in.

Playing Swap

Some people think crying is bad whereas others think it is good. One person's lazy is another person's 'not being a stressed out executive'. Being selfish is bad for some people but meeting our own needs first is essential for a well-balanced, cup-full life. You can be too good, too clever for your own good, 'honest to a fault' and so on. If we go through our 'not OK' column and our 'OK' column, really anything can be swapped from one side to the other. Literally what is 'right' is a heartfelt expression of the right thing being present in our life in the right quantity at the right time to inform right action, right thought and right speech.

Absolutely everything you can have on one list can be on the other list. Part of this exercise is just getting out of our mental constructs and expectations about how life is. It is letting go of what we might have been taught, so we can expand our paradigm of love and acceptance. When we think 'this is good' and 'this is bad', it is like being in a split universe, and we can only relate to half the universe and the other half we have to fight. Not until we can love our demons are they going to stop bothering us.

Accurate Perception

Mostly, when we are on the receiving end of unfairness, anger, violence etc, and we are upset about it, there is a tendency to think 'poor me'. This is victim consciousness. It is totally disempowering, and the sooner we get rid of it the better. It gets in the way of accurate perception: what is really going on is that our shadow is looming over us. As we learn to understand, accept, and finally to love that which we used to judge, sooner or later we set ourselves free and life improves. Love will heal all.

We see others not as the other person really is, but as a reflection of our own consciousness and issues. We judge others as though they will behave the same way as we do. Truly kind people see the kindness in others. Critical people see fault everywhere but in their own backyard. They create very difficult futures for themselves.

If we don't look at our shadow and we just pretend it isn't there, pretending that it is other people who have the problem, we disempower ourselves. Getting rid of a betraying friend or an abusive partner and not cleaning up our shadow is a recipe for repeated disaster. There is a high probability that the next person will have the same attributes because betrayal and disrespect are not *their* shadow attributes, they are ours. Thus, we will attract another friend or partner just like the last one.

When I am faced with any shadow characteristic, the most important realisation is that it is not the other person who needs to change, it is me. Despite how simple this is, it is a challenging concept to employ at first. When you get it, you will be amazed at how liberating it is. You will be able to turn around all kinds of difficult situations in your life and find inner peace, through enhanced self-knowledge.

Narelle

Narelle had been in a very dysfunctional marriage and the subject of domestic violence. Her husband had been outwardly a very nice, well mannered and courteous man, but when they were alone it was a different story. If he had been drinking he became very vindictive and violent. Narelle put up with this behaviour for years, each bad incident was followed by sincere apology and promises that he would change, but he never did. After 20 years she left.

While she left the physical violence and the marriage behind her, she had developed a serious hatred towards men. She was really angry and had bottled that anger up in her heart chakra. She could not forgive and forget. She was stuck and could not move on. She wanted nothing to do with men. Her life became bitter and lonely. She could not stop talking about her terrible marriage and her bastard of an ex-husband. I met her 10 years after they had split up. The way she spoke of her experiences, it was as if they occurred just yesterday.

Narelle had developed heart arrhythmia. She could not sleep properly and had started drinking heavily. She had also recently been in a dispute with a neighbour in which she was subjected to threats and verbal abuse. When she came to me, she was exhausted, unhappy and disinterested in life. Her heart chakra was very closed down. It was very black from all the hatred. Because of the vibration of hatred in her heart, she had attracted a series of abusive relationships, not in a romantic partnership (she had sworn off men) but generally.

The heart of Narelle's problem was that she saw herself as a good person and her ex-husband as the bad person. With a little encouragement, Narelle came to see that it was her own suppressed anger that had drawn violent action to her. Unless she unburdened her heart chakra, she would keep pumping out the same emotional signal of anger and hatred. This would attract anger and hatred towards her. It was stuck in her shadow.

Over several weeks of healing with the violet flame, we released more and more of the toxic energy, and each week she felt lighter and different. She also came to see that unless she could forgive her ex-husband, she would continue carting him energetically around with her the whole time.

Narelle did a deep and profound forgiveness exercise, and loads of black, tarry astral substance came out of her heart chakra. In the end, her heart chakra resumed proper functioning. The arrhythmia subsided, and she felt better.

Her neighbour had a change of heart and agreed to a peaceful solution to their dispute. She no longer felt like drowning her sorrows, and started to attend a book club where she met a nice man. They became friends and eventually she was able to have an intimate relationship with him.

Whose Stuff is It?

Whenever you are on the receiving end of any kind of unfair or hurtful treatment, just think, "Am I upset"? If the answer is yes, then it is your stuff, even though it might also be theirs. Their side of things is none of your business. You need to deal with your shadow. Acknowledging it and being aware is a good first step. If the answer to the question, "Am I upset?" is, "No, I am not upset", then you know that it is the stuff of the other person. While whatever is going on might upset someone else, it is not upsetting you, it just is. Send love and move on.

Often what attracts people to each other is their matching garbage. The angry or jealous person in our life might exhibit the characteristic at a volume of 9 out of 10, while in us it might only be 3 out of 10. It will however still be there. Finding where it is playing out in your life will save you from a lot of trouble.

Another way that the matching game occurs is when a person who judges anger as bad will attract another person who judges anger as bad. One of them will get angry "because you made me angry" and lash out. No one makes us angry. The anger is already inside of us. Both the giver and receiver of the angry energy are upset, and both get caught in a terrible dance of blame and accusation. Only when we take responsibility for the things that turn up in our lives can we find a lasting way out.

- *Our shadow is what we cannot yet love or accept*
- *It is what we were told was bad (even our beauty)*
- *Our shadow follows us wherever we go*
- *We cannot see it because it is behind us*
- *Others can see it*
- *Here we are unconscious*
- *Our shadow pulls unpleasantness to us*

Find Hidden Treasure

Shadow characteristics are not always bad. Sometimes the stuff in our shadow is amazing, but we have just never seen it. I knew a man who in all power games had been a persecutor. Because he had been a persecutor for so long and his wife had been telling him for 20 years what a bastard he was, he was able to own his inner bastard. He didn't like himself much, didn't respect himself much and he had lost sight of his light. To him it came as a great shock when his shadow was unpacked and out came all his beauty.

Have a look at your previous list of characteristics you admired in your friend. This doctrine says that every single thing on that list is already inside of you. Can you relate to that? It may be that someone else has the voltage on that thing turned up higher than it is in you, but if you are capable of seeing it in another person, it is in you.

If we cannot see the characteristic anywhere else in their world, then they are not ready for a teaching on it yet. For instance, if one cannot see love anywhere, we are not able to learn about love yet.

If I cannot see the Divine in another person then I am not ready to learn about the Divine in myself. If I can see the Divine in another human being, then I am ready to see it in me too. All of the qualities that one sees in a Guru are present in the disciple, and over time the realisation comes that this is true. An integral part of devotion is to realise that the Guru is a mirror. The Divine light and tremendous love I perceive in a Guru is actually in me.

It's Not About Them

The most important realisation is that it is not the other person who needs to change, it is me. When I realise how angry I am, how suppressed I am, and how much judgment I have, then I can decide to let it go. As I let it go, magically the angry/dishonest/manipulative people melt out of my life.

No Blame or Shame

When some people are presented with this information, they go into self-blame. They use this information on shadow to beat themselves up and their critical parent self goes wild. Truly, this is not about blaming anyone. It is about learning how the inner world works and how it affects our relationships. No one is to blame. Taking responsibility for our shadow is about empowerment. Now that we know, we can use this knowledge to make changes. The point is to love the self and acknowledge that we have always done our best, even if now we can see that our best can get even better. Quite frankly, if we cannot get over having to blame, we are better to blame our beloved than blame the self. Self-blame creates shame, which is even more debilitating and disempowering than blaming others.

On our journey of Divine oneness, it is easy to love that which is soft and fluffy but our task in mastering Earth life is to love the unloveable. Repeating the shadow exercise and continuing to look at the things we find challenging is an excellent way to achieve the masterful objective of loving unconditionally.

PART

8

ETHERIC BODY OF RELATIONSHIPS

Chapter

27

RELATIONSHIP ENTITIES

When people form any kind of relationship, subtle energy starts to form between them which not only helps the relationship establish, it also serves to assist there to be deep communication between them both on a conscious and unconscious level.

When people enter a close relationship and grow in love and friendship there is a pooling of energy between them. This pool of energy is what holds the relationship in place. It holds the understandings that the two souls have of each other, contracts of understanding and energetic patterns that drew the parties together. It holds love, attraction, as well as the spark and sparkle of that which brought us together and makes this relationship special.

However, it can also hold old, stale energy which keeps us stuck in old patterns. This stuck energy makes it difficult sometimes to move forward and create desirable change. When we have an argument, sometimes that energy hangs around for quite a long time, and small residues of resentment, stress and other difficult emotions can cause a cloudiness and denseness to permeate things. Relationships looked at from an energetic point of view can become quite congested and full of dirty or low vibrational energy. In fact they can become so stale that we feel that the only solution is to get out of it because it feels like a prison.

When we learn to care for the energy of our relationships we are able to avoid a lot of issues and clean up any conflict or misunderstandings more gracefully. So much energy that would support conflict and negative consciousness can be released simply by regular cleaning out of the relationship entity and cutting all cords of co-dependence that exist between the two people concerned.

The way we do this is to do 'Ignite Your Spirit' therapy upon the relationship itself, rather than on the individual parties to the relationship. This combines the information taught in our 'Ignite Your Spirit' seminars and our 'Empowering Relationship' seminars.

How?

We have a relationship healing tool which is a guided release meditation CD. This has proven very effective in helping people to manage the energy in their relationships and is recommended for use whenever you want to improve, upgrade or heal a relationship. The absolute best thing that we can do is to consult a properly trained and qualified Ignite Your Spirit therapist who will tailor the healing precisely to your circumstances.

The healing is then done either with just one, or with both parties present. The client sits comfortably on a chair, and the therapist will tune in and perceive where the main weaknesses and strengths are in the relationship entity, and give feedback based upon their assessment to the client/s. Then they will begin using release commands, counselling skills and blessings to cleanse, clear and support the level of consciousness within the energy of the relationship. This generally provides instant relief and can set the scene for greater clarity and the cultivation of more love than ever before.

Which Coloured Glasses

The relationships that you inhabit will have a chakral configuration that will reflect your thoughts, beliefs, issues and energetic patterns about it. If you were to scan the beloved's relationship entity with you, it would be from their perspective and therefore reflect their own thought forms, beliefs, issues and energetic patterns. It is to be expected therefore, that the relationship entity looked at from the perspective of the beloved will be different from how it will look if we look at it from our own perspective. The world is how we perceive it to be, and that is not how it actually is. If you understand something of the Sanskrit notion of Maya, you will understand what this is about.

Our entire world is an emanation of our own consciousness. This includes our experience of relationships. If we scan the relationship of two people, say Clare and Dean, we can do it either through her consciousness or through his. If they present together for the healing, then the combined creation can be worked upon.

We have often had situations where for instance, Clare presents with issues in the throat chakra, which are about communication and the navel chakra, which is about empowerment, whereas her husband Dean might have issues in the base chakra in his relationship entity with her.

This is because what we are seeing is how the consciousness of each party is impinging on 'reality' to create certain experiences for them.

Paradox

Logically, it may seem impossible that each person in a relationship can be one hundred percent responsible for it themselves. However, my experience working multi-dimensionally is that reality on the inner plane is sometimes upside down and inside out from what we think it is in the physical plane alone.

Paradox is an important doctrine, and basically says that through the law of paradox, two things that cannot possibly exist at the same time, in fact, do. Two things that are entirely contradictory can at the same time be true. For example, God is inside us and no where else, but yet God is outside of us as well. The Divine is the alpha (beginning) and the omega (end) which are opposite ends of the spectrum. The disciple surrenders to the Guru which on the face of it might seem like they give their power away, when in reality through that surrender the disciple actually gets spiritually empowered, like in the stories of Hanuman, the Hindu monkey God of power who was the disciple of Rama. These things are mysteries, which through meditation and observation we can come to understand. So it is that we can come to understand and appreciate the value of knowing that we, and our partners, are each 100% responsible for our experience of our relationship.

I am convinced that my relationship with others is entirely one hundred percent my own creation. This belief is derived from a background in metaphysics and 20 years intensive study of multidimensionality.

How I think, speak, react and analyse things is a function of my consciousness, not my beloved's. He may be having quite a different experience of the relationship than I am, even though it is supposedly the same relationship.

The fact of the matter is that when looked at from an energetic point of view, it is not the same relationship at all. The relationship entity is a giant thought form about the relationship of myself and my beloved. It is *my* relationship and each of us are 100% responsible for our own relationships. This is an empowering way to look at it.

If it is only a 50-50 deal, then I can only affect half of it. I have to give my power to my beloved in respect of the other half. This is going to lead to a raft of control strategies and co-dependence. When I know that the whole thing is my own responsibility, I have the power to make changes. By getting in tune with my soul, by changing myself and my mind, and by changing the energy in the relationship, I can transform it. This is something that allows me to take responsibility, dig deep into my spiritual tools and build the very essence of my light body, which is why we are here in the first place.

Jade and Guy

Jade and Guy were married for several years. Guy was a tools man, and he showed a lot of love by doing practical things, and looking after Jade and their home in that way. They ended up getting divorced and as usual in a divorce there are some hurt feelings. About a month after the split up can be worse than the actual time of separating. Anyway, one day they had a discussion on the phone and Jade was not very skilful, it got quite heated and was not nice. She was annoyed that she had let it get that unskilful but she went home and did a relationship healing. The next day Guy came over and fixed several things in the house. This is not what divorced husbands usually do. She didn't ask him, but it was clear that he somehow felt the cleaning out and the love that she put into the relationship healing and he responded. She did not do it so that he would do something for her, but that was the response. When you give love you open the door for someone else to give love.

For months whenever anything went wrong between them Jade would zap it straight away, and their relationship continued to evolve. They ended up with a friendly and respectful relationship even though they knew that they were better off apart. It was very easy for their children to go back and forth between them because of the clean way the relationship was energetically managed. Jade took 100% responsibility for the relationship with her ex, and was able to achieve an outstanding result in her life by never giving into the feeling of wanting to blame her ex if things went a bit askew. She held her potency, and knew that she had the tools and capacity to bring positive change to her circumstances. She used many of the tools in this book, including the relationship healing CD.

We are all affecting our relationship entities all the time by everything that we think, do and say.

Alice

Alice had married quite young and had three small children. She loved her husband Simon, who was a successful professional working for a large international accounting firm. He was very busy with work, and she had given up a very successful career in accounting herself to stay home with the kids. They were fairly stable financially and had a good life. However, Alice was increasingly concerned about the fact that he assumed he had the right to make all of the big decisions that affected both of their lives. He was offered a job, which would mean that they would have to live in Japan for three years, away from all of Alice's support networks, family and friends. She was upset and anxious about the move.

Since they had been in a relationship, Alice had deferred to Simon's wishes. She did this automatically, a habit that had become ingrained even when they were still dating. Deep down Alice doubted herself. She harboured an unconscious thought that if she didn't agree with him he would leave.

As Alice got to know herself through her spiritual studies, she realised that she had internalised quite a lot of resentment, anger and frustration about his seeming inability to see things from her perspective. She also realised that she had not been very good at speaking up at the right time, fearing his reaction and not really knowing how to say what she wanted to say.

When Alice first started to come to the Harmony Centre she copped a lot of resistance from Simon. He called it 'claptrap' and was derisive of her interest in spirituality. We did some work on the relationship entity. The navel chakra was virtually non-existent. The navel chakra has to do with personal power and this is different to the ability to force someone to do something that they don't want to do. Power enlivens and seeks harmony through energetic, mental, emotional and physical means. It creates dialogues through which truth can emerge and is a mechanism for growth, evolution and the life force.

We cleaned up the relationship entity and discussed how Alice could use different kinds of communication styles to get through to Simon.

She needed to do the inner work first, including working on her own self esteem.

After a few weeks of diligent use of purification meditations and affirmations as to her worth, and repeated use of the relationship clearing meditation, she spoke with Simon. She reported to me that the conversation went well and that he listened to her more than he had really done in years. She stuck to how she felt rather than what he had done or not done.

After the discussion Alice felt that, while they held different opinions, they were now actually discussing them. Over the next couple of months they had a number of talks about things that had to be said. To Alice's amazement, Simon was relatively open and actually listened to her. Alice learned to start to speak up in an assertive (not aggressive) way and to stop being so passive. She was able to do this because her self-esteem and sense of self worth were improving on account of her spiritual practices.

We also cleaned up any attachments that Alice had to where they lived. We asked that the highest decision be made that would be in the best interests of all members of the family. Through her meditations and purification, Alice became non-attached to where they lived, trusting that support would be available wherever they were. The couple ended up moving to Macau, and while there was the usual stress of moving, it turned out very well for them.

Alice had been feeling so disempowered and frightened previously that she could not have imagined that things would work out as they did. She knew things would have been very different if she had not done all the inner work before they left. She continued with her purification meditations while she was away and used the relationship healing meditation whenever it was required.

The work of keeping our relationship energy clean gives us a freedom and a capacity to come to grips with things, make changes and grow in love in a very refined and rapid way. It is a gift to ourselves and also to our beloveds that we heal our relationships.

Chapter

28

CHAKRAS IN THE
RELATIONSHIP ENTITY

Just as our own energy fields have chakras, over time energy vortices coalesce in the relationship entity and chakras form in it as well.

Chakras are energy centres, like filing cabinets for experiences, each of which holds different files. Together they have responsibility for various different functions of our body, mind and spirit. One can often perceive the strengths and weaknesses in a relationship just from scanning its chakras. Below is a simple summary of the energies of the chakras as they affect our relationships.

This chapter provides a summary of the types of issues that can arise in the chakras of a relationship entity. You may notice that the issues arising are much the same as they would be in the energy centres of an individual person. To deeply understand the spiritual, psychological and physical aspects of the energy field is the work of a lifetime and is the subject of a separate book. In *Ignite Your Spirit* (published 2004) I wrote in more detail about the chakras. Further information is to be found in *Child of God* (published 2006) and *Dimensions of Wealth* (Published 2009).

Who is the Captain?

As we go through the various chakras here, the aim is to simply reveal the filing cabinets of consciousness for each of the chakras. Each chakra is a centre of a particular quality of will inside of us. As well as looking at the basic issues, we will look at the way a person or relationship would be motivated if a particular chakra was dominant. To understand this, we are also going to imagine that each chakra in turn is the captain of a ship, and assess its competencies, tendencies and weaknesses for that role as a light hearted way to hopefully aid us in understanding what can happen when our chakras, or the chakras of a relationship entity, are out of balance.

Crown Chakra

The crown chakra, situated on top of the head is the front door to the Divine. How our relationship deals with matters to do with spirituality, God, the inner world generally, beliefs about Angels or spiritual guides, teachers and helpers will be governed by the crown chakra. When the crown chakra of a relationship entity is strong, the relationship is being fed by Divine energy. Love is a Divine gift, and the energy of that love enters our being through the crown chakra before being expressed through the heart chakra.

Stress and anxiety can build up in any of the chakras either of a person or a relationship, but is most noticeable in the crown chakra. Releasing that helps to bring a sense of peacefulness back into things.

If the crown chakra is weak, then the relationship might be suffering from a relative lack of connectedness to spirituality. When spirituality is missing from any area of life it becomes flat and lifeless. A strong spirit gives rise to a strong relationship.

Captain Crown

Captain Crown always agrees with the Higher Soul. She can have a tendency to want to bliss out, and totally ignore the reality of physical life. People who become spiritually developed and end up abandoning their family or worldly obligations are generally crown heavy. This gives rise to the monastic model of life. Sometimes it can be a problem when Captain Crown is too domineering and big, because then we are unable to wrest our life force energy away from the option that says to sit in a cave, on a mountain, in a spiritual community, or somewhere, and meditate because you have to save the world.

Someone with an overly big crown chakra will be most at home when they spend time in prayer and meditation. This can be at the expense of worldly things. The crown has no concept of timing, patience, planning or the slow speed at which things can occur in the physical plane. It just knows the whole, from the loftiest pinnacle. Captain Crown could be so busy blissing out at the beauty of the sea and the Angels singing that the ship gets stuck on the rocks. Captain crown needs support from the other chakral officers to help her to be part of the overall project of bringing heaven to Earth.

Ajna Chakra

The ajna chakra, situated between the eyebrows, is sometimes called the third eye. It is a centre of higher consciousness and holds the bigger picture of life. It governs our capacity for conceptual thinking, our higher will, and gives us entry into concepts which are new and which may alter our entire paradigm of life.

A strong ajna chakra gives us direction and the ability to see our overall path in life. When a relationship entity has a strong ajna chakra it would indicate that the parties to the relationship have a common sense of their life direction and purposefulness in attaining that together.

A weak ajna chakra could indicate that the parties to the relationship lack a common vision of their future. Each of them may be anticipating quite a different future, a different direction and the two of them might not be on the same page about what they expect life will have in store for them.

A congested or weak ajna chakra in the relationship may also suggest that there are issues to do with a clash of wills. How this is playing out can be seen by quickly scanning the ajna chakra of each of the parties to the relationship, and the odds are that the one with the strongest ajna chakra is dominating the person with the weaker ajna chakra. This pattern of domination and submission is not what relationships are meant to be about, and will cause a blockage and weakness in the ajna chakra of the relationship. The person with the stronger ajna chakra can assist the beloved to cultivate an understanding of their own uniqueness and direction, rather than dominating them. Respecting the will of each other, and getting out of our Egoic standpoints and looking at our life from a higher perspective will help the ajna chakra to become stronger.

Sometimes when the ajna chakra is weak, the parties just don't understand each other. There is a lack of ability to understand abstract concepts and find a common philosophy of being. This makes things generally feel uncomfortable or difficult.

If an ajna chakra is completely weak and congested, then it could be that the relationship is totally out of order and that there are many different kinds of systemic dysfunctionality at play.

Captain Ajna

Captain Ajna is used to being the captain of the ship and likes to be in control. Captain Ajna is a natural leader and has a will that takes into account many different factors. He can give us a full picture of how we can invest our energy in a concerted way. Captain Ajna hears the voices of all the other chakras, and balances them all, operating from a big picture perspective. He can think strategically and plan, and is able to make sense of spiritual stimuli. Captain Ajna is definitely loyal to his employer, the soul. He is able to take the subtle impulsing from our Higher Soul and operate in a manner that is based upon its objectives. Captain Ajna does not get bogged down in detail, but will chart a course that will give something to every part of our potential. Captain Ajna is likely to be the most highly qualified, effective and balanced captain we could have.

Throat Chakra

The throat chakra is located at the front of the neck in the hollow of the throat. This chakra has a lot to do with the way we bring order and structure into our lives by planning, analysing, applying logic, following directions, implementing decisions and generally being orderly. Whereas the Ajna chakra is about conceptual or higher order thinking, the throat chakra is about implementation and operational thinking. If the ajna chakra is the forest, the throat chakra is the individual trees and the details of all of the things that live under and in the trees.

How a couple orders their life, whether they have ever sorted out how to get chores done, budgeting and the day-to-day planning of getting themselves to work, the kids to school and the dinner cooked are all part of the jurisdiction of the throat chakra.

Communication is the other major subject that the throat chakra governs. Audible speech is made by our mouth and throat, and these body parts are energetically fed by the throat chakra.

When the throat chakra is in good condition, strong and robust, the parties most likely enjoy good communication and have the details of their life reasonably well organised.

When the throat chakra is weak or very congested, these same areas might be bones of contention or areas in which the parties lack very much skill or application. When the throat chakra is prickly and overstuffed with energy, this can signify that communication between the parties is very judgmental. Criticism and judgment can infuse our speech and leave an invisible impression of low vibrational and disempowering toxic residue in our chakras, particularly our throat chakra. Cleaning this out is a tremendous relief to everyone.

Captain Throat

Captain Throat can get a bit obsessive, fail to view the big picture, and be stubborn and opinionated. Captain Throat finds it impossible to understand anything much that the heart is trying to say. Captain

Throat is good friends with the sex chakra, quite likes the solar plexus, and usually always wants to get along with the base chakra. She has a natural tendency to want to speak out and to communicate with others. While highly creative, Captain Throat lacks vision. Captain Throat thinks she knows everything and cannot conceive of there being anything at all beyond its existing paradigm. Decisions made by Captain Throat usually end up being caught up in too much focus on details and the small picture rather than being able to conceptualise the overall plan. Captain Throat has no ability to understand abstract thought and conceptual thinking. She is good at organisation and management, but overall is not a good choice of captain, although is a great second officer and a good relief captain.

Heart Chakra

The heart chakra is found in the centre of our chest. It is our emotional centre where feelings of love, compassion, empathy and kindness live. A healthy relationship will have a strong heart chakra.

Sometimes people are together for reasons of convenience or codependence. If that is the case the heart chakra is likely to be weak. If there have been lots of fights and issues that have remained unresolved, this hurt can be buried in the heart chakra and block the flow of love. When things need to be forgiven, the low vibrational energy of non-forgiveness is visible to a clairvoyant as black lumps of coal in the heart chakra. This etheric debris weakens the heart chakra and makes it difficult for love to be expressed cleanly. In a weak heart chakra, loving kindness and compassion are not evident in the interactions between the parties.

Where the heart chakra is strong, the parties will have the tenacity, founded and fuelled by love, to stick together through thick and thin and make it work. Longevity in a relationship has a lot to do with the capacity of the heart chakra to ensure that the lives of the people concerned are founded in the bedrock of the love that infuses the relationship. The interaction between the heart chakra and the crown chakra, the effect of forgiveness and what it does to the chakras is more fully explored in my book *Child of God* and in our *Yoga of the Mind* seminar.

Captain Heart

Captain Heart just wants everyone to be happy. He wants to feel love, help others, and be considerate and compassionate. Captain Heart knows we are all Divine beings and loves God. He is a vehicle for peace and is very generous, warm and kind. Captain Heart is good, but is not a planner. Captain Heart doesn't care what happened in the past or future, and lacks a sense of context. He just wants to express and be love, right now. Captain Heart trusts that all will be provided for and takes no steps towards self-preservation. He has no boundaries. Captain Heart cannot say no to a beloved, or indeed to anyone. He has no sense of self-protection, a tendency to be walked on and is a bit of a pushover. Everyone loves the heart but it's important to recognise that Captain Heart does not achieve very much alone. In terms of living on the Earth plane, Captain Heart is too idealistic and through lack of interest in planning for the future could end up diminishing all resources.

Captain Heart is also very emotional, highly intuitive and lacks logical thought processes. He has profound connection with the soul, who is the beloved mother and father. He has trouble with things to do with the world. If Captain Heart runs the ship, everything might feel good while the ship goes around in circles. However we do need Heart to be expressed somewhere on the ship so that life on board is lovingly and compassionately lived.

Solar Plexus Chakra

The solar plexus chakra is found just under the heart chakra where the ribs meet at the front of the body. The solar plexus chakra is a centre of courage and self-esteem. Issues to do with self-respect, self-love and self-trust are generally reflected in this energy centre. The purpose of our incarnation is to help us evolve into our highest potential and blaze like the sun as an illumined soul. We cannot do that if our solar plexus chakra is oozing blackness and holding the dead energy of shame, lack of self worth and lack of belief in the self. Our task is to move through these things. This pain can become the fertilizer on the roses of our unfolding spiritual nature, helping us to come into radiant full bloom, in all of our innate beauty.

When the solar plexus chakra is functioning well, the person is confident and able to get ahead with projects and situations. In a relationship entity, this energy will allow the couple to act in dynamic ways with courage of their convictions.

When the solar plexus chakra is too strong and out of balance with the other chakras, the person becomes somewhat too selfish and egotistical. The balance between the heart chakra and the solar plexus chakra is very important.

Whereas the heart chakra is about our capacity for giving, the solar plexus is about our capacity for receiving. When we do not believe in ourselves it is very difficult to accept love, help, support or anything else. A weak solar plexus in a relationship entity would suggest that there are blockages to receiving love evident in this relationship, and perhaps issues to do with low self-esteem playing out in all kinds of negative and disempowering ways.

If we store a lot of anger, bitterness and self-loathing, this is often a place where it is to be found. Cleaning this out of the relationship entity allows a fresh start for the parties to move forward with some personal development work through which they learn to appreciate and value themselves more.

Weakness in the solar plexus chakra may also have to do with lack of courage. It takes courage to love, because love makes us vulnerable. The people that erect shields around themselves to keep pain out often have weak and congested solar plexus chakras, and this will show up in their relationship entities.

Captain Solar Plexus

Captain Solar Plexus has no boundaries. He thinks everything is his. What is his is his. What is yours is his. What is ours is his. He believes in separateness and in obtaining an ever-increasing slice of whatever action is going down. He is very territorial and selfish, and can be jealous and judgmental. Captain Solar Plexus gets angry easily and is prone to throwing tantrums. He is not really interested in what you might want, except if it affects what is in it for him.

Captain Solar Plexus only understands the astral and physical world. He has trouble conceiving of other dimensions, his God is the 'goodies' in life. He has great courage and strength, and a very loud voice when needed. He is quite reluctant to back down, even when everyone else is in agreement. Captain Solar Plexus expresses his will forcefully, without much, or any, deliberation beforehand. He is not a good captain for our energy ship, but is the captain of more ships than anyone else on Earth right now. He will lead us up the garden path and into all kinds of physical and emotional entanglements in the bid to protect his physical self, his own assets and wellbeing, and so that he can maintain his separateness from going into unity.

Quite often Captain Solar Plexus has low self-esteem. This is dangerous because it causes a retraction of energy, whereby only separation is experienced, which is his specialty. He becomes defensive, aggressive with the other chakras, and protective of his patch. Captain Solar Plexus is motivated by the fear of losing what he has, and of others finding out how insignificant he is. He cannot be truly generous with what is close to his heart because he does not understand that by giving he will receive. He thinks Captain Heart is a fruitcake. He is cut off from an ability to understand or apply Divine Law because he has no faith. He is suspicious of others and ready to undermine an opponent or competitor to secure his own position. He is not in touch with the soul, and his choices tend to be of a low vibration, thus the doors to heaven start to close and the doors to suffering open wider.

Continued choices based on fear over a long period of time will cause a downward spiral of vibration of which Captain Solar Plexus is blindly unaware. Eventually, there is a downfall and no understanding of how it came about. Usually, he will blame others and consider that he has been a victim of circumstance, or other people.

When Captain Solar Plexus finally develops self-esteem, which may take many lives, he is a pillar of strength, self-love and courage. He is a wonderful support to ajna, and respects Captain Ajna's incredible insights. In times of war and adversity, Captain Ajna can call on Captain Solar Plexus's strength and courage, so that heart and others are protected. Solar plexus is a good second officer but not a great captain, even when he is very developed.

Navel Chakra

The navel chakra is found at the belly button. It has to do with our relationship with power, and how we digest the energy of life and utilise it.

When the navel chakra is weak, chances are that the parties have poor boundaries. If the navel chakra is congested there are likely to be lots of power games going on, which need to be unpacked, explored and healed.

When the navel chakra is strong, the parties have a dynamic and empowered relationship in which both can derive support and yet be largely intradependent rather than co-dependent.

Captain Navel

Captain Navel is very powerful and very fast on her feet. She makes a great warrior; is quick with a sword or a shield. She is good both at attack and defense. She becomes impatient with the slow speed of the other potential captains, even Captain Ajna cannot keep up with Captain Navel. She is a good dancer and very balanced physically. Whenever agility is called for, Captain Navel comes to the fore. Captain Navel has a strong sense of aesthetics and understands energy at a profound level. She loves action, has plenty of power, but needs the other captains to direct where that power ought to be employed. Captain Navel is probably not our choice of captain, unless we are in a race!

Sex Chakra

The sex chakra is found at the top of the pubic bone at the front of the body.

In a sexual relationship the sex chakra will reflect the state of the sexual relationship between the parties. If the sexual attraction is very strong, this chakra will be highly energised. If the sex chakra is very weak, there may be poor libido or level of attraction and chemistry between the parties. They may have more of a brother/sister kind of relationship.

If the relationship being scanned is not a sexual relationship then the energy we are looking at is the creative energy. What do we do together that is fun and creative? How do we enjoy being with each other? A relationship where there is little or no creative energy will be boring and perhaps not terribly satisfying. A relationship with strong creative energy is a joy to be in, and the sex chakra has a lot to do with the quality of joy.

Captain Sex

Captain Sex frequently jams reception into and out of all other chakras. Captain Sex takes over completely and causes the ship to engage in manoeuvring that is often costly, and not always successful, to achieve sexual union. Captain Sex can steer the ship into reproductive activity regardless of what the other captains might have to say about it and regardless of the merits of the other ship.

Captain Sex has a huge repository of energy and is very bubbly. Captain Sex is a rousing leader and very magnetic in character. She can pull support from other humans and sell ice to an Eskimo. She has marvelous leadership skills and is a good motivational speaker. She wants to merge with others in a sexual way. She yearns for sexual partnership and to reproduce herself, and all other priorities are secondary to this. She has a deep understanding of the soul and God, but what she desires to create is *herself,* over and over again. Captain Sex is too distracted to be captain.

Base Chakra

The base chakra is found at the base of the spine. This chakra has a lot to do with our groundedness and practicality, as well as our ability to manifest. A relationship with a firm foundation will have a strong base chakra. If the base chakra is weak, then the relationship is not on solid ground and needs help.

Included in issues pertaining to security are issues to do with money and abundance generally. When we have a weak base chakra, we are not capable of grounding the energy of abundance into our lives. In relationships which have weak base chakras the parties may be experiencing financial issues or inadequate supply of resources. If there has just been a retrenchment or business failure then the energy may not be strong in this area.

Our security is also to do with our position in our family and society. The base chakra can become drained if we have ongoing issues with family members, or with our in-laws.

Captain Base

Captain Base is motivated by personal safety and survival. He will make every choice based upon these parameters. Captain Base wants desperately to belong to a tribe and be accepted. He insists on a firm foundation and understands the Earth and the physical dimension in a deep way. He is excellent at making money. However, he can shut down in a crisis and cause the ship to have structural problems. He likes to put down roots and values stability. He looks at how things have been done in the past and emulates them. There will be no lateral thinking or innovation here. He gets flustered by change. In a dynamic world, Captain Base will cling to the past in a way that can be detrimental.

Who is the captain of your relation-ship? Possibly you can discern which chakras might be calling the shots in your life. IYS therapy and relationship healing is a way to rebalance things, and to get the ship in order so that it will operate optimally.

Working with the Relationship Entity

In our seminars we choose a relationship that we would like to renovate energetically. We then go through a series of release affirmations and receive blessings which go straight into the chakras of the nominated relationship to lift its energy and provide a scaffolding for more love to be built.

If you are unable to attend a seminar, we highly recommend the Relationship Healing CD, which was recorded live and which will guide you through a relationship cleanse. Repeat the affirmations out loud, and allow yourself time to meditate if possible at the end, while you are in an uplifted state of consciousness.

PART

9

SOME NOTES IN CLOSING

Chapter

29

GETTING OVER
OLD RELATIONSHIPS

Getting over an old relationship can involve more than just physically splitting up. Long after we have moved into separate homes and even re-partnered, we can wake up in the middle of the night feeling upset about something that might have happened 5, 10 or 20 years ago. This is because the energy and the thought forms which were a part of that relationship are still with us. We are still energetically tied to our former beloved, even though this may not be what we want to be the case at all.

Falling Out of Love

When we are at the end of a relationship quite often there has been a lot of conflict and a lot of pain, we can seldom find much to admire in our ex. There can seem to be a lot to find fault with and we wonder why we were ever with them in the first place. Our memory is clouded by our feelings, which at the time may be fairly negative.

Sometimes we get a bit obsessive about old relationships, and find that our ex partner comes to dominate our mind. This drains our energy in a spiral dance of anger, negativity, frustration and exhaustion.

When a partnership ends, very few people terminate the emotional and spiritual links that have been created between them and their partners. The very same energy lines that helped the relationship to take form are now a trap that can be difficult to end, without some help in the form of energy healing, to release the ties that bind you.

Get Out of My Head

Do you ever feel like your ex is sucking your energy dry? Do you get tired having to deal with him or her? Chances are that you are in the category of people that have not yet really actually energetically separated, even through you may have been divorced for a long, long time. If you are still upset about a split up that happened years ago, then energetically and emotionally you may be still joined to that person. Your etheric or energy body is still busy interacting with them, and big fat chords of energy are joining you together. Through these, loads of energy in the form of thought and emotion is being sent and received.

Failing to recognise and release energetic ties to our ex-partners can seriously undermine any new relationship that we may wish to establish, and can cause either or both parties in an old relationship break up to feel drained or stuck in old patterns.

When relationships go wrong, the lines of energy get jumbled, and the disputes that have occurred stay trapped in the lines of energy. It holds us in the past and stops us from being able to get free and move on. People join with each other through their chakras, and these old ties that bind us can extend even to relationships that have been dead for years. This is really uncomfortable, as each would rather not be continually caught in a thought loop which involves the other.

It is possible to experience an almost miraculous change for the better that can be achieved when you understand that your energy field holds conflict, and that you can release it. By cutting lines of energy to your past relationship and freeing your energy from the conflict, you take the weight off your shoulders, the dispute seems much less important, you stop thinking about it all the time, your mind becomes free of it and you can move forward with your life with much more ease and grace. Very often things take an unexpected turn for the better.

Moneybags

A lovely schoolteacher from Sydney called Kate came to one of my workshops where we were looking at energetic ties that bind us to our ex-partners. She had been very angry and filled with resentment and rage about her ex, who had stolen money from their joint bank account to feed his gambling habits. He took $30,000 which was their whole life savings when he left her. She could not think about him in any other way except through the painful miasma of old energy patterns that had grown up between them. During the seminar Kate was asked to forgive her husband and to cut the ties which had kept him bound to her. She did this and she felt a lot of energy release from her heart chakra and from her solar plexus area.

Later *that same day*, her ex rang her. He had not spoken to her for over 12 months. He said that he had been thinking about their situation and that he was sorry for what he had done. He asked if he could meet with her for lunch soon so that he could return the money. Within two weeks he had done so. Because Kate changed, her whole world changed.

Barrister Blues

Another woman I know, Eva, was married to a very powerful and willful barrister who she found to be overbearing and sometimes downright threatening. Their marriage had been stormy and their separation was no better. The problem was they had a very young child and access was a real issue. Eva did not trust her ex to care for the child and he felt aggrieved that Eva was resisting him seeing their baby.

Eva, like Kate, was led through a forgiveness exercise and then we cut the energetic ties that bound her to her husband. Eva called me a couple of weeks later and said that there had been a remarkable transformation in his behaviour. He was now treating her with courtesy and respect, and she felt less intimidated. She allowed him to have access to the child and they were able to sort out a workable arrangement, which had its ups and downs but was basically friendly from that time onwards.

It is Up to Us

No one can take our power or our energy but often we give it away without even realising. If this is the case, see a reputable healer and ask them to help you to forgive and cut so as to cleanly release the past.

Completing with Dignity and Love

If it comes to a stage where you know that your relationship with a person is complete, then endings can be filled with love just as much as beginnings for the spiritually empowered. We are able to keep our hearts open and parent ourselves, as well as protect ourselves as we settle into a new way of being on the Earth together. Splitting up can be done with consciousness and grace. Your ex can become a very close and loving friend, there can be new and excellent boundaries and even when one or both of you re-partner, there can be happiness and joy in each other's company.

Re-acquainting ourselves with our inner child is a fabulous way to begin the next phase in our lives, of being connected and developing a meaningful relationship with ourselves, that is not based on criticism and continued feelings of not being good enough. Instead we start to really accept, respect, love and trust ourselves. As we do, our entire life and all of the relationships that we have start to mysteriously change.

Mastering this paradigm makes bad relationships better and it makes good relationships heavenly. It is a skill that all of our disciples need to learn, and forms the vessel into which 'new wine' can be poured: when we become robust in self-respect and self-love, we can withstand the down-pouring of the holy spirit without crumbling.

Over the page you'll find my best ten tips for a happier divorce.

Following these will lead to happier outcomes for all involved.

Ten Tips for a Happier Divorce

1. Act, don't react. This is the sadhana (spiritual practice) of divorce. Every word or deed needs to be able to stand on its own, is it reasonable? Would you normally behave like that with someone else? If not, don't do it that way with your ex either.
2. Have good manners even if they don't. Be empowered to be pleasant.

3. If you screw up say you are sorry.

4. Watch your communication style, make requests not demands, be assertive, not aggressive.

5. Reward every try, don't be super critical, be OK with individual differences and remember that no one is perfect and everyone makes mistakes, even you!

6. Rewind where you are at with Intimacy. Sometimes it is hard to know how to be together when there has been such great intimacy and now there is not. Find a new category or place to park them in your mind, no longer are they as close as a beloved spouse, but they are not distant from us either. In your mind park them from now on as family members, like cousins or other family who are part of your life every now and again and with whom you would be civil and pleasant.

7. Try very hard to ensure that the relationship your ex has with your kids is a good one. Do not white ant or undermine this relationship as your child only has two biological parents. Knit a tribe, a family *forest* not just a tree, with lots of great grown ups who love them. Remember your kids chose you both. Help both families to have a chance to love your kids.

8. Build and honour basic agreements. Be considerate, it's about you not them.

9. Do not dramatise. Do not tell everyone when your ex acts badly, just have a mentor or therapist or close friend to talk to, and definitely don't discuss this with the kids.

10. Get energy healing to break the ties still binding you together.

Chapter

30

10 Relationship Mistakes Not to Make

Have you ever noticed that sometimes our really nice friends choose partners seemingly from hell? Why do they do this? Have you ever done it yourself? What is it that makes normal sane people choose partners that their friends can clearly see are trouble? Over the years I have witnessed this phenomena many times. If we are looking for long term happiness, choosing the ones who '*treat us mean*' is a recipe for disaster. Below are ten reasons why this might occur, and ten tips on how to avoid going out with Godzilla again next time.

1. I Like a Challenge

I have met many young people who are not interested in the nice thoughtful considerate people that they meet, preferring instead the bad girl/boy. When you ask them why, they say "I like a challenge'.

What we are attracted to in others is sometimes based on something unresolved or unexpressed within ourselves. Compliant 'good girls' have a tendency to judge lots of things as 'bad' and therefore disown their rebellious side. In an effort to be approved of they are always pleasing others and behaving as they are expected to behave. They project the rebel outwards and end up attracting someone who will carry that energy for them. In some deep secret way we fear that we are a challenge. As we come to peace within ourselves, our attraction to the bad boy/girl wanes and we wonder how we ever thought that we could be with them. The real challenge is to get to know the self, to explore the inner recesses of our own being and take responsibility for what it is that we attract.

Tip: *Reflect upon whether you are a 'people-pleaser' who sacrifices authenticity to gain approval. Call back your spirit. Find your challenge within.*

2. Conditioning: Early Role Models

Whether we love them or they drive us crazy, our parents (or first caregivers) are our original and most influential role models. How often have you heard someone say, "I will never be like my father/mother" and the older they get the more they become exactly like their parent! If we do no work upon ourselves we can be pretty sure that we will emulate our parents, like it or not. Chances are we will not even know we are doing it, the behaviours are so ingrained they are invisible to us because it is what seems 'normal'.

Without any personal development training, we are likely to choose a partner who is just like one of our own parents as well. Usually it is the parent of the opposite sex, but not always. It may be dysfunctional, but it is familiar.

Tip: Notice when you react like your mum/dad, and when your partner behaves just like their dad/mum. Don't blame them, do some inner work yourself and learn to become empowered to be the person you want to be in relationships.

3. What do I Believe about Men/Woman? Thought Forms

As we are starting to realise from the Law of Attraction (discussed in the recent film 'The Secret' and in my *Spiritual Mastery* book) we actually attract to ourselves situations and people who somehow vibrationally resonate with us. Most of this has to do with how we think. Usually our partners will be in accord with our deep beliefs about the opposite sex. I met a man who believed all women are fickle. His insistence that women are fickle meant that he viewed people through the lens of his own belief. Not only did he attract fickle women, but he would see fickleness regardless of how reliable and honest the woman might otherwise be. With his belief system, he would pull the energy of 'fickleness' even from a woman who was a saint. Likewise, if you think *'all men are bastards'*, then good luck finding a nice one. You won't.

Tip: Examine your thoughts, and prune the garden of your mind. Get a good affirmation about women/men and use it a lot: e.g. (wo)men are kind, considerate, romantic, loving, funny, witty, intelligent.. and so on.

4. Falling in Love with Potential: Rescuer Syndrome

When we fall in love with a person, we are often able to discern the potential that our beloved holds. We fall in love with that rather than the reality of the person as they are right now. This is all very well, however unless we can love what is, we are in for a long and difficult journey.

Sometimes we try to rescue people, believing that if they just had our help, they would be able to achieve all of the greatness within them. Generally, rescuing others no matter how good our intentions is a messy business. The rescued usually end up resenting their rescuer and blaming them if anything goes wrong.

As a spiritual teacher I believe that every person is born with a potentially great spiritual destiny. But the road is long and winding with many side roads that mislead us or at the very least take up our time, often diverting us from the latent potential that we have.

While it is wonderful to hold a vision of our beloved attaining all that makes their heart sing, it is really important that we accept and love them *as they are*.

Very often we want to mould people into our own perception of perfection. This is not very respectful of the free will and individuality of our beloved.

Sometimes it is very tempting to try to change people particularly when they are stepping on our toes and squishing our boundaries as to what is acceptable and what is not acceptable to us in our relationship. As we will see in point 6 below, the problem is not really all about them 'out there' rather it has to do with how we process life internally.

Being a saviour is a recipe for disaster in a relationship and if you are thinking that you need to rescue a person, my top tip is: *Don't!*

5. Rescue Me!

The other side of the rescuer story is that we ourselves may want to be rescued. If we have come from a difficult background, if life seems uninspiring or to be heading nowhere, the temptation to find someone else to run our lives can be strong. Like Cinderella we can quickly surrender to Prince Charming, exiting the drudgery of our ordinary life and entering the interesting, or at least different drama of someone else's.

The trouble with Cinderella is we never find out what happens next.

Was she happy? Did she exchange one tricky situation for another? Was Prince Charming as good as he seemed or was he controlling and codependent? If we are pretty needy when we meet our Prince(ss), chances are that in some way, (s)he will be too.

Tip: Ensure that we develop the capacity to meet our own needs. Finding inside of ourselves the resources, skills, attitude and energy to provide our own security, approval, self-love, and a stimulating life will ensure that we attract someone who is able to do the same.

6. Low Self-esteem

People actually treat us in a manner that matches the level of our own self-esteem. If you are being treated disrespectfully by your man/woman, then instead of trying to change them, change yourself by raising your self-respect and self-esteem. It is miraculous what happens when we start to respect ourselves. Suddenly others start to change their behaviour towards us and life becomes far more pleasant.

I once counselled a woman in her 60's who had been enduring putdowns from her husband for over 30 years. He was forever telling her that she was too fat, too stupid, that her spiritual beliefs were flaky and so on. This particular woman was a lawyer, a gifted dancer and a very elegant woman. She wanted him to do some personal development work. I asked her instead to look at her own self-esteem. She did and within months he was *complimenting* her for the first time in their married life. She changed herself, began to really respect herself deeply and this caused a change in the behaviour she pulled from him.

Try this affirmation as my tip for change: *"I accept, respect, love and trust myself just as I am: I am love on legs."*

7. Past Life Attachment: Karma Baby!

Sometimes when we meet people we feel an instant like or an instant dislike. This is a soul recognition of unfinished business from another incarnation. We might not remember the details, but our soul remembers the other being. The laws of karma will continually throw us together until we sort out our differences and learn to love each other. As one of my spiritual mentors used to say, "If you cannot love them in this life, then they may incarnate as your child and you will be wiping their backsides in your next life." Graphic, but *oh my God* is this what we want? I have never heard a better reason to sort out our relationships than this.

Tip: Practice forgiveness. It happens in layers, but you know you are really doing it when beneath all of the pain and anger, and all of the stories of what they have done to you, once again you feel love for them.

8. Your Soul's Agenda

We might think that the object of life is to get married, have kids and live a comfortable and enjoyable life. The soul may think otherwise. The soul's agenda has a lot to do with us developing the strengths and virtues that the soul requires for its ageless, deathless, immortal existence. Thus we are here on Earth practicing kindness, tenacity, forgiveness, calmness, development of inner strength, compassion, service, assertiveness, understanding, humility, diligence, consideration, peacefulness and so on. If we are able to practice these in relationships they will pay rich dividends as our vibration will lift and so will our experience of 'reality'.

The patterns that we experience in our life are visible in our astrological make-up. The position of the planets relative to each other at the date, time and place of our birth have been pre-chosen by the soul so as to give a context to our incarnation. Find out what our soul has in mind and work with the energy that is coming instead of forever going against the tide.

Tip: Get your natal horoscope professionally done, check out what the planets are up to and start to 'surf' the waves of energy that are coming your way instead of getting dumped. Find out by looking at Venus, Mars, the Moon and your seventh house what your relationship profile really looks like and the qualities that would be important for you in a partner.

9. In Too Deep Too Fast

Loneliness, the need for love and the desire to merge with another can lead us to make unnecessary haste when choosing a partner. Instead of getting to know each other, we now jump into bed with people at the drop of a hat. Health issues aside, we need to ensure that we are practicing selflove and self-respect in our sexual activities. Sexual involvement brings with it a host of emotional and psychological issues that can cause us to become entangled long before we really know the person we are with. By practicing a little restraint in the early stages and enjoying the rituals of a good old fashioned flirtatious courtship, we can deepen the eventual ecstasy of sexual union and genuine love. Develop good boundaries early in relationships and things will flow better forever.

Tip: *Take your time – be friends first.*

10. Notice the Good

As a former family lawyer I used to see the very worst in couples as they came to end their marriage in the divorce courts. People who had once cherished each other enough to get married now hated each other, and the stories in the affidavits would make your hair curl. Otherwise sane and normal people were doing and saying out of control things, reacting to each other and engaging in 'tit for tat' warfare.

When we are in our 'stuff' it is difficult to retain accurate perception about the other person. All of the good qualities that attracted us in the beginning are still within them. We are just now focused on their faults. Everyone has faults including us, or we would be enlightened already and living in some other plane of existence.

To bring the best behaviour from our partners, don't wait until they get 'it' perfect according to your standards. Instead, turn the energy right around: shock them by 'rewarding every try'. Encourage every move that is made in the direction you would like things to go. If your partner never helps you clean up but they actually wash a few things one day, thank them. The approval and attention trains people into better behavioural patterns. You need to keep this up for a while and simultaneously work on your own self-esteem. Nicely ask for the help you need. We can often assume that 'they must know what I need' but unfortunately few people possess advanced telepathic ability! Remember that the more we respect ourselves the more others will too.

Tip: Don't just criticise. Give positive feedback as often as you can and notice the good in your partner. Don't wait until there is perfection as you perceive it but reward every try.

Signs of Empowerment

When we utilise relationships as a spiritual pathway, the kinds of development we will encounter are many and varied. When we become empowered in relationships, we can live in peace, even when there are challenges. Imagine if we all learned to be like this, what a wonderful Golden Age we would bounce into!

Here are some signs of an empowered person in an empowered relationship. They can:

- Maintain healthy boundaries.
- Have good, healthy, assertive communication (not passive or aggressive).
- Respond with wisdom rather than knee jerk reactions to challenges.
- Manage their energy and time productively and happily.
- Be open.
- Own their shadow.
- See that everything in their world must have something to do with them – taking 100% responsibility.

- Keep their minds clear and fresh, not fixed on negatives.
- Feel and experience appropriate vulnerability.
- Answer demands with: "Yes", "No" or "Not now".
- Be unaffected by other people's negativity.
- Maintain a high vibration even when under pressure.
- Exhibit strength and courage as well as authenticity.
- Be virtuous.
- Be confident.
- Be surrendered from egoic positions.
- Hold trust and faith.
- See conflict as a pathway to deeper understanding, intimacy and harmony.
- Respect the self and others, seeing the Divine in all.
- Meet their own emotional needs through healthy self-parenting.
- Convert judgment to compassion and accurate perception. Show forgiveness.
- Be joyful.
- Be a peace ambassador.

In Shanti Mission we train peace ambassadors. They strive to be walking embodiments of these capacities. Will you join us?

We are forever a work in progress,

But how magnificent, Empowered and blazing we can become, And how tremendous our contribution can be.

With what refinement and beauty can our thoughts shine,

And how elegant become our actions,

That we dance in the light of the sun And are comfortable in the dark of the moon.

We know in all places and in all things

There is the perfection of Divine creation.

Whether I like it or not,

Whether I understand it or I don't understand it, I surrender to its truth and wisdom.

With relationships sublime, the Golden World is created.

The Kingdom of Bliss is mine.

In ecstasy I surrender, Not my will but thy will be done.

I visualise the world I seek to inhabit I am Eternal hope and salvation.

My faith is inviolate.

Holy Shekinah, Prakriti, Gaia, I see you only as my reflection. I am the World to Come: It is within me.

I offer my thoughts,

My words

And my actions to the Divine.

And to you, My Beloved!

In full faith, so be it.

Namaste, Shakti Durga, April 2012

SUGGESTED READING

Bach, Richard, *Johnathon Livingston Seagull*

Bach, Richard, *Illusions: The Adventures of a Reluctant Messiah*, Dell Publishing 1977, Reprinted Delacorte Press 1998

Bach, Richard, *The Bridge Across Forever*, Pan Books, 1984

Capacchione, Lucia, PhD, *Recovery of your Inner Child*, Simon & Schuster, USA, 1991

Fraser, Kim, *Ignite Your Spirit*, Higher Guidance Pty Ltd 2004

Fraser, Kim, *Child of God*, Higher Guidance Pty Ltd 2006

Fraser, Kim, *Spiritual Mastery*, Higher Guidance Pty Ltd 2008

Shakti Durga, *Dimensions of Wealth*, Higher Guidance Australia, 2009

Goyo, Franziska, *Push my Buttons Baby*!, Australia (self-published), 2002

Hawkins, Dr David R., *Power Versus Force*, Veritas Publishing Arizona USA 2001

Hawkins, Dr David R., *The Eye of the I*, Veritas Publishing Arizona USA 2001

Hay, Louise, *You Can heal your Life*, Hay House, Inc. 1984, 1987, 2004

Jampolsky, Gerald, *Love is Letting Go of Fear*, Celestial Arts, 1979

Jansen, David & Margaret Newman, *Really Relating*, Random House 1998

Jeffers, Susan, *Feel the fear and do it anyway*, Arrow Books 1991

Lerner PhD, Harriet, *The Dance of Connection*, Harper Collins 2001

Lerner PhD, Harriet, *The Dance of Anger*, Harper & Row 1985, 1997

Lerner PhD, Harriet, *The Dance of Intimacy*, Harper & Row 1989

Parampara, *Introduction to Astrology*

Miller, J. & P. Laut, *Love Sex & Communication: skills for recovery*, Vivation Publishing, 1990

Redfield, James, *The Celestine Prophesy*, Bantam Books, 1994

Redfield, James, *The Celestine Vision*, Bantam Books, 1997

Roman, Sanaya, *Living with Joy: Keys to Personal Power*, H J Kramer 1986

Roman, Sanaya, *Personal Power through Awareness*, H J Kramer 1986

Roman, Sanaya, *Spiritual Growth: being your Higher Self*, H J Kramer Inc., 1989

Tebo, Barbara & Terry, *Free to be Me*, Bantum, 1993

Viscott, David, *How to Live with Another Person*, Simon & Schuster, 1974

Westheimer, Dr Ruth, *Guide for Married Lovers*, Bantam, 1986

RELATIONSHIP HEALING

Relationships benefit in tangible ways from one or both parties engaging in Ignite Your Spirit energy healing, developed by the author over the past 30 years and practiced in various countries.

On our website www.igniteyourspirit.com you will find help with more information. Below is some information to help you on your journey of love.

What is Ignite Your Spirit Healing?

Ignite Your Spirit therapy is a no drug, no touch healing modality developed by Shakti Durga which has helped thousands of people to experience better health, peace and happiness.

Energy healing, whether it be Ignite Your Spirit Healing or other modalities, is very powerful and life changing for those who are open to it. It works whether you believe in it or not, but can be blocked by adamant use of will that it will not work. So be it.

What Happens?

You sit in a chair with your feet on the floor, hands palm up for receiving energy and your eyes closed so you can go within. The therapist will scan your energy field and assess its strengths and weaknesses. They may give you feedback about your energy anatomy and what they see a need to focus on, and discuss with you what you wish to attain from the session.

Sessions take no more than 45 minutes and during that time the therapist will focus on your physical, mental, emotional and soul bodies.

What Happens Afterwards?

Sessions might only take 45 minutes but the healing will continue to unfold over the coming few days. Some people experience spiritual ecstasy during healings and for some period afterwards. Meditation becomes easier and deeper.

Sometimes people feel tired or a bit emotional immediately after the healing, and that is evidence of the releasing a lot of stuck energy that has been trapped inside the etheric and physical body. That passes, and you will feel lighter, cleaner and more filled with hope. Pain is often lessened and in some cases permanently removed, even where one has serious pathological reasons for assuming there would be a continuing pain issue. Divine energy is stronger than any bodily malfunction and miracles sometimes happen in our healing rooms.

Can You Guarantee a result?

No. A medical practitioner who is going to operate on you cannot guarantee that the surgery will be successful, but they can tell you that it is likely to be successful. Similarly we can tell you that IYS is likely to help you overcome your problems.

Your own personal grace bank account is relevant to what you will experience. If you have good karma you can expect miracles, and if you don't then not much will happen. However, we can help you learn to develop grace, and we have had instances where initially we have been unable to help people but after a year of following our advice about lifestyle issues or other specific matters, things have dramatically changed and the healing session has been profound, resolving the issues that had previously been unresolved..

Is This a Religious Thing?

No. People of all religions or none, enjoy IYS therapy. Every person has a spirit whether they go to church or not, and every person has the capacity to experience Divine connection and self-realisation. Religions are like fingers pointing the way to God, and you can learn something from all of them. It is irrelevant to us which religion you practice, so long as it is supporting your spiritual awakening we encourage you to go deeper with your faith. We will fit in with your beliefs.

Some Examples:

Miraculous turn around in health can occur. Tim had an amazing escape from the surgeon's knife when he had IYS therapy instead of spinal fusion. He went from being unable to walk, let alone work as an engineer, to being back at work with no surgery required. We have helped those diagnosed with cancer to recover wellness, including in some cases those who have been told that their condition is not treatable. Col had prostate cancer which had metastasised through out his body and he had been told he only had a short time to live. Now 10 years later he is still well after a series of IYS therapy sessions over a 6 month period.

Asthma, diabetes, allergies, blood pressure, kidney problems, heart issues, headaches, sports injuries and many other issues respond well to ignite your spirit therapy.

What About Depression, Anxiety, Addiction, Eating Disorders and Stress?

We have had great success with the diminution of depression, anxiety and stress, all of which are spiritual ailments as well as medical ones. You will also receive encouragement and training in how to meditate if you want to learn, and in techniques to ease your problems. In most cases we are able to assist people to wellness and to non-reliance on medication, in conjunction with the medical profession. We have helped anorexics and also those suffering from pain, to recover and flourish in life. When you ignite your spirit you will find that you are enjoying a natural high, and drugs, alcohol, or other forms of addiction seem pretty boring by comparison.

Post Traumatic Stress Disorder is a problem with the energy field and astral body, and pills can only put a band-aid over it. We work to remove the traumatic memory over time and teach clients how to build wellness.

Well and Happy

For long term change, energy healing is most effective and personally empowering when it is combined with a well constructed program designed to expand the awareness and insight of the person receiving the treatment. Thus, we also recommend that you start the path of Ease and Grace seminars.

Seminars
by the Author

☐ the Path of Ease and Grace©

Shanti Mission offers a path of awakening, healing, illumination and self-discovery designed to help you to Ignite Your Spirit and get more out of life. The Path of Ease and Grace© interactive courses are taught in easy-to-understand steps that allow you to learn at your own pace through a series of inspiring seminars, designed for everyone. Be supported on your journey through optional one-on-one IYS Energy Healing sessions with a registered, qualified IYS Therapist. A range of books and CDs and a friendly, welcoming and open community comprise a treasury of resources available to support your personal progress. We know that there is an endless potential for increased self-fulfilment, love, joy and peace, as well as a wealth of opportunity sitting untapped right under your nose. Our job is to help you find it.

The Path of Ease and Grace© shows you how to connect to a deeper level of your own consciousness, so you can take the next step towards a happier, healthier, wealthier and more fulfilled life.

Seminars include:

☐ Ignite Your Spirit - Energy Healing Made Easy

Learn about your own energy body and how it is affecting your life every day. Learn simple energy healing techniques to help you manage your energy and your health. Appreciate the interaction between your energy field and your physical body. Learn how to cut from negative people and heal adverse situations. Meditation and easy exercises that will help you feel brighter and more balanced and that will ease pain and reduce stress.

☐ Ignite your Spirit – Centres of Consciousness

This is a fascinating, inspired yet practical opportunity to learn more about your own energy anatomy and spirit.

Learn how we are interconnected with all of life through energy centres. Experience powerful guided healing meditations, and let your energy be replenished through wonderful transmissions of light and grace. Discover how to anchor more vitality and healing capacity, and have some fun as our teachers share their warmth, humour and personal stories of transformation. As you practise, your own energy will be enhanced – something you are likely to notice straight away, with continuing changes in the weeks ahead.

Discover more powerful ways to heal the mind and body, and safe effective use of light and sound for healing. Perceive the unique shape of your own energy field.

☐ Yoga of the Mind

The mind is an instrument of our soul, and when we learn to connect with our soul our consciousness transforms. Yoga means union and can be used to help us to attain peace and enlightenment. Yoga of the Mind is a companion to Ignite Your Spirit and helps us learn to still our minds, using ancient techniques to erase negative thought patterns, fears and self-defeating beliefs and ideas. Astounding changes in consciousness frequently occur during the seminar, and life changes afterwards are often profound. Break free of old grudges and negative habits and put in place new healthy foundations. Learn more about how to care for your developing energy body and add more healing techniques to your repertoire.

❐ Dimensions of Wealth

In Dimensions of Wealth we learn the art of Natural Manifesting. This is a method which aligns us with Universal design, which is Benevolence and Abundance. Wealth is both tangible and intangible. It includes having enough money to do whatever we want, as well as having the capacity to enjoy the earth, care for our families, have great friends, and a real sense of who I am and why I am here.

In this seminar we look at the way in which we either attract or repel good things in our lives. We learn potent affirmations to change our reality, study the five dimensions of wealth as well

as spiritual laws that bind us, whether we like it or not. Knowing them makes life a lot easier to understand.

Activations of the base chakra, learning how to self-assess our individual capacity to manifest wealth, and exercises to improve wealth creation are imparted.

❑ Empowering Relationships Emotional Liberation

Being empowered to have great relationships is an important key to a fulfilling life. Learn about your eight core needs and how to beat co-dependence. Experience an amazing healing meditation that you can practise any time. See how your mind, your energy, your soul and your speech can all become assets to anchor more love, joy, peace and intimacy, trust and security in ourselves and in our relationships. This transformative and experiential seminar will bring relief and freedom as well as a raft of ways to turn around difficult relationships and make good ones even better.

❑ Empowering Relationships from Conflict to Connection

It is easy in the honeymoon stage, but how do you keep the energy high and stay committed, retaining the zing and the intimacy? Rediscover the golden flow of deep togetherness. Learn simple ways to handle conflict, be more assertive and experience greater love. Find out how to gracefully transition relationships from one form to another, so that peace and authenticity, respect and trust are possible even when they may not have been in evidence till now. Practical and inspiring, we help you let go of old wounds, heal the past and get your energy into present time. Attain peace and happiness even in challenging relationships.

❑ Empowering Relationships Spirit and Soul

We live in a relational universe. Relationships are a portal for self-realisation and can be utilised as vehicles for the transformation of our consciousness. Rather than being stuck in old, habituated patterns, we can lift ourselves and our relationships into new paradigms. In this class, we learn tools of the spirit and soul for this exact transformation. You will be astounded by how liberating and transformative this is, and by how much freedom, light, love, clarity, and connection you can create in your life.

❏ Spiritual Mastery Laws of the Soul

Learn the rules of the game of Life!

The twelve spiritual laws are part of the fabric of creation itself. We cannot avoid them, so we need to learn to understand and embrace them. When we start to work with the Law of the Universe, the Universe starts to work with us and then anything is possible!

Spiritual Mastery —Hallmarks of Awakening

Explore 12 hallmarks of Spiritual Masters, with practical examples to help understand how Mastery can be lived. What should we be aspiring towards? What will bring us the greatest change internally and externally?

Measure your own progress in each of the 12 Hallmarks of Awakening. For each hallmark, you will clearly understand what we are seeking to attain, as well as how to avoid the pitfalls on the path. Practices which support each hallmark of spiritual mastery are explained and vibrant spiritual energy helps us to absorb the teachings to transform our experience of life.

❏ Living Truth and Purpose by Dr Gayatri Anderson

Introducing Shakti Durga's daughter, Dr Gayatri has been living the Path of Ease and Grace, healing and teaching spirituality since her teenage years. Her program Living Truth and Purpose is part of the Path of Ease and Grace seminar series.

Everyone has a spark inside that yearns to be expressed. When we are in touch with the essence in the world, we feel alive, uplifted and inspired. We feel motivated even in the face of challenges.

When we are not in touch with that essence, we can feel like the spark inside has gone out. We can feel like the world is grey; like life is repetitive and boring. We can feel a sense of not being enough, even if we are hitting all our targets. We know deep inside that there is more to who we are, but we don't know how to find it. In Living Truth and Purpose, we will be exploring the multi-dimensional nature of purpose and soul-identity. We will be exploring soul-based, mental, emotional and physical techniques to connect with and live the truth of who we are.

OTHER PRODUCTS
BY THE AUTHOR

SPIRITUAL MASTERY

Spiritual Masters exist in every religious and mystical tradition, and their job is to guide us home, each one taking us a little further on our evolutionary journey. Mere knowledge or theory is only helpful when we actually embody it in our day to day existence.

Spiritual Mastery entails the capacity to generate

inner peace, personal power and prosperity in whatever range of circumstances are presented to us.

This book covers the many tools and life changing ideals that have helped thousands to find peace, power and prosperity on the Path of Ease and Grace©. Witty and sparkling, practical and easy to read, it will help you to recognize the spiritual laws, hallmarks, pitfalls and practices that bring us closer to Spiritual Mastery. This book is also the text for the seminars Spiritual Mastery Laws of the Soul and Spiritual Mastery Hallmarks of Awakening.

DIMENSIONS OF WEALTH

Have you ever used affirmations until you are blue in the face, yet some areas of your life stubbornly stay the same? Have you worked at the Law of Attraction but still experience the same old problems? Chances are you have done part of the work needed to change your life, but the most powerful part of your wealth anatomy, your soul, may still remain a mystery.

Beyond anything you have read before, *Dimensions of Wealth* takes us on a spiritual journey of discovery into how to attract wealth and opportunity. Natural manifesting is a spiritual science and art, creating powerful life change. It requires energy as well as thought, stillness as well as action, soul as well as mind. Affirmations can set the scene, but our powerful soul must be in really good shape for natural manifesting to succeed in anchoring the Kingdom of Heaven on Earth, for ourselves and for others. Discover the five Dimensions of Wealth and the 12 Mansions of the Soul. Come on an amazing journey of the spirit as the means to attract miracles is revealed.

CHANT, MEDITATION AND SEMINAR, LIVE CDS

A large range of live recordings, including audio files of seminars and presentations made by Shakti Durga over the past 20 years are available from Shanti Mission centres and online www. shaktidurga.com and www.shantishop.org

STRENGTH OF THE SOUL CARDS –

TRANSFORM YOUR CAPACITY AND POTENCY OF THE SOUL

Shakti Durga has created this set of 54 cards, designed to assist you to attune with the amazing power of your soul as a means to transform your life, facilitate healing and blaze through the obstacles in your life.

MORE STRENGTH OF THE SOUL CARDS –

TRANSFORM YOUR CAPACITY AND POTENCY OF THE SOUL

Accessing the power of your soul is an incredible gift that is available to everyone. Shakti Durga has created this second set of 54 cards, designed to assist you to attune with the amazing power of your soul as a means to transform your life, facilitate healing and

blaze through the obstacles in your life. This stand alone deck is a companion to Shakti Durga's first Strength of the Soul deck. They are designed to be used together or independently.

WEALTH WISDOM CARDS –

NATURAL MANIFESTING WITH EASE AND GRACE

Wealth Wisdom is a multidimensional approach to leading an abundant life. Shakti Durga has created a series of cards based on her teachings to assist everyone to gain clear soul guidance on a daily basis. Card decks are available to buy from Shanti Mission Centres and online www.shaktidurga.com. Beyond affirmations, learn to align with the strength of your soul and the Archangels to enter the flow and anchor real goodness in your life. There are 72 beautifully designed cards in this deck.

ABOUT THE AUTHOR

Shakti Durga

Shakti Durga (Kim Fraser) is a mystical yogi, spiritual teacher and healer, sacred musician and a seeker of the Eternal Wisdom from both Eastern and Western sources.

She established the energy healing modality Ignite Your Spirit and Shanti Mission, a School for the Soul, in Australia. Shanti Mission now also operates in the USA, UK and India. Shanti means peace and the mission is to find peace within. Only then will we start to develop more peace in our world.

Shakti Durga's courses and seminars teach practical, grounded tools and approaches to resolving conflicts, financial issues, health issues and feelings of emptiness. Because she teaches beyond the mind, and helps students release and let go of blocks to creating better lives, people's lives transform rapidly. Common spiritual concepts and practical tools suddenly become much easier.

Prior to commencing her vocation in spirituality, Shakti Durga was a practising lawyer. She has two grown children and lives with her life partner in Cooranbong, north of Sydney in NSW, Australia

Discover more about Shakti Durga:
www.shaktidurga.com

For mystery school go to
www.shantimission.org

Email: info@shantimission.org
Phone: (02) 49773300

 facebook.com/shaktidurga

*This is the beginning of the adventure
of the rest of your life!*

Imagine if work was joy

Relationships were bliss

And education developed the soul

As well as the mind and body?

What if hospitals were temples of healing

And prosperity was for everyone?

The Shanti vision becomes real.

Each of us holds tremendous, untapped power

To transform our world.

We have forgotten how to use it.

Come and find yourself,

Ignite your spirit and

Discover your Path of Ease and Grace.

NOTES

NOTES

NOTES